Digital D.C.

Digital D.C.

*How Information Technology
Is Transforming the Hub
of American Politics*

Wilson P. Dizard, Jr.

McFarland & Company, Inc., Publishers
Jefferson, North Carolina, and London

Publisher's note: Wilson P. Dizard, Jr., died on August 31, 2009, shortly after completing the manuscript for this book.

LIBRARY OF CONGRESS CATALOGUING-IN-PUBLICATION DATA

Dizard, Wilson P.
  Digital D.C. : how information technology is transforming the hub of American politics / Wilson P. Dizard, Jr.
     p.   cm.
  Includes bibliographical references and index.

  ISBN 978-0-7864-4469-4
  softcover : 50# alkaline paper ∞

  1. Information technology — Washington (D.C.)
  2. Information services — Washington (D.C.)   3. Political campaigns — United States.   4. United States — Politics and government — 21st century.   I. Title.
  HC108.W3D59   2010
  303.48'3309753 — dc22   2009039614

British Library cataloguing data are available

©2010 Lynn Wood Dizard. All rights reserved

No part of this book may be reproduced or transmitted in any form or by any means, electronic or mechanical, including photocopying or recording, or by any information storage and retrieval system, without permission in writing from the publisher.

Cover images ©2010 Shutterstock

Manufactured in the United States of America

McFarland & Company, Inc., Publishers
  Box 611, Jefferson, North Carolina 28640
    www.mcfarlandpub.com

For Lynn

Table of Contents

Preface   1

1. Washington in the Information Age   7
2. In the Beginning   29
3. Silicon Valley East?   48
4. Digital Bureaucracy, Bit by Bit   74
5. The Last Colony   99
6. Hip DC   120
7. Arts and Ideas: The New Meld   139
8. Washington's Digital Future   157

Afterword: Washington in the Obama Era   179
Chapter Notes   189
Bibliography   201
Index   203

Preface

The United States is the leading force in determining the shape and direction of the emerging information age. Though it may someday have to cede this role to another society, for the present its role is unchallenged.

Digital D.C. is a survey of the political center of this new American era: Washington, D.C. The capital city follows the pattern of other digital-age cities in many ways, but it also has a special impact on the form and direction of the changes taking place throughout the nation and beyond. Its role as headquarters of a far-flung federal bureaucracy is clearly a major factor. Further, a new generation of commercial firms has moved into the region, heavily focused on providing digital goods and services to the government and other customers. By one estimate, almost ten thousand companies, large and small, have migrated to the Washington area in recent years. As a result, Washington has joined San Francisco's Silicon Valley, Boston, Frankfurt, Osaka, and other global centers as part of what urban planners have begun to identify as "knowledge economy regions."

The city plays a unique role among these digital centers. Its main activity since its quill pen origins has been the production, storage, and distribution of government information in paper formats. Today, its bureaucracy is slowly getting rid of documents stuffed in file cabinets and on storage shelves. The National Archives is currently engaged in a project to digitize nine billion pages of old government records at a cost of over $300 million.

These changes add up to what Washington officials have enshrined as e-government — "e" for electronic. It involves a complex pattern of computer resources, from laptops and BlackBerrys to the Defense Department's recent acquisition of an IBM BlueGeneL computer, which performs at 3.5 teraflops, a number that translates into a trillion floating-point operations per second. Important as computerization is to the government's day-to-day activities, its influence pales beside the impact of digital machines in defining the U.S. role in the information age. The Washington establishment is the single most powerful force in dealing with these changes. A critical part of this pattern is determining how to preserve and strengthen basic political rights, especially those represented by the First Amendment.

Other issues are less important, but equally pressing. One is how to regulate the safe disposal of older digital equipment as more advanced machines emerge. The federal government alone retires about ten thousand computers a week. Overall, Americans discard two million tons of electronic units annually, including 50 million computers and 30 million cell phones, according to the International Association of Electronic Recyclers. These throwaway devices often contain neurotoxins and carcinogens such as lead and beryllium metal that are leaching into waterways and entering the air through burning or dust. The social and environmental implications of regulating this toxic junk have only begun to be faced.

Once derided as a plodding bureaucratic enclave, Washington is now the center of a region whose economy is booming; its population is expanding, and its cultural life and other amenities are more diverse than at any time since it was founded on a swampy plain two centuries ago. An important new element in this mix is a generation of computer-savvy young professionals who have moved into the area. In the midst of these changes, traffic congestion, pollution, and inner city crime, among other issues, remain stubborn realities. The burdens of racial and economic discrimination have been eased but not ended. A new wave of immigrants from Latin America and Asia signals major social and cultural shifts. All this adds up to a city and a region in transition, with a mixed agenda of hopes and problems.

Washington's origins as a digital center trace back to the late 1940s when the government leased several of IBM's early mainframe computers, primitive room-sized machines whose operations were, by today's standards, slow, laborious, and expensive. By the late 1960s technical advances began to change the ways in which computers were used. A new technique, time sharing, meant that computer operations could be shared by multiple users. This was an important advance, but it still involved narrow applications. An informal network of computer pioneers scattered across the country challenged this limitation. One of the key actors was an MIT professor, Joseph Licklider, who saw computerization as the basis for what he called "thinking centers," a new form of human-machine interaction involving collaboration across networks to store and exchange information. The result, several technical generations later, was the freeform utility we call the Internet.

The ideas advanced by Licklider and other computer pioneers were picked up by an informal fraternity of young technical buffs grouped largely around universities on the West Coast. Many of them were, in the then current epithet, hippies. They were bearded, sandaled, bright, and disdainful of careers that involved a conventional climb up the corporate ladder. The group included Bill Gates and his colleagues, whose technical and marketing skills made computing available to hundreds of millions of users. A young engineer, Vinton Cerf, headed another group that developed the software that helped make the Internet possible. One of the first commercial personal computers, the Apple, was the brainchild of Steven Jobs and his partner Stephen Wozniak. Jobs summarized their attitude at the time: "We realized that we could build something ourselves that could control billions of dollars of infrastructure in the whole world.... We could build a little thing that could control a big thing." These West Coast pioneers were an unlikely group to start a cultural revolution but that is what they did. They turned the ideas advanced by Joseph Licklider and others into workable machines and networks.

Back east, the Washington establishment was generally slow to recognize the role of mass computerization as a new political and social reality. There were exceptions to this attitude, particularly among researchers at the National Science Foundation and other specialized government bureaus. A decisive breakthrough emerged from the Defense Department, which had created an Advanced Research Projects Agency (ARPA) to encourage cutting-edge inventions with military relevance. One of its projects in the early 1970s was to develop the technology which would provide a more secure network ("Arpanet") for military communications. The technique, known as packet switching, delivered messages across a widely dispersed network by breaking them into disparate chunks and attaching a label to each chunk before sending it off across the network to be reassembled at the other end. It was a breakthrough, with sophisticated trimmings, that made the Internet possible.

Meanwhile, political Washington was becoming increasingly engaged in the complexities flowing from Arpanet and other digital breakthroughs. Government bureaus and Congress came under pressure to adapt to the new technologies. In 1964, the Lyndon Johnson administration issued the first executive order mandating the introduction of computer-based operations in all agencies. By and large, information age issues were downplayed by other presidents until the 1990 elections when Bill Clinton and his vice-presidential running mate, Al Gore, adopted the subject as a major campaign theme. Their advocacy of a digital "information highway" was a direct appeal to younger voters involved with computers at work and in their personal lives.

Since then computer-based techniques have become a critical element in the U.S. political process. The Internet has played a decisive role in this transition. The turning point was the 2004 election campaign. By that time, almost two-thirds of Americans had access to the network. A post-election survey by the Washington-based Pew Internet and American Life Project indicated that there were over 63 million online consumers of Internet election data during the campaign, including 34 million who researched candidate positions on issues and 4 million who contributed to the candidates online.

These statistics were not lost on Democratic and Republican party officials in their plans for the 2008 election cycle four years later. Although they continued to rely heavily on general television coverage, their major focus was on the Internet's ability to reach specific target audiences, particularly young activists. Surveys since then have documented the decisive role computer-based electioneering played in Barack Obama's victory. The evidence is strong enough to suggest that the Obama administration is the first full-fledged presidency of the American information age.

The impact of this change in national politics has important implications for the nation as a whole and for Washington in particular. The federal structure has been transformed piecemeal by its adoption of digital practices, particularly in the last twenty years. It has, however, been a willy-nilly process, dependent on short-term solutions and uncertain appropriations. The Obama administration took office with plans for a more consistent long-range strategy, following up on its election campaign promise to appoint a cabinet-level "technical czar" to plan and monitor the operations of federal computer facilities.

In assembling this survey, I have drawn on many resources. The task involves a moving target — a city and a region in rapid transition. At times, neither stands still long enough to let a panting researcher pin down an elusive fact or trend. The daily press, notably the *Washington Post* and the *New York Times*, has been a stalwart resource in documenting current developments, as have two British publications, the *Economist* and *Financial Times*, both excellent recorders of the American scene in general and of Washington in particular.

I am also beholden to other research resources, including the Brookings Institution's policy studies on Washington area issues and the publications of the Greater Washington Initiative, a trade group dedicated to promoting the region as a corporate center. Academic institutions, notably MIT, NYU, UCLA, and Brown University, have become important resources for the study of the information age's impact on urban centers. A new generation of scholarly journals, including *Government Information Quarterly* and the *Journal of Information Technology and Politics*, is making an important contribution to understanding the digital impact on the political process. In Washington, *Information Week, Government Computer News* and other trade publications are major sources of information on the subject, as well as the Historical Society of Washington, the National Capital Planning Commission and other federal agency resources.

Finally, special thanks go to Margery Boichel Thompson, my editor and agent, and to my wife Lynn and our four sons — John, Stephen, Wilson, and Mark — all of whom provided useful comments on the book's draft.

1
Washington in the Information Age

In the early years of the new century, Washington, D.C., is in the middle of a dramatic shift in what it is, what it does, and how it does it.

It is a town redefining itself, moving beyond its traditional political focus. If present trends continue, Washington is on track to become a leader among the world's major cities in making the transition to a digitally driven information age. In the process, it is shaking off its reputation as a plodding bureaucratic enclave, a "gummint town" in the local patois, a place memorably described by John F. Kennedy as having the virtues of Southern efficiency and Northern charm.

In a city where conversations are often punctuated with short cut acronyms, the trendy initials these days are IT — information technology.

This is an interim report on IT's impact on Washington and the surrounding region. The changes it describes are a work in progress. They are emerging slowly, a kaleidoscope of trends and events documented in small-print economic reports, technological surveys, and census charts. One measure of this transition is provided in a survey of worldwide IT developments issued annually by Robert Huggins Associates, a British economic research firm. Huggins's analysts track the course of 125 "knowledge economy regions," the leading centers of information-technology activities around the globe. American cities have dominated the survey since it was started: San Francisco's Silicon Valley has led the list every year, usually followed by Boston, Ann Arbor-Detroit, Seattle, and San Diego. In 2002, however, a new name appeared among the top half-dozen of Huggins's knowledge-economy regions: Washington, D.C.[1]

The Huggins survey relies primarily on business data in ranking knowledge economy regions. This formulation falls short, however, in defining Washington's role in the new global reality. No other metropolitan area, here or abroad, can match the city's impact — political, social, and economic — in the digital age. The obvious overarching reason for this is Washington's role as the seat of the United States government, whose strategic decisions shape and direct the changes taking place. Along the way, the federal government has embraced wide-ranging digital practices in its day-to-day operations, from automated post offices to NASA's weather stations on Mars. The annual congressional budget for expanding its digital operations exceeds $30 billion, not counting the billions of dollars built into individual agency budgets to operate these systems. Collectively, the Washington bureaucracy manages the biggest computer operation on earth.

The shift from a paper-shuffling bureaucracy to today's digitally based operations began modestly with the purchase of several room-sized IBM computers in the early 1950s. Computerization of federal operations was slow-paced for a long time, because of the cost of the new machines and the reluctance of many agencies to give up old practices. Challenging this early hesitancy, a 1967 decision by the Lyndon Johnson administration mandated a sharp increase in federal computer operations.

Slowly, then swiftly, computerization began to take hold throughout the government. With the introduction of small desktop machines in the 1980s, most federal agencies were well on their way towards computerizing their operations on a large scale. The significant exception was the Congress, which clung to many of its pen-and-pencil habits for another decade.

The digitization of federal agencies led to another change that bolstered Washington's status as an information center — the creation of a large information-services industry in the city's suburbs, as thousands of companies moved in to compete for federal contracts. The newcomers included all the major players in the sector, from IBM on down to startup outfits run by young digital innovators seeking government business. In chapter 3, we will look at the region's continuing attraction for U.S. companies, as well as for hundreds of their foreign counterparts who have moved into the area in recent years. This pattern has continued at a somewhat slower pace following the severe recession that dominated the national economy in 2008 and beyond.

Meanwhile, the overall impact of digital changes on the nation at large and in the Washington region continues to grow. The 2008 presidential election, much of the Democratic and Republican platforms, and the hoopla of the campaign itself confirmed and reflected this shift. To a striking degree, the contest came down to perceptions of how the two major parties dealt with the new digital realities shaping American life in general and the economy in particular. Computer resources dominated the election process itself. Although radio and television figured prominently in the parties' election strategies, new digitally based appeals played a crucial role for the first time.

In particular, the Internet came into its own as a powerful campaign tool in influencing voter attitudes and, ultimately, their choices. Postelection surveys indicated that the Democrats were particularly effective in reaching out to computer-savvy younger voters on YouTube, MySpace, Facebook, and other popular Web sites. These and other venues proved particularly useful as fundraising sources. Armed with a list of nine million e-mail addresses, Democratic campaign managers collected $150 million for Barack Obama's campaign in the last weeks of the contest — three times more than any other presidential candidate in history had raised in so short a time. In this and many other ways, the 2008 presidential campaign was a defining moment in the American transition to a digital society, leading some observers to suggest that it was the closing event of the first phase of the American information age.

The 2008 campaign is but one piece of the mounting evidence of the federal city's new standing as a digital-age center. Recognition has also come from the head of the information industry's biggest trade group, Harris Miller, president of the Information Technology Association of America, who notes: "Clearly this is the strongest information technology area in the country right now."[2]

The larger story is that Washington is a town with a new pace and style. The federal establishment still dominates much of the region's activities, but IT–oriented private enterprises are moving up fast. The area's economy grew by 20 percent in the early years of the new century, compared to 14 percent for the rest of the nation. While the major IT capitals of San Francisco and Boston suffered job losses in the first half of the decade (88,000 and 72,000 respectively), the Washington region added 287,000 jobs.[3] In 2005, the region accounted for more new jobs than did greater New York or Houston in the previous five years,[4] largely because of the thousands of IT–related companies that have settled in the area over the previous decade. One result is that information-technology activities have replaced tourism as the region's largest commercial sector. Few markers measure the flow of IT enterprises into the area. If a date had to be picked for the rise of this corporate migration, a useful one might be 1995, when Lockheed Martin, an industry giant, moved its headquarters from Sunnyvale, California, to

Bethesda, Maryland, just outside Washington. Lockheed's local presence has since expanded to the point where it owns or leases over seven million square feet of office space. The company's clear purpose is to be closer to its largest customer, the U.S. government. Its Washington presence has paid off handsomely for both its management and stockholders; in recent years, the firm has led the industry in winning over $5 billion in federal contracts for information goods and services.[5]

As a buyer of IT goods and services, the government is the main economic engine driving the industry's presence in the Washington region. The $3.1 trillion budget submitted to Congress in 2008 by the Bush White House was ten times greater than Wal-Mart's annual sales. Although IT goods and services are a relatively small part of this budget — about $60 billion — it is enough to attract Lockheed Martin and other companies to the region and to keep them there. As George Mason University economist Stephen Fuller points out: "Companies that work for the government want to be close to the mother ship."[6]

At first this presence involved only American firms. More recently hundreds of foreign IT companies have moved into the Washington area. In many instances, their presence is the result of aggressive economic-development marketing by state and local governments in the region. It is the exceptional scale of government spending in the region that commands their attention. More recently, a new trend has emerged within the local IT sector. It is a slow but steady shift from its almost total dependence on federal contracts to a growing share of commercial business. Increasingly, the region's IT companies are competing directly for private contracts against firms in Silicon Valley, Boston, Dallas, and other IT centers. Their Washington location offers special advantages to this new outreach; beyond its proximity to federal largesse is its proximity to strategic markets in the mid–Atlantic region and an economically resurgent South.

Furthermore, the region is home to some of the country's most advanced IT-based research facilities, including the National Institutes of Health, which operate on an annual budget of over $25 billion, and the private Howard Hughes Medical Institute, with an $8 billion endowment focused heavily on medical research. Government agencies with special technology needs, such as the code-breaking National Security Agency in suburban Maryland, work closely with academic research groups in the region. "There is no bright line between the University of Maryland's mathematics department and the NSA," one knowledgeable IT analyst notes.

Washington's new role as a digital-age center marks the city's third transformation since its founding in 1790. For its first sixty years, it was a muddy village inhabited by transients, including congressmen who convened in January, conducted their business, and went home before the miasmic summer heat set in. Unimpressed with their newly minted capital, the lawmakers debated moving it somewhere else. (St. Louis was a popular alternative.) Meanwhile, they ruled the city by legislative fiat. When Congress authorized street lighting in 1842, the legislation included a provision that the lights should be turned on only when Congress was in session.[7] It was an era of small government: the Bank of the United States began operations in 1830 with three clerks. Its lineal descendent, the Federal Reserve Board, currently has 20,000 employees on its payroll.

The city's first transformation took place during the Civil War. In order to fight a modern war, one that relied on mobilizing industrial resources and millions of men, the federal government expanded to a full-scale bureaucracy. Washington emerged from the war as the political center of a unified continental nation. In the following decades, the federal establishment expanded steadily, with only an occasional pause, into a complex web of departments, commissions, task forces, working groups and all the other bric-a-brac of modern government.

The 1930s witnessed the city's second transformation. Traumatized by an economic depression at home and the threat of war from abroad, the country voted for the Roosevelt New Deal and an era of interventionist government. Roosevelt's new "alphabet agencies," from the Tennessee Valley Authority to the Social Security Administration, required specialists in public administration, economics, and other academic disciplines. This expert cadre began to shift the intellectual and cultural identity of the federal city. The depression ended, the war was won, and Washington took on a new role, this time as a global capital.

Meanwhile, almost unnoticed, the stage was set for an even more momentous change in the city's prospects. It was the invention of the modern computer — machines that held out the promise of efficiently storing all human knowledge as well as their users' specific memories. During World War II, the War Department, predecessor of today's Defense Department, played a critical role in funding early research on computers that focused on the task of calculating the trajectories of artillery shells. After the war, the government bought its first half-dozen IBM computers without a clear idea of how or where they would fit in a paper-shuffling bureaucracy.

The technological descendents of those early room-sized machines have driven Washington's third transformation. In the process, they have changed the town politically, economically, and culturally. From small beginnings in the 1960s, this trend accelerated steadily as technology companies moved in from California's Silicon Valley and other IT centers to set up shop in the Washington suburbs. Other new arrivals were hopeful start-ups — teams of young engineers with a big technical idea for cracking the IT market, operating out of small offices, sparely equipped with rented furniture, fancy letterheads, and a few computers. Many of these early ventures failed, but others survived to become permanent fixtures in the local business scene. By the turn of the twenty-first century, IT companies in the region numbered in the thousands, up from several hundred fifteen years earlier.

Washington's digital transition is still in its early stages. Nevertheless, the current changes are an unexpected turnaround for a town once largely marked by gray bureaucratic pallor. The city's new role has not followed the pattern set by Silicon Valley (still the world's biggest technology cluster) and other early information-age centers, all of which boasted better resources for managing their transition from an industrial-era economy to the new digital order. These assets included aggressive local entrepreneurs, savvy corporate managers, and risk-taking investors, along with world-class universities and research centers.

Washington lacked many of these advantages as it began its shift into the information age. It has never had an industrial base. The District of Columbia's last big manufacturing enterprise, a naval shipyard on the Anacostia River, closed down more than a hundred years ago. The city's overarching advantage in the new digital environment is as the headquarters of the federal bureaucracy. From its quill-pen origins, Washington's major industry has been the production, processing, storage, and distribution of government information. The end products of this process have been stuffed into file cabinets, boxes, and shelves for most of the past two centuries. This pattern has changed dramatically in recent decades as computers have taken over the job. A few examples illustrate the point:

- The National Archives and Records Administration (NARA) is digitally cataloguing nine billion pages of government records dating back two centuries. In 2005, NARA awarded a $308 million contract to complete the job.[8]
- The Government Printing Office, the world's largest publisher, is shifting its printed products to digital formats, from its perennial best-seller,

Baby Care, to NASA maps of Mars. Its goal is to cut back and eventually eliminate most of its old-fashioned printing operations. One of its projects, the Future Digital System, will make available online key government documents, a total of 60 million pages tagged by easily searchable keywords.[9]

- The Library of Congress needs 530 miles of shelves and bins to hold its 120 million items, from books and music to classic Hollywood films. Its organizational passion for collecting encompasses the grand piano George Gershwin used to compose his songs. The library's long-term plan is to transform a large portion of its printed holdings into electronic bits and bytes. In 2005, it recorded almost 3.7 billion transactions on its public computer systems.[10]
- A National Sex Offenders Public Registry run by the Department of Justice provides real-time access to public sex-offender records to help parents safeguard their children. The site received 27 million hits in the first 48 hours after it was activated in 2005.[11]
- The Census Bureau will automate part of its 2010 population count with the help of handheld transmitters linked to global positioning satellites. Census takers will use the devices to store and transmit data from households that have not responded to mail surveys.[12]

The prospects opened up by this digitization have led the bureaucracy into strange and wondrous projects. In laboratories just outside the city limits, researchers at the National Institutes of Health in Bethesda, Maryland, have completed a major computer-driven study of the human body. It involved carving up two cadavers — dubbed Adam and Eve by irreverent researchers — from head to toe, one millimeter per slice. The slices were reduced to digital bits and bytes that contain the first detailed anatomical record of the human body, 42 gigabytes long. (A gigabyte is a billion bits.) The results of both autopsies reside in seventy compact discs available to medical researchers worldwide as part of the NIH's Index Medicus, an online database of global medical literature that processes millions of queries annually from doctors here and abroad.

The Adam-and-Eve project is an outsized example of how the federal establishment has adapted to the digital age. The process began modestly in the early 1950s with a half-dozen room-sized IBM computers. A half-century later, no one knows how many computers there are in the federal inventory, ranging as it does from millions of ordinary hand-held or tabletop PCs to the Defense Department's recent acquisition of an

IBM BlueGeneL supercomputer, which performs at 3.5 teraflops, a number that translates into 35 trillion operations per second.

The new computerization, and particularly the need to keep up with changing technologies, has become an increasingly vexing problem for federal planners. The International Association of Electronic Recyclers estimates that Washington agencies retire 10,000 old computers every week. Their disposition is so complex that Congress voted in 2005 to give the Environmental Protection Agency a special $8 million fund to help agencies discard their outmoded digital equipment without harming the environment.[13] This shift to digital operations in the government has taken place fitfully over the last forty years. In large part, the delays resulted from bureaucratic foot-dragging, a reluctance to change old habits. It was not until 1965 that the advantages of the new digital machines in government operations were fully acknowledged when the Lyndon Johnson administration issued its directive ordering agencies to speed up computerization of their operations.

Some agencies, notably the Defense Department and the Central Intelligence Agency, moved quickly to implement the directive. The State Department was among the laggards, continuing to rely primarily on paper files and slow-moving telegraph messages. It took thirty years for the department to warm up fully to the idea of computerized operations. The result has been a dramatic change in the way America handles its foreign relations. By one recent estimate, computer-driven e-mail traffic between State and its overseas embassies now outnumbers old-fashioned telegraph traffic by a ratio of sixty to one. Another result of the department's new emphasis on digital operations is a computer-friendly passport designed to improve border security. Among other features, the passports contain a computer chip that includes a digital photograph of the passport holder that allows machine verification by features such as eye socket depth and nose width.[14]

In recent years, the federal bureaucracy has moved more aggressively to embrace what is now enshrined as e-government—"e" for electronic. This rush to digitization has resulted in some spectacular failures, one of the largest an Internal Revenue Service plan to computerize its tax-collecting operations. The project collapsed in a tangle of technological mishaps at an eventual cost to taxpayers of $4 billion. The program's errors were eventually corrected, and over 60 million citizens now file their tax returns electronically. The federal computerization program has seen other setbacks, but the basic structure of a digitized bureaucracy is now largely in place. The Congressional Research Service has estimated that by the turn of the century 75 percent of all transactions within the government and with the general public were electronic.[15]

Although many information technologies have contributed to this record, none has been more pervasive than the Internet and its offshoot, the World Wide Web. Its basic technology, known as packet switching, was familiar to electronics researchers by the 1960s. Its potential as a mass medium was not grasped until the Defense Department created an experimental packet-switching network in 1969 to test its possibilities. The project, called Arpanet, had fewer than a dozen terminals when it began operations. Today's Internet has over 200 million registered links throughout the world, the lineal descendents of the original Arpanet terminals.

Beyond the federal bureaucracy, Washington, D.C., has embraced digital living. It is, by any measure, one of the most plugged-in tracts of real estate on earth. Over three-quarters of the city's homes possess a computer, ranking it third in the nation behind two more populous towns — Salt Lake City and San Francisco. Washington has consistently led the nation's cities in the number of Internet users, with over 70 percent of its citizens connecting to the Web. The Internet also pervades the city's suburbs. Companies based in the region process over half of the world's Internet traffic.[16] One of the largest public networks of Internet users, America Online, bases its major operations in the Washington region.

Over and above its technical and economic implications, the Internet has had a powerful political and cultural impact. An American aura pervades the entire global network. Although it is growing rapidly abroad, almost half the network's users are American. About 90 percent of the most active World Wide Web sites are in the United States. Increasingly, these sites are operated by a new generation of commercial information providers. Google, the largest of them all, had over six billion items in its Mountain View, California, computers by 2005 and was processing more than 100 million search requests a day from its global audience.

From its 1970s origins as a Defense Department project, the Internet has played a special role as a multiplier of American global influence. Don Heath, former head of the Washington–based Internet Society, notes: "If the United States government had tried to come up with a scheme to spread its brand of capitalism and its emphasis on political liberalism around the world, it couldn't have invented a better model than the Internet."[17] If the Internet suits the American character, the new digital environment suits the way Washington does business. The U.S. government is the biggest producer, storer, and distributor of electronic information on earth. Its annual budgetary outlay for information-technology goods and services rose from modest hundreds of millions of dollars in the 1970s to the $60.9 billion voted by Congress for IT operations in the 2006 fiscal year. When all expenditures, direct and indirect, for IT resources are factored in, this figure more than doubles to $155 billion annually, according to a survey by Input, a Washington-area consultancy. Input estimates that direct federal IT spending will continue to grow steadily for the rest of the decade, topping $91 billion by 2010.

These dry statistics have fueled a steady migration of technology firms into the Washington area, attracted by the fiscal honeypot that is the government's annual budget. In part, this represents an extension of the private sector's long-standing interest in federal goods-and-services business, from aircraft carriers to pens and pencils. Although a few of the bigger firms have always maintained outposts in Washington to monitor government business opportunities, most companies relied on their trade associations and law firms to keep them informed about potential federal contracts.

This pattern began to change thirty years ago as federal IT budgets expanded. Ivan Selin, one of the region's digital pioneers, recalls setting up shop in Rosslyn, across the river from Washington, in the early 1970s with the aim of bidding on government IT contracts. He and his partners named the venture American Management Systems (AMS). "There was nothing on my desk," he recalls. "No phones were ringing. There was nothing in the in-box." Three decades later, the company posted annual revenues of nearly a billion dollars, with 8,000 employees worldwide, selling complex software systems to both government and private customers.[18]

As with other local IT-based firms, American Management Systems' primary focus was on tracking government business. By 2007, the federal government was spending over $25 billion a year on IT products and services in the region, which added up to about half of its annual outlays nationally in this category, according to the Greater Washington Initiative, a local trade-promotion group sponsored by the Washington Board of Trade.[19] From several hundred small enterprises like AMS, the region's IT enterprises have expanded steadily in the past twenty years. About half of these firms have fewer than five employees, working on the fringes of the industry, hoping to transform a bright technical idea into a big moneymaker. Ivan Selin's start-up company was one that succeeded. Many other small firms have fallen by the wayside, victims of inadequate capitalization or a too optimistic faith in a technology that did not live up to its initial promise.

The region's current growth and prosperity derives from the companies that survived. MCI Communications and America Online were two early examples. In the early 1970s, MCI set up shop in Washington as a maverick phone company with the aim of challenging AT&T Corp.'s longstanding monopoly. At first, MCI's success depended on Federal Communications Commission (FCC) permission to compete with AT&T. Accordingly, the firm's founder, William McGowan, set up the fledgling firm's headquarters across the street from the FCC's headquarters at 20th and M Streets Northwest. After MCI and AT&T's other potential competitors prevailed in their regulatory fight, MCI moved its headquarters to Northern Virginia to take advantage of lower rents and better commuting for its technical staff. Its lawyers, however, stayed downtown to protect the firm's political interests.

A decade later Steve Case, a former Pizza Hut executive, came up with the bright idea of marketing an all-purpose consumer information archive and e-mail network based on Internet technology. The result was America Online (AOL). It took ten years for Case and his colleagues to sign up their first million customers and much less time to reach the twenty-million mark. Larger companies have since absorbed both MCI and AOL, but their operations remain an important part of the Washington IT complex. AOL moved its corporate headquarters to New York City several years ago, but its major day-to-day operations remain in the Washington region.

Although AOL and other start-up firms have been a critical part of the Washington area's growth as an information-age center, the trend was sealed when older established firms moved into the region. These included IBM, Hughes, Hewlett-Packard, Northrop, and Lockheed Martin — all of whom now have major operations in the region. As noted earlier, Lockheed Martin is a major player in the new regional IT boom. Its involvement in government contracts stretches from the Pentagon to the Postal Service. In addition to being the nation's largest military contractor, it sorts the mail, cuts Social Security checks, tabulates the United States census, runs space-flight operations, and monitors civilian air traffic. To make this happen, the company writes more computer code annually than does its larger commercial rival, Microsoft.

The IT industry's skill in lobbying its interests within the government is a typical example of what Washington insiders call the Iron Triangle — the long-standing alliance between the military services, the defense industry, and their congressional advocates. The three-way arrangement is a critical factor in the IT sector's Washington presence, since the Defense Department is its largest single customer.[20] None of the participants plays the game better than Lockheed Martin. In a typical example, when the Pentagon proposed to cancel one of the firm's major aircraft products, the technology-laced C-130J Hercules transport in 2005, Lockheed's lobbyists quickly rounded up two dozen senators to criticize the proposal, assuring that the proposed cuts would be eliminated or at least modified. "It's impossible to tell where the government ends and Lockheed begins," says one critic of the company's outsized role in Washington politics. "The fox isn't guarding the henhouse. He lives there."[21]

This combination of start-up and old-line firms has fueled the region's new role as a digital-age center. Among other outcomes, it raised the area's population of IT-related technical workers by the turn of the century, matching such earlier entrants as Silicon Valley, Boston, and Los Angeles.[22] For the first time, private-sector workers in the Washington region outnumbered government workers, according to Scarborough Research, a Washington consultancy. By the middle of the decade, the federal government directly employed only 10 percent of the Washington region's workforce, down from 20 percent two decades earlier. Private information technology firms and the services trades grouped around them were largely responsible for the change.

This trend has held despite the continued expansion of the federal government in recent decades. During the 1992 presidential election campaign, Bill Clinton declared that the era of Big Government would end if he were elected. It was a promise he could not keep. The bureaucracy continued to grow during his two terms, as it has for every recent president. It is another proof, if one is needed, that the federal government operates on autopilot. Short-tem projects that start small routinely take on a life of their own, despite "sunset laws" designed to close them down. The process supports the old Washington proverb that the closest approach to immortality on earth is a temporary government bureau.

The federal establishment's reputation as a steady source of business was tested in the late 1990s when the information-technology sector across the country went into a painful downward spiral — the bursting of the "dot-com bubble"— following a decade of steady expansion. The NASDAQ stock index, a leading indicator of technology-sector activities, plunged 74 percent in 30 months. IT firms in Santa Clara County, the heart of California's Silicon Valley, shed nearly a fifth of their employees. Other regions suffered similar losses. By contrast, Washington area firms prospered, adding tens of thousands of workers throughout the lean years.

Government contracts helped the IT sector in the Washington region thrive as the rest of the industry languished, with the added effect of sharpening the region's competitive edge in the larger IT market for commercial work. Diversification into the industry's private-sector markets has strengthened local firms by reducing their dependence on government contracts. This factor became more important as the pace of growth in federal IT budgets, particularly for big-ticket items, began to level off in recent years after two decades of spectacular growth. Overall, the Washington-area IT sector emerged from the dot-com bubble years stronger and more diversified, a development with continuing ripple effects throughout the local economy. More recently, local firms have managed to maintain and even expand their operations in the face of recessional pressures.

Washington can no longer be defined as a federal enclave surrounded by a narrow ring of residential suburbs. It is now a large-scale region, pushing out in all directions: east-west from the Chesapeake Bay to West Virginia, and north-south from the Pennsylvania border to Richmond.[23] By mid-decade, Virginia's Loudoun County, a rural area twenty years before, led the nation in population-growth rate, followed closely by nearby Prince William and Stafford counties in Virginia and Calvert County in Maryland. Despite this local population surge, the Washington region ranks only forty-third in urban density nationally, according to the U.S. Census Bureau, with less than half the density of the two most crowded regions, Los Angeles and San Francisco.

The Washington region's prosperity and growth are tilted heavily to Northern Virginia, which accounted for 45 percent of the area's economy at mid-decade, double the District of Columbia's share and a third more than suburban Maryland's.[24] One result is sprawl, particularly in the outer ring of Virginia counties, which are expanding in population at a blazing rate, an exurb on growth hormones. The predictable results are traffic jams, crowded schools, rising crime, and high-priced housing. Despite these handicaps, regional employment is forecast to grow by 50 percent in the next quarter-century. This prospect has led some professional region-watchers to advocate the politically unappealing course of greater density in the inner suburbs and in Washington itself. "The only way we'll really add to our prosperity is to add to our density," says economist Richard

Florida. "And we have to because we've almost reached the limits of carrying capacity and infrastructure."

Meanwhile, the outer counties are setting the pace for the region's growth. By mid-decade, Prince William County added jobs at a faster rate than any other large county in the country, thanks to new IT businesses. In part, this suburban expansion is the result of local governments' aggressive efforts to court new businesses, both at home and abroad. Fairfax County has marketing offices in London, Tokyo, Frankfurt, Tel Aviv, and New Delhi. By 2005, 250 of the 4,000 firms in the county were foreign-owned.[25]

In short, the region is redefining itself with a new pace and style, sometimes too swiftly for Washington's buttoned-down establishment. A recent controversy surrounding the proposed addition to the Corcoran Art Gallery, two blocks west of the White House, typifies this clash of tastes and temperaments. The gallery's proposed extension is a shamelessly modern building with an undulating stainless steel façade, designed by world-class architect Frank Gehry. The city's Fine Arts Commission approved its design after much throat-clearing and debate about the threat of creeping modernity in the city's monumental center. The proposal, much less the commission's decision, would have been unthinkable a decade earlier. Unfortunately, the Corcoran's more cautious trustees put the Gehry project on hold because of funding problems.

Outside critics have long derided the city as a cultural backwater. Surveying Washington's prospects, the London *Economist* noted:

> [Washington] did not, like other cities, evolve gradually. It was invented. Conceived as the political focus of the nation, [it] was superimposed on a huge expanse of swamp, scrub and forest, fully planned out before anything was built.... This means that there was little about Washington that lent itself to creative ferment. It was not a hub or crossroads like Paris or Constantinople. Nor, like New York or Los Angeles, was it a point of entry for immigrants who seeded their adopted habitat with traces of their own culture while responding to the one they stepped into.[26]

Despite these criticisms, the town is changing in ways that evoke mixed feelings beyond the Beltway. The old image — the Greco-Roman-temple capital of the nation — had a certain stability to it, along with populist doubts. The new ambivalence is reinforced by some of the town's local customs, including the way its inhabitants talk among themselves. Washington-speak is a special patois, as *Washington Post* columnist Anne Applebaum has noted: "Thanks to acronyms, neologisms, euphemisms and other forms of government jargon, small groups of people in the nation's capital have a private language that is incomprehensible to the rest of the country."[27]

This local jargon is a special problem for outsiders. The president of the United States is POTUS. His first-lady wife is FLOTUS. On any given day, he may deal with FLPMA (Federal Land Policy and Management Act) or FERC (Federal Energy Regulatory Commission) or meet with PFIAB, the President's Foreign Intelligence Advisory Board, pronounced "piffy-ab." At times the local acronyms get light-years ahead of reality. In 2004, President George W. Bush announced a Greater Middle East Initiative, which was promptly reduced to "Gimme." However, the political situation changed, and the project was renamed the Partnership for Progress and a Common Future with the Region of the Broader Middle East and North Africa. The result was the unpronounceable PPCFRBMENA.

This semantic confusion seeps down through the bureaucracy. In 2005 the Defense Department found it necessary to issue a manual listing the hundreds of acronyms and abbreviations used in its day-to-day operations. The Pentagon's corkscrew vocabulary often descends to the incomprehensible. One of the more exotic examples of this in recent years is its Non-Obvious Relationship Awareness Program, a part of its Horizontal Fusion initiative. Whatever the project's role in defending the nation, it cost American taxpayers $156 million in the 2004 fiscal year.

Overall, the new age of digital connections has done little to lessen the differences between a big government and the people who pay its bills. As Arthur Cotton Moore, a local civic activist and architect, once summed up general attitudes about Washington:

> Let's face it: DC is not popular. That's because Washington makes the rules. Like a scolding parent, DC tells you what kind of stepladder you can use, what kind of bug killer you can use, what kind of drugs you can consume. Americans have never taken to this kind of control. And for these services, you have to send DC a slice of your hard-earned income. If you don't do it, you go to jail. But like a teenager who smashes up the family car, you go running back to Daddy for help. Whenever there is a calamity, Washington is the first place people go. It was the first place New York went to after 9/11.[28]

The comparison with New York is a telling factor in defining Washington, including its role in the information age. Trashing the nation's capital is a blood sport for New Yorkers, who see their city as the intellectual and business capital of the nation as against Washington's world-capital claims. For *New York Times* cultural critic Frank Rich, Manhattan is "the real national seat — and Washington is an island off the coast of America. After dark, it's more like Paducah than Paris." Donald Trump, the real-estate tycoon, adds: "New York has all the money, and money decides who goes to Washington. Washington is just a place people happen to be. It's New York that gets them there."

The late senator from New York, Daniel Patrick Moynihan, who had a foot in both camps, added a moderating tone in the debate when he declared: "In the past half-century, the power of New York has declined almost in proportion to the imperious, if not imperial, ascent of Washington.... New York is still a great city but, inexorably, Washington becomes a greater one."[29] Arthur Cotton Moore, quoted above, adds to the defense of the nation's capital by noting its cultural riches, including the Library of Congress, "which makes the New York Public Library look like books-on-wheels."[30]

The debate goes on. Meanwhile the city's evolution as an information-age hub continues. An important part of this change is the impact of new demographic forces — race, gender, economics, religion, and geography — at work in Washington and its surrounding region. This shift is taking place at a faster pace than at any time in the past two centuries. Among the varied reasons for the change, high on the list is the region's expanding IT-based economy. Along with a slow, steady shift away from dependence on the federal establishment has come a new pattern of emerging private-sector enterprises, located mainly in the surrounding suburbs and heavily weighted towards digital activities.

The vital center of this change is the new prominence of what Toronto University's Richard Florida calls the Creative Class — talented, young, digitally oriented professionals who have moved into the region in increasing numbers in the past twenty years.[31] Professor Florida's research builds in part on the theories propounded in economist Michael Porter's seminal 1990 work, *The Competitive Advantage of Nations*. Porter popularized the cluster-based theory of economic growth, suggesting that innovation is derived from specialization and dense networks of motivated, highly educated professional workers. These "agglomeration economies" have strong comparative advantages when they cluster in a limited geographic space. In modern America, the prime example of this in recent decades has been California's Silicon Valley. Professor Florida has focused his cluster-based research heavily in the Washington region and specifically on the local Creative Class. Overall, he ranks Washington first among large U.S. metropolitan areas in this group's impact in strengthening the local economy in recent years. Beyond the Creative Class's professional talents he adds another factor — the group's easy acceptance of ethnic and lifestyle differences.[32]

The region's current infusion of bright young professionals brings new stability to a city long known for its transient character. Speaking about Washington, Richard Nixon once complained that everybody there is from someplace else. This was certainly true in the first three-quarters of the city's history, with its shifting population, most of it involved in doing business with the government and then going back to where they came from.

More recently, Washington demographic trends involve newcomers who are staying put. The white-black divide that has dominated the region's demographics for over two hundred years is still a disturbing reality, but it is being modified by new arrivals, including the young careerists described above. Washington and its suburbs have a higher share of residents with graduate degrees that any other large American region. The city's black and Latino residents, although less likely than whites to have a college degree, are also educationally well ahead of minorities nationwide.[33] As a result, Washington now ranks in the top tier of the nation's "brain-gain" cities.

To a considerable degree, the new careerists are a transient lot. "They are fickle movers," says demographer William Frey. "They are bright young people who have a lot of options and a lot of opportunities." Many of them move on after testing career prospects in the city and surrounding suburbs. Despite occasional dips, job growth in the private sector has been steady since 2000. At mid-decade, the region's households had the second-highest income and least poverty of any of the nation's major metropolitan areas. Virginia's Loudoun County emerged as the country's wealthiest jurisdiction, with a median household income of $98,000. Next in line was Fairfax County, with Maryland's Howard and Montgomery counties not far behind.[34]

As noted, the new Creative Class tends to be footloose, moving on to other cities as job opportunities and other factors dictate. But this pattern has been changing in information-age Washington. Today more and more of the Creatives are moving in and staying put. Traditionally, those who stayed opted for marriage, kids, and a house in the suburbs. The newer trend is to settle in the city. The District of Columbia government has encouraged this trend with a campaign promoting "City Living — DC Style." The resulting steady increase in the number of younger residents has helped reverse a thirty-year trend in which the District annually lost population.

Another result is that the city is taking on the trappings of a hip community. The ultimate acknowledgment of this change may be found in a 2004 *Men's Health* survey of American lifestyles. The magazine proclaimed Washington the sexiest city in the nation, based in part on its having a high percentage of college-educated single women.[35] Such an accolade (if that is what it is) would have been unthinkable a few years earlier.

Another factor in the region's gentrification has been the professional opportunities newly opened to women. The era of "government girls" recruited by the Civil Service Commission at high schools across the nation to work as clerks and secretaries is over. Political scientist Julie Dolan of Macalester College has documented the stepped-up role of women as Washington careerists in her analysis of the gender makeup of the Senior Executive Service, the government's top managers. A generation ago, Dolan points out, women were a distinct minority among senior executives. By the beginning of the twenty-first century, women represented over a quarter of the pool, a ratio that is expanding steadily.[36] The trend has extended into the lower ranks of the civil service. By 2008, women accounted for almost half of the professional federal work force.

Chapter 6 takes a closer look at the town's young new careerists, who form a critical part of a complex pattern in a city moving away from its buttoned-down past to more swift-paced and open-ended lifestyles. High on the list of reasons for this new presence of young careerists is the city's emergence as the hub of an information-age region.

The other significant demographic reality influencing Washington's digital-age role is a new generation of immigrants, largely from Asia and Latin America. From small neighborhood enclaves a generation ago, their presence has spread rapidly. According to a report by the Center for Immigration Studies, the Washington-Baltimore region had nearly 1.3 million recent immigrants in 2004, a figure that had increased by almost 380,000 in the first four years of the new century. By mid-decade, one in five persons in the metropolitan Washington region was an immigrant, compared with one in six at the turn of the century. Overall, Hispanics are leading the trend: their numbers will triple by 2050, representing nearly 30 percent of the population, according to projections made by the Washington-based Pew Hispanic Center in a 2008 survey.[37]

Moreover, the region's newcomers intend to stay there. Almost half of foreign-born families in the area own their own homes. They are also setting up new businesses. Ying Lowrey, a Small Business Administration economist, points out that minority-owned firms are the fastest-growing segment of both the national and local economies. Asians currently account for the largest number of businesses and employees, but Hispanics are starting up firms at a faster rate, according to Lowrey. In the Washington area, Hispanic-owned firms increased by two-thirds in recent decades to over 32,000 establishments.[38]

Meanwhile, Washington has joined six other major metropolitan areas — New York, Los Angeles, Miami, Chicago, San Francisco, and Dallas — with immigrant populations of a million or more. "This is a significant benchmark," demographer Audrey Singer points out. "It clearly demonstrates that Washington has emerged as an immigrant destination."

The pace of racial and ethnic change in the region has stepped up dramatically in recent years. Five of six new residents in the Washington area since 2000 have been people of color, according to a 2006 report by the U.S. Census Bureau. The region added nearly a half-million residents in the first five years of the decade, an 8 percent increase in total population, with racial minorities growing at a much swifter pace. In recent years, the number of Hispanics in the region increased by 34 percent, Asians by 27 percent. In one outer suburb, Prince William County, the Hispanic population doubled, while in adjoining Loudoun County the Asian population quadrupled.[39]

The new arrivals and their children may grow to a quarter of the region's population within the next generation, according to other urban specialists. Further down the road, they are on track to becoming the dominant element in the area's population mix. By some estimates, almost half of all babies born in the region now are Latino — a statistic with major demographic implications for Washington's future, including its status as a digital-age center. The region is among the major U.S. metropolitan areas that now have a "majority minority" child population: fewer than half of under-15-year-olds are white. Demographer William Frey predicts that the Washington region's overall population will have a majority made up of minorities after 2010. It will then join thirty-five of the country's fifty largest cities in which the non–Hispanic white population will be in the minority, according to demographic experts.[40]

These projections are skewed by the unreliability of census estimates on the newcomers, particularly those involving Latinos. The Mexican embassy sets the size of the Mexican community in the region at a quarter-million, more than twice the official census count. Census estimates put the number of Salvadorans living in the area at about 125,000. The Salvadoran embassy in Washington suggests that a half-million is more realistic, part of that nation's diaspora that adds up to one-fourth of El Salvador's total population.[41] The need to service the passport and other needs of the local Salvadoran community has forced the embassy to take the unusual step of opening a satellite office in nearby Woodbridge, Virginia, with its heavy concentration of newly arrived families. Overall, the gaps in estimates of immigrant numbers in Washington and other American cities are accounted in part by the Census Bureau's definition of the immigrant population as persons born outside the United States. This ignores the rapid growth in the number of Latino children born locally, as noted above. Each of them is legally a U.S. citizen at birth.[42]

Overall, minority groups are affecting the pace and look of the entire region. Commenting on this change, Jonathan Rauch, an *Atlantic Monthly* editor, notes:

> Washington, for so long a lagging indicator of American social life — far behind edgy New York and buzzy Los Angeles and brazen Chicago and even upstart Atlanta and Houston — is now, of all things, a harbinger. Increasingly, the Washington area is the post-racial America that we have all been told to expect. A member of Congress who wonders what a genuinely multicultural country might look like need only rustle up taxi fare to Arlington and walk around. My immediate neighbors include a black-white couple, a Filipino psychiatrist, a Korean accountant, and two Indian families, whose kids' names I can't pronounce. I have never lived in a more neighborly neighborhood. If this is the future, it seems to work.[43]

The newcomers differ dramatically from the legendary huddled masses that crowded through Ellis Island a century ago. They now arrive in small groups or families, by car, bus, or plane. Once here they tend not to settle in large ghetto districts, as past immigrants did. A 2001 survey by the Brookings Institution's urban studies unit found that the new arrivals were spread more or less evenly across ten metropolitan Washington zip-code districts. Meanwhile, the region is moving closer to the day when it joins Miami, Los Angeles, and other metropolitan areas where minority communities collectively constitute the majority of residents.[44] This prospect adds an intriguing cultural aspect to Washington's evolution as an information-age center.[45]

The area's immigrant mix is diverse, representing nearly two hundred countries. As noted above, Latino migrants dominate. However, all global cultures are represented, with a heavy concentration of Indians, Koreans, Ethiopians, and Filipinos. The Indians, both immigrants and long-time residents, are a strong presence in the local information-technology sector. Another important group are Iranians, including many who fled to this country after the 1979 revolution at home. They form part of the region's growing Muslim community, which has spawned its own technology outposts and a string of Halal food stores. More troubling is the number of illegal immigrants crowding into the area, which increased almost 70 percent, from 300,000 to almost half a million in the early years of the new century.

Another distinction points up the difference between the new wave of immigrants and earlier ones. Although many recent arrivals were at or near the poverty level when they came, they were in a hurry to move on economically. The Center for Immigration Studies notes that immigrants accounted for 15 percent of working people in the region in 2000. Three years later, the figure was 20 percent. Increasingly they are taking their place in the region's booming information-technology sector, moving beyond their original reliance on work in the construction, hospitality, and other low-income industries.

The Brookings studies cited above also note that the Washington region has the lowest immigrant poverty rate of the ten U.S. metropolitan regions with the largest foreign-born populations. In part this reflects the higher educational level of the new arrivals. The 2000 census found that 21 percent of the region's Hispanic population, both old settlers and new arrivals, had a college degree. Among Asians, the figure is an impressive 54 percent. (The U.S. average is 24 percent.) The census report also noted that in affluent Montgomery County immigrants have a higher percentage of advanced degrees than the native population. This trend is particularly striking in Loudoun County, a magnet for IT firms, where over half of recent immigrants hold college or advanced degrees. Overall, this makes these newcomers a welcome addition to the region's information-age enterprises.

In summary, Washington and its suburban ring are in fast-paced transition, with a mix of new hopes and old problems. An expanding information-based economy is transforming the city beyond its traditional dependence on the federal establishment. "It is one of the few central cities in the United States that is economically necessary," says Edward Hill, a researcher at Cleveland State University's Levin College of Urban Affairs. "In Youngstown, Ohio, the economy could move to the exit ramps. Who cares? In DC, New York, possibly Chicago, it's in the national interest to keep it alive."[46]

Notwithstanding this justifiable optimism, the region has its problems, including an economic and social disconnect between the booming suburbs and the central city. As we shall see in chapter 5, there are many hopeful indicators of progress within the District of Columbia, including a spectacular downtown building boom and the new infusion of bright young professionals. Nevertheless, the city has to deal with stubborn facts, including long-standing racial divisions. New factors in play help moderate these problems: the region's immigrants and younger career settlers have reduced the ratio of African Americans in the District of Columbia to under 60 percent, the lowest in many decades. Meanwhile, more blacks live in better economic circumstances in the city and its surrounding suburbs than ever before.

Old divisions are easing in the District, largely as a result of the civil-rights gains of the past half-century. Nevertheless, disparities remain. The Fiscal Policy Institute has estimated that, in recent years, the income of the top fifth of the city's households was thirty-one times higher than that earned on average by the lowest fifth. Unemployment in the city at mid-decade was double that of the surrounding suburbs. Job prospects for many blacks are still low, with unemployment at 25 percent in some neighborhoods. In recent years, the city has had the country's highest incidence of AIDS, ten times the national average. Washington's unwanted reputation as a "murder capital" is only slowly being modified. District of Columbia police dealt with 194 slayings in 2005; it was the first time since the 1980s that the city recorded fewer than 200 homicides in consecutive years. Morgan Quitno, a Kansas City consultancy that issues an annual urban-crime survey, continues to list Washington among the most crime-ridden cities in the country.

Beyond these stubborn realities, other trends point to a hopeful future for the city and its surrounding region. To put this prospect into perspective, it is useful to recall the events that led up to Washington's emergence as an information-age center. The story begins with a deal cut in the backroom of a Georgetown tavern over two centuries ago. The dealmakers, all veterans of the recent revolutionary war, debated the details of where the capital city should be and how it should look. Despite many disagreements, they were united on what to call the new town. It would be named after one of the tavern's backroom conspirators: George Washington.

2

In the Beginning

Washington's origins as an information-age center trace back two centuries. The city was the creation of an extraordinary group of men in wigs and satin knickers who gathered in Philadelphia to negotiate the constitutional ground rules for a new country. In the process, they defined the ideological premises for today's information age and, by extension, Washington's role in it.

A distinctly American idea drove their decisions: to create a new Eden through the melding of nature and technology. This machine-in-the-garden was a persistent vision from the beginnings of the nation.[1] At once utopian and pragmatic, millennial and immediate, it saw society as progressing towards an earthly ideal, rather than as a static set of unchangeable conditions. Benjamin Franklin personified this vision when, kite in hand, he took that famous first step toward an electrically powered society. Thomas Jefferson, following the convention's proceedings from his diplomatic post in Paris, regarded America as sufficiently removed from the evils of European society to be the model for fusing libertarian values with technology-based prosperity. Both men actively promoted constitutional protections for information freedoms. A half-century later, Ralph Waldo Emerson, the quintessential national philosopher, wrote: "Machinery and transcendentalism agree.... Our civilization and these ideas are reducing earth to a brain.... See how by the telegraph and steam the earth is anthropoligized."

This theme has been given further expression in modern times in the writings of, among others, Marshall McLuhan, a Canadian scholar who proposed, in his folksy image, a global village transformed by digital technology. In a metaphysical flight, McLuhan once declared that the computer promises by technology a Pentecostal condition of universal understanding and unity. This is the rhetoric of the technological sublime, in sociologist Leo Marx's phrase, and it runs like a golden thread through the American experience. It remains a powerful force today, the secular theology of the information age. The talented men meeting in Philadelphia to debate a constitution had little inkling of these outcomes. Nevertheless, they approved a national charter that set the standards for an open information society, the first time that this had ever happened.

The constitution makers took several practical steps to promote information freedoms. One of their first decisions was to include a provision for a post office system in the new government. Thirty years later, Alexis de Tocqueville, traveling along the frontier in his survey of the new American republic, was struck by the high political literacy among farmers and others far removed from the big East Coast cities. The reason, he discovered, was the availability of newspapers delivered by the national postal system.

Another of the constitution's innovations favoring information freedoms was the provision for a patent office. Its premise was simple: if you have a useful new idea, particularly a technical one, and you could demonstrate that it was unique, you could register it with the government and potentially benefit from it. For a period of time, no one else could claim it or, equally important, prevent you from making money on it. It was a stunningly simple concept, which was expanded to nontechnical property, including books and other written materials and, in modern times, electronic information.

The other decision at Philadelphia that laid a foundation for today's information age was an afterthought. It was the first of ten amendments tacked on to the constitution after the delegates had completed the basic document. It proposed the then-startling idea that, among other rights, the public expression of ideas should be protected from government interference. The First Amendment focused on speech and on print publications — the only mass medium available at the time — but it defined a right that has since been extended to every information technology. In the process, it established the ideological basis for the American information age.

The constitutional convention also mandated the general location of the new nation's capital. That decision involved a lobbying effort as energetic as any conducted by the best of today's cell phone–toting Washington lobbyists. The stakes were high, and the outcome defined the site of the new city as well as its political, economic, cultural, and demographic dimensions. Each in its way contributed to today's digital environment.

The site-selection story is a tale of two taverns. Negotiations began in the back room of Fraunces Tavern at the eastern edge of Wall Street in

New York City and concluded two years later at Suter's Tavern in Georgetown, on the western edge of the new capital site. The decision about the city's location was part of a package deal that involved Alexander Hamilton's bold proposal that the government assume the debts of the thirteen former colonies in order to establish the new nation's fiscal credibility.

In debating the site for the new national capital, the New York negotiators considered a number of possibilities. Philadelphia, the largest and richest city in the country, was a leading contender but it was also a Quaker stronghold with attitudes on slavery that were anathema to the convention's Southern delegates. New York was another contender, but it was suspect, then as now, because of its general brassiness, including its easy acceptance of British occupation during the recent revolution. After considering other sites, the negotiators accepted the fact that the new capital had to be located somewhere along the political fault line that separated the commercially minded Northern states from the slave-owning South. It was, as historian Carl Abbott has noted, a compromise based on the need to moderate the tug-of-war between the economic influence of the North and the cultural staying power of the South. The eventual result was the selection of the unpromising tract of land south of Baltimore that was ambiguously neither Southern nor Northern.

The details of these New York negotiations were later refined at Suter's Tavern, 230 miles to the south in the Potomac river port of Georgetown. The village's commercial activities were no competition for the down-river city of Alexandria, the third largest seaport in the colonies. Georgetown was a thriving town nevertheless, robust enough to support fifteen taverns, including Suter's, located near the present-day junction of Wisconsin Avenue and M Street.

Suter's was a drinking place, a hotel, and a social center. George Washington slept there, as did Thomas Jefferson, the Marquis de Lafayette, and other worthies. As a stagecoach terminal, it included a branch office of Benjamin Franklin's postal network. Tavern patrons and other Georgetowners made use of its small lending library. Suter's was also the site of a slave market, a Masonic meeting place, and temporary quarters for circuit-riding doctors and dentists. It had a theater of sorts where shows were mounted, including *The Beggar's Opera* by John Gay, the best-known British dramatist of the day.

Suter's played a unique role in planning the new city in the swampy plain south and east of Georgetown. When Pierre L'Enfant, a Frenchman and revolutionary patriot, was chosen as the town's planner, he set up his office in Suter's. It is not difficult to imagine Washington and other members of the planning committee poring over L'Enfant's charts in the tavern's back rooms. What they saw was a grid pattern of diagonal avenues and circles, reflecting the Frenchman's Cartesian turn of mind, together with landscaped squares and plazas, and a monumental central mall, along with meandering wooded parks. Two centuries later, the plan remains one of the world's great urban designs, flexible enough to still be a work in progress and a model for present-day planners. It provided, among other attributes, a worthy setting for the city's current emergence as an information-age center.

Disputes arose about the city plan. Thomas Jefferson, a self-taught architect, crossed swords with L'Enfant, resulting in the Frenchman's withdrawal from the project before its completion. Whether or not he left of his own accord is unclear, but the historical record shows that he had confidence in his design. He told George Washington that it was "drawn on such a scale as to leave room for that aggrandizement and embellishment which the increase of the wealth of the nation will permit it to pursue at any period, however remote."[2] Despite this grand goal, implementing the town plan proceeded slowly. In 1791 when the final details were approved, there was no immediate rush to realize L'Enfant's vision, including the Grand Avenue — today's Pennsylvania Avenue — linking the "Congressional house" and the "Presidential Palace." L'Enfant saw one of the city's prominent hills as a pedestal waiting for a monumental building where the Congress would meet, a vision that took over a half-century to realize.

There was no rush to populate the new town. Many of its founders and their followers preferred the cosmopolitan delights of Philadelphia, New York, and Boston to the spare amenities of a swampy village. President George Washington, writing from the temporary capital in Philadelphia in 1796, directed one of the city commissioners to remove himself from the high life in Georgetown and settle in the new city. "I have always thought," he wrote, "that buildings between the Capitol and the President's house ought to be encouraged as much as possible — and that nothing would have a greater tendency towards accomplishing this than the Commissioners making that part of the City their residence and compelling all those who are under their control to do the same.... Measures of this sort would form societies in the City — give it éclat."

Despite these efforts, Washington in its early decades was a town of transients lodged in boardinghouses, some of them owned by George

Washington himself. He never lived in the city: his term of office was over before the White House was ready for occupancy. He died in 1799, a year before his successor, John Adams, rode into town to take up residence in the "President's House."

Meanwhile, the new government took its first steps towards implementing the Constitution's commitment to an open information society. A patent office and a post office department were created. The Library of Congress, that unique political expression of information freedoms, was created, based on an initial purchase of 1,600 books from Thomas Jefferson's personal library. Equally significant was the political battle over the 1798 Alien and Sedition Acts, an attempt by the incumbent Federalists to punish their opponents with fines and a two-year jail sentence for speaking or writing against the government, Congress, or the President. This led to the prosecution of a group of journalists that included Benjamin Franklin's grandson. This early threat to First Amendment freedoms ended with the inauguration of Thomas Jefferson in 1801. Jefferson pardoned the convicted journalists and persuaded Congress to refund their fines.

The new District of Columbia was a rootless town, a transient place, in its early decades. Its pace was set largely by its location, sandwiched between two states that were Southern in attitudes and practices. Slavery was never officially condoned in the new federal city, although racial segregation was a daily reality within its borders. The town's white citizens were also politically constrained, although less harshly. Their right to vote for a member of Congress (albeit one from Maryland) was revoked within a decade after the city was founded.

L'Enfant's plan included a district for manufacturing plants, but the project was soon forgotten. The city's main business from the start was the federal government, whose chief activity was the production, storage, and distribution of information. For a long time, the new bureaucracy was a very small enterprise; during the Andrew Jackson administration in the 1830s, the three branches of government had a total of 665 employees.[3] The available information technology, beyond quill pens and paper, consisted of flat-bed presses, which differed little from the fifteenth-century Gutenberg machines until the introduction of steam-driven presses in the 1820s.

The center of gravity for information production in the new republic was in the Northern cities — New York, Boston, and Philadelphia — with their lively newspaper, book, and magazine enterprises. Washington was, by comparison, a provincial backwater. "Few people would live in

Washington, I take it, who were not obliged to reside there," Charles Dickens grumbled after a visit to the capital in the early 1840s. He complained about almost everything he saw, from the lack of fine buildings to the behavior of the natives. What struck him most during a visit to Congress was the failure of the legislators to take proper aim at their spittoons.

Washington's prospects as a grand capital city emerged slowly. The pace picked up in the middle decades of the nineteenth century, in part as the result of a series of technological breakthroughs that hastened the city's evolution as an information center. The first of these innovations was Samuel F. B. Morse's "electro-magnetic telegraph" in the 1840s. Morse was a portrait artist and political activist in the anti–Catholic Know Nothing party. He is remembered today, however, for the telegraph, a concept that other men had tinkered with for decades but one that he turned into a technical and commercial success.

The city of Washington played a central role in fostering the new invention. Morse lived there for a while, and his early experiments were carried out on a one-wire line that ran from the federal city to Baltimore. Morse was adept at lobbying for government support of his project, deploying a vision that foreshadowed the Internet and other information-age technologies. "It will not be long," he told a congressional committee examining his telegraph proposal, "ere the whole surface of this country will be channeled for those nerves to diffuse with the speed of thought, a knowledge of all that is occurring throughout the land, making, in fact, one neighborhood of the country."[4]

If members of Congress were skeptical about these blue-sky promises, it did not stop them from appropriating $30,000 for the Washington-Baltimore experiment. In 1844, Morse tapped out his famous first message: "What hath God wrought?" Whatever his personal ideas about the role of the deity in the project, it was a good question, worthy of any modern-day Washington lobbyist seeking federal funds. The reverential tone helped persuade Congress to appropriate another $4,000 to keep the experiment going. From its original Washington-Baltimore axis, the telegraph network expanded with astonishing speed. New York, Boston, and Buffalo were soon linked to the original line. Significantly, most of the networks were located in the Northeast. When civil war broke out a decade later, this was a critical factor in giving the Union forces a strategic advantage over the Confederacy. Western Union, the largest of the new telegraph companies, profited handsomely from its largely northern operations, which included 44,000 miles of wire networks by the end of the war.[5]

Beyond its military significance, the Morse telegraph forced the federal government to face up to the political implications of electrically powered information technology, notably the telegraph's role in the nation's westward expansion. A transcontinental line to California was authorized in the Pacific Telegraph Act, passed by Congress in 1860, which provided an annual subsidy of $40,000 for its construction. At the same time, the California state legislature voted a $100,000 subsidy to the state's local telegraph company to link up with the transcontinental line.

Not the least of the issues raised by the new network was its ownership. As telegraphy expanded across the world, particularly in Europe, it was quickly turned into a government monopoly, usually as an extension of the national postal system. In the United States, this pattern took a different turn: the telegraph (and, by extension, all electronic communications systems since) was developed and operated as a private enterprise.

By 1851, seven years after the Washington-Baltimore line was set up, fifty separate private telegraph companies operated along the Eastern seaboard. Most of these were absorbed in an epic corporate battle for monopoly control of the entire network involving two companies — Western Union and American Telegraph. Western Union won, largely through its superior lobbying efforts in Washington, which included giving free access to its network to congressmen friendly to its cause. By 1866, Western Union had bought out or otherwise dominated its rivals, establishing itself as an entrenched monopoly throughout the country.

The completion of the national system raised another issue for the federal government. It involved the First Amendment guarantee of the right of free speech and, by extension, the legal basis for open access to the new electrical networks. The immediate issue was a secret trust agreement between Western Union and the Associated Press, the newsgathering cartel of the country's leading newspapers. The agreement forbade the AP's members from receiving telegraphic news reports from any source other than Western Union, making it impossible for any would-be competitor to enjoy similar economies of scale and scope. This exclusion provoked calls for federal regulation; but the issue was settled at a lower level in a Supreme Court of Illinois 1900 decision, which invoked the First Amendment in declaring the agreement null and void. The ruling was crucial in defining the right of free information flow through the new electrical grids, a decision that resonates in today's environment of the Internet and other public networks.[6]

The next breakthrough involved the Bell telephone. Although he invented (or, more correctly, stumbled upon) the device in a Boston loft, Alexander Graham Bell had strong connections with the federal city. He lived and worked in Washington on and off from 1879 until his death in 1922, lobbying for his new invention and conducting research related to his lifetime interest in electrical devices to help the deaf.[7] His newfangled telephone changed the ways in which the federal government, private firms, and ordinary citizens went about their business.

The telegraph, the telephone, typewriters, carbon paper, cash registers, phonographs, and wireless radio — all the early artifacts of today's information society — formed part of what communications scholar James Beniger has called the "control revolution." Beniger was characterizing the American effort from the nineteenth century on to apply electrical technologies to the task of producing, storing, and distributing information. The effort prefigured the introduction of the culminating technology: computers.[8]

Computerization, the hallmark of the new age, has strong roots in Washington's past. One of its early applications was the brainchild of a young engineer, Herman Hollerith, who had a chance encounter in 1881 with John Shaw Billings, chief of the Census Bureau's vital statistics section. Billings thought there had to be a better way for the bureau to record statistics than by manual hand counting. Hollerith was intrigued by the challenge. Three years later he patented a tabulating machine that relied on encoded holes punched into cardboard cards. Metal pins in the machine sensed the holes and kept a corresponding count. Hollerith later claimed that the idea came to him while observing a railroad conductor punch tickets.[9]

Hollerith's machine was a primitive computer, first used to tabulate statistics about the 63 million Americans counted in the 1890 census. His data-processing experiment was a critical step towards the digitization of U.S. society. Hollerith left the government soon after and set up his own firm, the Tabulating Machine Co., in Georgetown. He later retired, leaving the details of the company's operation to a young manager he had hired to run the tabulating-machine division. The manager, Thomas Watson, made a number of changes in the operation, including a decision to rename the firm in 1924. The new name was the International Business Machines Corp., better known today as IBM.

The Hollerith punch-card machines were part of the new wave of American industrial expansion based on electrical resources in the last decades of the nineteenth century. Predictions of onward-and-upward prosperity were laced with the rhetoric of the electronic sublime. Popular fiction writers like Jules Verne and Edward Bellamy reinforced the idea; naysayers like Mark Twain and Henry Adams were outnumbered. New technologies poured out of the research labs, many of them financed by big corporations. AT&T's Bell Laboratories in New Jersey proved a major source of technical breakthroughs, producing a series of innovations that set standards for today's information age. Despite occasional economic setbacks, this feel-good era, based increasingly on new technological innovations, extended well into the twentieth century, until it came to a screeching halt in the Great Depression of the 1930s.

The halt was temporary, thanks in large part to Franklin Roosevelt's New Deal initiatives and activism, which included national policies and programs promoting electric-powered technologies. The dams built by the Tennessee Valley Authority and the wiring of remote farmhouses by the Rural Electrification Administration, among other programs, represented a new phase of government involvement in technology, establishing critical precedents for today's digital environment.

To get a perspective on the roots of Washington's information age, it is useful to look back to that era's early research experiments in what were then known as "thinking machines," the ancestors of today's computers. The story is largely a tale of two cities, Washington and Cambridge, Massachusetts, as partners in the science and politics that created an agenda for a new age. In Cambridge, a small group of academics led the way. Their names — Norbert Wiener, Claude Shannon, Vannevar Bush, among others — cause few nods of recognition today, even among reasonably informed people. But it would be difficult to exaggerate their impact on shaping postindustrial America and, by extension, the rest of the world. Working in the esoteric academic area known as information theory, they understood the need to define information and its characteristics more accurately. Their pursuit of this goal in Cambridge laboratories and faculty-club discussions left an indelible mark on American society and Washington in particular.

A powerful force among the Cambridge academics was Norbert Wiener, an MIT mathematics professor and authentic genius who had earned his Harvard PhD at the age of nineteen. His contribution was to explore the concept of self-regulating mechanisms akin to the human brain's feedback capabilities. Meanwhile, in another MIT department, a young graduate student, Claude Shannon, examined the practical applications of Wiener's approach by studying the design of electrical circuits.

After graduation, working at AT&T's Bell Laboratories in New Jersey, Shannon and a fellow researcher, Warren Weaver, drafted a report, published in 1948, that described a general communications system based on the electronic transmission of binary digits.[10]

These "bits," made up of symbolic ones and zeroes, represented the lowest common denominators of information, each a unit resolving uncertainty or doubt between two exclusive alternatives, such as yes or no, on or off, up or down. Meanwhile, at Princeton University, mathematician John von Neumann added a vital theoretical element to their concept with his idea of a machine that could control its calculating sequences by modifying its own instructions. This concept moved computing technology beyond simple storage and calculating devices to digital stored-program machines, dramatically expanding their capabilities as intelligence extenders.

These academic probings needed a dramatic application to take them out of the realm of theory. The 1941 attack on Pearl Harbor and the resulting need to mobilize American scientific resources for wartime purposes had provided the catalyst that quickly engaged the federal government in the development of a broad range of new technologies. A key player in this transition from academia to government was Vannevar Bush, a flinty New Englander, who was an MIT professor of electrical engineering familiar with the idea of computers. Bush had designed a primitive computer in the late thirties at the MIT labs. It was an ungainly mechanical monster that filled a large room and required days of adjustments to program a simple experiment.[11]

As the threat of American involvement in the European war loomed, President Roosevelt had persuaded Bush to take on the job of coordinating national scientific research to support the defense effort. At the time, the United States seriously lagged behind Germany in developing technical and production capabilities for weapons and other wartime needs. Bush became head of a new White House Office of Scientific Research and Development (OSRD), which became the command center for an unprecedented effort to promote advanced technical projects. It was the beginning of the federal government's involvement in supporting Big Science. Vannevar Bush worked to establish the subject as a major public-policy issue and to lobby for the bureaucratic changes needed to deal with it.

Bush's ideas on Big Science resonate six decades later. Instead of relying solely on a massive network of government research facilities, he focused on private academic and industry resources to develop critically needed technologies. Through this approach, two-thirds of the nation's physicists were soon working on wartime OSRD projects, including the technical upgrading of radar systems pioneered by the British. Bush was also a key White House adviser in the decision to build an atomic bomb.

A lesser-known Bush project, ENIAC, was the government's initial involvement in computer technology. An Army-sponsored project built at the University of Pennsylvania, ENIAC'S task was to measure the trajectory of artillery shells. The ENIAC machine weighed thirty tons, filled a large hall, and was powered by seventeen thousand radio tubes, requiring round-the-clock replacement maintenance. Despite its bulky operations, ENIAC worked and went into the record books as the world's first operating computer. As science writer Michael Shrage notes about Vannevar Bush's role in the project: "The same man responsible for launching the Atomic Age helped define the insights and vocabulary of the Information Age as well."[12]

With the war's end in 1945, Bush turned his attention to what he regarded as the next great challenge for Big Science — the management of information based on emerging advanced technologies. It was the first organized attempt to lay out a political strategy for the digital age. At President Harry Truman's request, Bush drafted a paper, "Science — The Endless Frontier," in which he laid out a blueprint for a federal initiative to promote Big Science as public policy, including the reorganization of the bureaucracy to implement it.[13] The initial result was the creation of the National Science Foundation to guide the effort. The report's recommendations were approved, and Bush returned to Cambridge to finish out his career as president of MIT.

The following decade saw the creation of a network of digitally based research facilities, including the Defense Department's Advanced Research Projects Agency (ARPA) that carried out the first experiments in what later became the Internet. This focus on new technologies had other impacts on the way Washington did business. As one observer noted at the time, scientists began roaming the corridors of bureaucratic power, accorded a deference and respect similar to that enjoyed by Jesuits in the royal courts of Europe centuries before. Meanwhile, the prospects of bigger government budget outlays for information goods and services encouraged business firms to set up operations in the Washington area. They were the forerunners of the thousands of companies who have since made the region a digital-age center.

The adaptation of wartime Big Science policies to peacetime pursuits took a new turn in the late 1940s with the emergence of the Cold War. Science again went to war, this time to assure U.S. superiority over a massive Soviet attempt to catch up with American technical advances. The ability of Soviet scientists to create a nuclear bomb in the late forties, years earlier than expected, came as a shock. The launching of Sputnik, the first orbiting space satellite, followed a decade later. These politically traumatic events triggered a strong American response, including stepping up government efforts to outmatch Soviet technical advances, a strategy that resulted in increasingly bigger budgets for advanced technologies. Such Cold War competition dramatically advanced Washington's transformation as an information-age center.

Technological breakthroughs made during World War II attracted private industry as it retooled for postwar consumer markets, though the changeover often proceeded cautiously. In the early 1950s, IBM estimated that the market for its new computers would absorb about fifty machines worldwide, a miscalculation it later ruefully admitted in a 1980 advertisement in the *New York Times*.[14] Despite these early doubts, change was in the air, stimulated by advances in information technology, most of them developed by private-sector research groups, often with government subsidies. AT&T's Bell Laboratories achieved the first breakthroughs in transistor technology, dramatically upgrading the capabilities of electronic devices. This was followed by a leap forward in semiconductor-chip research by engineers at Texas Instruments and other firms. In California, the Rand Corporation, a think tank funded by the Defense Department, took the lead in developing packet-switching technology, the technical foundation for today's Internet.

Other research breakthroughs changed the ways Americans did business in the early postwar decades. Three such innovations were the telephone-answering machine, the Xerox plain-paper copier, and digitally based messaging. Collectively, they transformed the nation's office culture in and out of government. Among other distinctions, they resulted in the near-extinction of the traditional boss's secretary. In the new digital order, most bosses answer their own phones and type out their own e-mail messages.

The political and economic implications of these technologies drew the attention of a new breed of information-age academic observers. Harvard political scientist Karl Deutsch posited, in his masterful 1963 book *The Nerves of Government*, that information is power. Moreover, he added, it is a multiplier of political power, more important than control by traditional forces such as the police or the military. He argued for a reorganization of government to deal with this reality, using computers and other information technologies that would allow greater sharing of the resources needed for American society to thrive in a new digital environment.[15]

Another Harvard professor, sociologist Daniel Bell, created a stir with his 1973 book *The Coming of Post-Industrial Society*, which predicted a major shift in the economy from goods production to information-based services. In his view, technology-oriented professionals would replace industrial entrepreneurs as the preeminent business class.[16] A young Stanford graduate, Marc Uri Porat, who had written his doctoral dissertation on the evolving information economy, gave Bell's theories statistical underpinning. Porat later expanded his thesis as editor of a nine-volume 1977 Department of Commerce survey of the subject.[17] His research indicated that, by the 1960s, information activities accounted for almost 50 percent of gross national production and employment. He projected a continuing expansion of these activities in ways that would make the production of information goods and services the country's major economic sector. This outcome is now taken for granted, but in the 1970s many old-line economists regarded Porat's conclusions with suspicion.

These academic studies, among others, provided important backing for a new wave of public policies dealing with information-age realities. Slowly they had an impact on Washington across a range of interests, from White House decision-making to congressional legislation and the ways in which the government bureaucracy was organized. For the first time, federal budgets increasingly reflected a focus on information technology in ways that had ripple effects throughout the Washington region. The capital area was not ready to challenge California's Silicon Valley or Boston's Route 128, but pressures were building for a long-term shift in the region's economy. It was the beginning of a steady transition from almost total dependence on government operations to one that, in recent years, includes the expansion of private-sector opportunities in information goods and services.

Two technologies played a special role in this shift, one old and one new. The old technology was the telephone: the new one was the communications satellite. Between them, they hastened the emergence of the Washington region as a major information and communications hub in recent decades.

The idea of using space satellites to relay messages around the world was a theoretical prospect until 1962 when AT&T successfully launched

"Early Bird," an experimental satellite that transmitted voice messages between earth stations in Maine and England. Early Bird could only transmit a few hundred phone calls simultaneously or a single video transmission. These physical limits to high-speed, high-volume satellite services were soon breached, well beyond the then-current capabilities of wire-based networks. Within a few years, the new "comsats" were relaying tens of thousands of voice messages and dozens of video programs simultaneously. This achievement triggered a massive change in communications networking at home and abroad, requiring major political, economic and technical decisions. More than any other single factor, satellites and other new communications technologies advanced Big Science decision-making in the federal government.[18]

The result was to widen the Washington region's prospects as a major player in the information age. Shortly after the first successful Early Bird flight in 1962, the Kennedy administration made a decision to sponsor a global satellite network whose facilities would be available to all countries. The project took ten years to negotiate, resulting in the creation of Intelsat, an international consortium that eventually included 145 governments as its owners. The organization's headquarters were located in a modernistic office complex on upper Connecticut Avenue in Washington. To manage American participation in the network, Congress chartered a public corporation, the Communications Satellite Corporation ("Comsat"), which was also headquartered in the city.

The other technology to play an early role in Washington's digital-age transformation was the old-fashioned telephone. The United States was the first nation to achieve near-total telephone penetration. By the 1950s, half the world's phone communications originated or terminated in this country. This was largely the result of a government decision in 1934 to authorize a regulated monopoly of a national system operated by AT&T, the so-called Bell System, replacing dozens of smaller local systems. Given the technology of the time, it was a good decision. For the first time, universal telephone service was available to almost all Americans.

By the early 1960s, however, technical, economic and social patterns were shifting in ways that called for changes in the telephone system and, by extension, the entire national communications structure. As with the global satellite system, Washington was the center for the political and economic decision-making that brought this about. In the process, the conditions were created that led to the city's present role as an information-age center.

A key player in this transformation was a scrappy young entrepreneur who decided, against the conventional wisdom of the times, to challenge the Congressionally mandated AT&T national telephone monopoly. The challenger was a feisty Irishman from upstate New York, William McGowan. While working as a college student for the local railroad company, the Lackawanna, he was intrigued by the fact that the company, like other railroads, owned and operated its own telephone network, which it used to coordinate train operations. Why, McGowan asked himself, couldn't there be other telephone networks, independent of the AT&T monopoly?[19]

McGowan teamed up with a partner to petition the Federal Communications Commission, the overseer of government telephone policies, for permission to operate a competitive long-distance service between St. Louis and Chicago. Despite objections from AT&T lawyers, the proposal was approved. McGowan moved the new firm, MCI Communications, to downtown Washington in 1972. Within a few years, MCI had installed more than a million miles of fiber-optic cable across the country. The firm's success set the stage for the dissolution of the AT&T monopoly in 1982 as the result of a Justice Department legal decision.

McGowan was an original among early information-age entrepreneurs in the Washington region. His strategy of standing up to the AT&T giant was based in large part on aggressive marketing campaigns. One of his favorite aphorisms, repeated regularly to his staff, was: "The meek shall inherit the earth but they won't do anything for your bottom line." When employees entered the MCI building each day they were confronted with a display listing the firm's stock price from the previous day, and a notice that today's price would be up to them. "MCI served almost as the Harvard/Yale in terms of educating telecommunications executives," according to Washington attorney Andrew Lipman, whose law firm represented MCI in the early days. "It was really an incubator for dozens and dozens of other companies. If you look across the competitive telecom industry, you find many companies in the region that are populated at the executive level with MCI grads."

McGowan's success gave a special impetus to Washington's evolution as an information-age center. This included his decision to locate MCI's headquarters in the city, the last place that most telephone-company executives at the time would pick as a corporate base. It was a smart move for more reasons than the one recognized by his competitors: he wanted to be close to the Federal Communications Commission and other government agencies regulating his business. More important, McGowan had a feel for the town's growing importance as a digital-age center. His instinct was later shared by more than a dozen other telephone companies who moved their headquarters into the city and its suburbs in the seventies and eighties. Many of them have since been merged into or bought out by larger firms. MCI itself was acquired by a rival company for $30 billion. It was a bittersweet moment for a maverick firm that had begun operations two decades earlier with a single wire connection between St. Louis and Chicago.[20]

MCI and the other phone companies that set up shop in the Washington area accelerated the region's transition to digital-age prominence. Beginning in the 1980s, however, their economic influence began to be displaced by other corporate newcomers that focused on advanced information-technology goods and services. Nevertheless, the telecommunications sector is still an important part of Washington's digital infrastructure. Sprint Nextel Corp., headquartered in suburban Reston, became the area's largest company based on stock market valuation, following a $35 billion merger of the two telecom giants in 2005. AOL moved its corporate headquarters to New York in 2007, but its major operational activities remained in the Washington region.

Many of Washington's new IT enterprises had migrated from Silicon Valley and other West Coast centers. They were the professional descendants of an informal fraternity of young computer buffs who had pioneered California's high-tech digital industries in the 1960s. Bearded, sandaled, well educated and generally disdainful of careers that involved a conventional climb up the corporate ladder, their goal was to develop digital products and services for mass consumption.

The best known of these self-styled techies were Bill Gates and his colleagues in a new venture they named Microsoft. Another group, led by Steven Jobs and his partner Stephen Wozniak, produced the first personal computer, Apple. "We realized," said Jobs, "that we could build something ourselves that could control billions of dollars of infrastructure in the whole world.... We could build a little thing that could control a big thing."[21] Within a short time, their influence and their attitudes spread beyond the West Coast to eastern cities, including Washington. This early influx of young IT entrepreneurs added a new dimension to the region's resources. In part, the area's attraction for them was its new economic promise as a communications center, thanks to Bill McGowan's MCI and other phone companies. Ambitious entrepreneurs were also drawn to the area by the federal government's interest in expanding its digital resources and the new business opportunities that went with it.

The other factor that attracted new IT enterprises to Washington was its growing importance as a research center. The region had long enjoyed a respectable reputation in this area, with such scientific groups as the Carnegie Institution and the National Bureau of Standards. In the postwar era, however, Washington had fallen behind California's Silicon Valley and Boston's Route 128 in information-technology innovation, with their proximity to major research universities such as Stanford and MIT.

By the 1960s, Washington began to catch up as a major research hub. This was largely the result of a new flow of federal money into government laboratories and other technology centers. Chief among these was the National Institutes of Health whose annual budgets, heavy with digitally based research projects, had expanded to over $20 billion by the end of the century. Other major research facilities were grouped within the Defense Department, including the Advanced Research Projects Agency (ARPA). The region also became a magnet for private research groups such as the Howard Hughes Medical Institute whose $28 billion endowment funds a range of digital disciplines, with a special focus on biotechnology. Among the new information-services firms moving into the region at the time, one stands out. It was a small start-up venture, originally called Quantum Computer Services. By the mid–1980s, Quantum had developed a technologically primitive set of online services for personal computers. The company changed its name to America Online and set up shop in the Washington suburbs, an unusual move at the time for a consumer-based technology company.

A key player in AOL's early years was Steve Case, who came to the company from a job as a product development manager for Pizza Hut. He and his AOL colleagues transformed the way information of all kinds was made available to a mass public. "Steve was the first person to understand that cyberspace could be a consumer product, and like any other brand, it needed to be sold," financial analyst Rick Martin points out. "That may seem obvious now, but that is what made his company special."[22] It took the company nine years to sign up its first million customers. A decade later it had over 20 million. AOL's marketing strategy relied heavily on mass mailings of free software disks; once the newcomers signed on to AOL, they were usually hooked.

AOL's decision to settle in Washington boosted the region's role as an information-age center. By the turn of the century, over sixty Internet providers were located in the area, making Washington one of the world's leading locations for such services. According to the Greater Washington Initiative, a local trade-promotion group, sixty percent of the world's Web traffic flowed through companies based in the area at the time. Meanwhile, AOL had expanded to the point where it became the focus for what was at the time the biggest merger in American corporate history — a takeover of Time Warner, the nation's largest media company, in an all-stock transaction that was worth $183 billion. The deal eventually soured when the economic "dot-com bubble" burst at the turn of the century. Despite the setback, AOL remains an important, though diminished, factor in the highly competitive consumer information field.

Meanwhile, federal IT spending played an increasingly important role in the Washington region's digital expansion. The old pattern of dealing with the political implications of new technologies one at a time has given way to more multifaceted approaches. This change began tentatively in the Nixon administration in the 1970s and gathered speed during the Reagan presidency a decade later. The result was a new federal policy approach in dealing with digital-age developments in general and with Washington's role in particular.

The political impetus for this change gathered force in the run-up to the 1992 presidential election campaign, which pitted the governor of Arkansas, Bill Clinton, against the incumbent George H. W. Bush. The Clinton campaign focused heavily on digital-age issues. It was a shrewd move, targeted at millions of younger voters whose job prospects were being affected by a fast-changing information economy. These "knowledge workers" (in economist Peter Drucker's phrase) belonged to the first computer-literate generation, increasingly drawn to careers in digital workplaces. In the 1990s, young people were beginning to equip themselves with laptop computers, Internet addresses and cell phones. Although this trend had been brewing for years, both Democratic and Republican strategists had largely ignored its political implications. This changed after the 1992 Clinton victory, with major implications for Washington's role as a digital-age center.[23]

It is a long distance, chronologically and otherwise, between the bewigged statesmen who crafted the world's first democratic constitution in Philadelphia two centuries ago and the men and women who are managing the current transition to a digital environment. But the vital connection is there: the promise of a society that places a special value on the principles of open inquiry and freedom of expression. Quill pens and computers may be far apart technologically, but they remain closely linked in American political ideology and in the evolution of Washington as an information-age center.

3
Silicon Valley East?

The 1990s were a time of giddy growth for the information technology sector in Washington and across the country. Politically, they were the years of the Clinton administration, the first presidency to promote major policy and program initiatives dealing with information-age issues. The mantra of the 1992 Clinton presidential campaign staff was: "It's the economy, stupid." Although the slogan cut across all parts of the economy, it had special relevance for the IT sector, caught up in a rising wave of electronic breakthroughs, from small computers to the Internet. The consumer phase of the digital age was underway.

At the time, Moore's Law, a rough rule-of-thumb proposed by computer industry pioneer Gordon Moore, famously defined these changes. Moore described the industry's evolution in terms of the steady rise in the digital capabilities of silicon chips, the basic modules of the early information age. The fingernail-sized chips, he pointed out, became twice as powerful and twice as cheap every eighteen months, thanks to a steady series of technical breakthroughs.

Moore's formula, though subsequently modified, set the tone and direction of information-technology development at the time, a mood Clinton campaign advisers capitalized on to win the presidency in 1992. Given the national penchant for reducing big ideas to bumper-sticker simplicity, the Clinton campaign staff trumpeted the information highway as the road to a new era of high-tech prosperity. The theme, repeated with metronomic regularity during the campaign, targeted a newly important constituency: digitally savvy young people. It resonated strongly among this group as a contemporary expression of the traditional American faith in salvation-through-technology.

The Clinton campaign based its information-highway proposals on policy initiatives developed by the outgoing George H. W. Bush administration. Bush policymakers had developed plans for a massive increase in electronic information resources within the government and throughout the economy. They were slow, however, in making their proposals public before the presidential election campaign got underway in 1992. This gave Clinton campaign officials an opening to adopt the issue as their own. Once in office, the new administration distributed the Bush proposals almost without change as an Office of Management and Budget paper. The document became a working charter for the Clinton approach to digital-age politics.

Having ignored information-age themes in the 1992 campaign, the Republicans sought to catch up with the Clinton initiative. Representative Newt Gingrich, a self-styled conservative futurist, belatedly announced: "We are beginning to invent the information age." In his enthusiasm, Gingrich suggested that laptop computers should be a deductible expense on income-tax returns, a proposal he later dropped in the face of opposition from fellow legislators.

Vice President Al Gore took the lead in implementing the Clinton administration's IT initiatives. His office became the command post for organizing the effort. The Commerce Department set up an Information Infrastructure Task Force with strong private-sector participation. Together with rising federal budget expenditures for IT goods and services, the task force drew national attention to Washington's new role as a digital-age center. By the end of the Clinton administration, a local business publication, *Washington Technology*, could hail the change with a banner headline: "From a government town to a high-tech hub," pointing out that employment in IT–related enterprises in the area was overtaking that of federal agencies.[1] It was a shift that put Washington in the same league as older technology centers such as Silicon Valley, Dallas–Fort Worth, and Boston.

It was also the beginning of a radical change in the region's overall prospects. Washington for the first time was something more than a "gummint town." Moreover, the transition involved more than a shift in workplaces. It also included the changing nature of the local workforce, in and out of government. A 2007 survey by the Greater Washington Initiative (GWI), an affiliate of the Washington Board of Trade, claimed that the region had attracted a higher concentration of "knowledge workers" than any other large metropolitan region, including New York, Los Angeles, Boston, Chicago, and San Francisco's Silicon Valley. The GWI report noted that Washington's knowledge workers accounted for a third of the area's labor force.[2] Their presence was a major factor in giving the region the lowest jobless rate of any U.S. metropolitan area by 2007, at a time when the American economy was beginning to cope with the effects of a general business downturn.[3]

"Regions are becoming much more specialized in what they do and companies are moving to where the human capital is," Steven Pedigo, GWI's research director, declared when the report was released. "This study says we have the workforce to serve a wide variety of sectors.... Basically, if you're educated and have general skills, you're going to be very employable here."[4]

Despite the cushion of knowledge workers, the region was not immune to the overall impact of the national recession that followed. Bloomberg, the business news agency, reported in April 2008 that over two-thirds of the Washington area's leading firms, including many of the high-flying IT companies, reported significant declines in their stock prices.[5]

The expansion of Washington's IT sector began taking form in the 1980s as the first big wave of technology companies moved into the region. As noted earlier, a pair of start-up firms — MCI Communications and America Online — highlighted the change. More than any other factor, they helped form the two pillars — telecommunications and information — supporting the region's new role as a high-tech economy. In the 1970s, MCI had sparked a revolution in the telephone business by successfully challenging the mighty AT&T telecommunications monopoly. For its part, America Online played a major role in transforming the Internet, then a play toy for scattered groups of computer geeks, into a populist information service.

The presence of AOL and other high-tech firms in the region began to attract the interest of corporate America. Older industries had long viewed Washington as primarily a place to protect their economic, political, and legal interests. The arrival of IT firms in the area changed this perception. Their most direct motivation was to take advantage of rising congressional budgets for information goods and services. The U.S. government was, by any measure, the industry's largest single customer, and it was clearly good business to be close to such a profitable market. Within a decade, over twenty IT firms in the region were earning more than a billion dollars each from federal contracts, according to FedSources, a local business-research group.[6]

Beyond the lure of federal contracts, the need to monitor Congress and government agencies on a wide range of legislative and regulatory issues important to the sector at home and in overseas markets drove the

IT industry's new presence in the region. These issues could no longer be negotiated effectively from New York, San Francisco, and other corporate centers. The new IT companies needed help from Washington professionals who knew how to navigate the town's complex ways of doing business, a group that included lawyers, lobbyists, political consultants, think-tank gurus, and assorted other wheelers and dealers. Together they added a new dimension to the importance of a "Washington presence" for the industry.

This trend accelerated during the prosperous years of the Clinton presidency, which benefited the U.S. economy in general and the IT sector in particular. Rosy predictions were the order of the day, fueled by the White House's promotion of information-highway programs. It was a digital version of the California gold rush, although this time the action took place in new suburban office parks and factories across the country.[7]

Inevitably, in the late nineties, a pause in the good times occurred, as warning signs signaled a slowdown in the digital boom. The turn-of-the-century recession hit the IT sector hard across the country, resulting in the bursting of what had come to be known as the "dot-com bubble," a digital variation on the boom-and-bust pattern of previous economic cycles. Overall, information technology companies suffered less than old-line industries. Nevertheless, the decade-long expansion of the IT sector slowed down. California's Silicon Valley, the sector's iconic birthplace, lost tens of thousands of jobs, as older established firms cut back and many newer ones closed down.

The dot-com recession had less impact on the Washington region's IT activities. Despite cutbacks, particularly among start-up companies, the general trend was one of slower but continued growth. The local IT sector actually expanded its job base, at a time when the jobless rate in Silicon Valley stood at around 6 percent. Overall, the Washington region's IT sector maintained its forward motion during the dot-com-bubble years.[8]

Steadily expanding federal outlays for IT goods and services accounted for this economic cushion. At the turn of the century, the Greater Washington Initiative estimated annual government IT spending in the region at $39 billion, a significant portion involving information goods and services. Federal spending also helped moderate the economic downturn for the IT sector across the rest of the country. Government outlays accounted for one-third of total national spending on information goods and services during the dot-com-bubble years, increasing at a rate of 7 percent annually.

The new attention paid to homeland security after the September 2001 terrorist attacks in New York and Washington accounted for some of these increases. By 2004, the newly created Department of Homeland Security had a budget of over $26 billion, a large portion of which went to contracts for IT goods and services. Washington–area companies were major beneficiaries of the agency's programs, which included a $10 billion multi-year contract for tracking foreign visitors as they entered and left the country, a project managed by Accenture, a major IT contractor in the region.

In addition to profiting from business generated by rising federal budgets, local IT firms benefited from increasingly lucrative contracts in another sector — state and local governments. Although tightening budgets often constrained these jurisdictions, their investment in IT goods and services grew during the dot-com recession. Given the fiscal restraints imposed by the recession, many states turned to outsourcing their IT services to the private sector. In the Washington region, both Virginia and Maryland outsourced some of the work involved in setting up computer-based programs to modernize state government functions.

State and local outlays for IT goods and services across the country increased to over $44 billion a year by 2005, according to Gartner Inc., a Connecticut consultancy that tracks the IT sector.[9] This was within hailing distance of matching the federal government's overall spending in the sector at the time. Although state and local funds for IT goods and services are spread throughout the country, the Washington region absorbs a disproportionate amount, in part because a large share of local government spending involves federal grants.[10] Increased spending for IT products by both federal and local governments during the dot-com bubble years added to the Washington area's overall economic stability.

In summary, the Washington–area IT sector has been able to ride out the harshest effects of recent economic downturns because of the rising level of federal, state, and local government spending for its goods and services. These governments mounted campaigns to attract IT firms to the region through aggressive promotional campaigns, including the lure of financial incentives. In a typical case, DataStream Content Solutions, a data management firm in the Maryland suburbs, got its start with a $260,000 grant from the state's Industrial Partnership program. IBM was persuaded to open a new facility in Virginia's Fairfax County in part because the county and the state government pledged $1.2 million toward the move. The result of this particular deal was to add over twelve hundred high-paying jobs to the county's workforce.[11]

State and local governments have since expanded their efforts to attract IT firms to the region, concentrating on those that deal in promising technical breakthroughs. Biotechnology companies have been a special target. Virginia's Loudoun County gave $6 million in tax breaks to the Howard Hughes Medical Institute when it opened a research campus, betting that it would be a magnet for commercial biotech firms. Maryland appeals to biotech companies, as well as a Howard Hughes Medical Institute in Chevy Chase, by touting the advantages of being near the National Institutes of Health in Bethesda, with its $25 billion in annual research outlays.

Recent efforts to bring new firms into the area have been directed specifically towards firms in older IT centers in California, Texas, and Massachusetts. In a typical project, the Greater Washington Initiative sent a recruiting delegation to Silicon Valley in 2004, which lobbied 130 firms to consider transferring all or part of their operations to the Washington region. State and local development agencies in Virginia and Maryland also mounted promotion campaigns aimed at attracting international investors. Virginia's Fairfax County Economic Development Authority maintains offices in London, Frankfurt, Tokyo, Seoul, and Bangalore, an effort that has helped lure over 300 foreign firms to the county in recent years.[12]

Almost all of the region's IT expansion has taken place in the Washington suburbs, outside the capital city itself. In his plan for the new capital, Pierre L'Enfant had set aside space for what would today be called an industrial park. It never happened. The District of Columbia is too small, only ten miles square, to accommodate both industry and an expanding government structure. One estimate of the city's prospects as a high-tech center found that the IT sector accounted for less than 3 percent of its gross product. The suburbs offer plenty of room as well as other advantages. "For the kind of businesses that make sense to locate in Washington, it comes down to an educated workforce, quality of life, and cost of living," says Dennis Donavan, a location consultant for firms considering a move into the region. In the effort to attract new IT firms to the region, these advantages tipped heavily in favor of the suburbs.

Above all the suburbs offered plenty of room, a critical factor for IT entrepreneurs who saw their future in terms of expansion. Beyond the small circle of traditional "inner suburbs" around the capital city — the so-called bedroom communities — a wider circle of small towns and farmland are getting an economic boost. New digital industries settle into what they like to call campuses, complete with shiny glass buildings, broad lawns, and plenty of room to park.

The opportunity to fashion this kind of work environment prompted America Online to move its operations from the inner suburbs to open land near Dulles airport in the 1980s. Hundreds of other firms have since joined the trek to what was formerly farmland.

The airport has played a special role in this westward migration of IT firms across Northern Virginia, along what is now called the Dulles Corridor. It was a surprising turnaround for a transportation hub that was an architectural triumph and an economic failure for many years after it opened in the 1960s. As late as 1982, Dulles had only ten international flights a week. Satirized by Washington pundits as "Doolie's landing strip," the airport was surrounded by farmland and small housing developments. "This was Simple Town," according to regional economist Stephen Fuller. Today Simple Town has become Boom Town, home to hundreds of companies, most of them focused on delivering IT goods and services.[13]

As a result, Dulles has been transformed from a white elephant into one of the busiest airports in the nation. By 2005, it was servicing 27 million passengers a year, including 5 million boarding international flights.[14] One result was a $3 billion project to expand the airport, underwritten in part by state and county funds. The airport's role as a magnet for IT firms was underscored by the successful efforts of local entrepreneurs to persuade Postal Service officials to create a special Dulles ZIP code for an area that was neither a village, a town, nor a city. Dulles, VA 20166 became a symbol of the region's status as a digital-age center, leading some regional planners to describe the surrounding area as an "aerotropolis."

After fifteen years of steady expansion, the Dulles Corridor now stretches westward a dozen miles beyond the airport to the Blue Ridge hills of western Loudoun County.[15] Overall, Northern Virginia accounted for about half of the regional economy at mid-decade. This migration from the inner suburbs to the outer counties has spawned a range of new problems, including the need for schools and other civic facilities for the thousands of families that have moved into the region, many of them attracted by job opportunities in the IT sector. Prince William County, south of Dulles airport, led the nation's large counties in job growth in 2004 with 8 percent employment growth. Neighboring Loudoun County ranked sixth with 5.5 percent growth. Loudoun's population growth was the fastest among the nation's counties in the early years of the new century. By mid-decade, it recorded the highest household median income — more than $98,000 — of any county in the nation.[16]

More recently, IT companies have been expanding southward in Virginia towards the North Carolina border. Northrop Grumman built a high-tech research center in Russell County, an area previously known for coal-mining operations. The firm's decision was aided by state and federal local-development grants, together with the prospect of avoiding the traffic jams, high-priced housing and other suburban-sprawl obstacles that have affected industry recruiting efforts in Northern Virginia.

Meanwhile, Maryland's problems in dealing with regional sprawl reached as far as the Pennsylvania border, seventy miles north of Washington, by the turn of the century. In 2003, the Wornold Development Co. announced plans to build 1,200 homes in Liberty, Pennsylvania, just north of the border, with the intention of marketing them to workers in the fast-growing industrial parks of Maryland's Frederick and Montgomery counties to the south.[17] IT firms moving into the Washington region ranged from corporate giants to small start-up firms, many of them little more than a pair of Alpha-type young entrepreneurs in a small office with a bright idea and a business plan written in information-age jargon, all in the hope of repeating the success of earlier start-ups such as AOL. The corporate mortality rate among these new ventures is alarmingly high, even in the industry's best times.

Others survived, usually by identifying and exploiting a promising niche market. One such firm was Edge Technologies, Inc., a Fairfax start-up that built a business on dairy farmers' dreams of breeding the perfect milk machine. Using a technology called Web-MGI (Mating for Genetic Improvement) the firm offered farmers a computer-based service that measures the breeding performance of individual cows and bulls, a procedure that can involve over a thousand calculations for each pairing. The calculations replace earlier hit-or-miss methods, which often involved flipping through trade journals for ads about bulls with desirable traits. The sex lives of cows and bulls may seem far removed from high-flying information technology, but the subject is a critical one for the $20 billion dairy-farming business, and the reason why Edge Technologies thrived.[18]

When start-up firms fail, it often involves a combination of flaws in the technology and poor management or simply because they run out of money. Successful firms are often the target of takeover bids by larger companies. The early years of the new decade saw a rash of such deals, particularly by big companies such as Lockheed and Northrop Grumman that were under pressure to invest in new IT products and services. Although private-sector revenues are growing, most IT firms in the Washington region still focus on winning government contracts. Most of this money is appropriated to a handful of federal agencies that in turn distribute a large share of it to an equally small list of megacorporations.

Heading the list of big-spending federal agencies is the Defense Department, with the Department of Homeland Security and the National Institutes of Health close behind. Defense's annual information technology budget dominates the list. Most of its funds were allocated between developing advanced weapons and updating of the department's communications systems. The sums involved are staggering by any measure. Defense spending on the fiscal 2009 budget submitted by the White House to Congress totaled $515 billion, a sum that did not include the prospect of supplementary budget requests that have become standard practice in recent years.[19]

A large share of these funds goes to support Defense's digitally based operations. The effort has created its own bureaucratic lexicon — cyberdeterrence, digital battlefields, netwar, and information warfare, among others. A Pentagon study notes: "The computer chip and digital systems for ground combat are as radical as the machine gun in World War I and the blitzkrieg in World War II; they will permit standoff attacks rather than closure at rifle range, decreasing U.S. casualty rates and increasing the tempo and breadth of the battlefield."[20] The Defense Department's sweeping changeover to digital technologies produced a new strategic doctrine in the 1990s, dubbed the Revolution in Military Affairs (RMA) by defense planners.

Many of the technical breakthroughs spawned by the new doctrine have originated in the Pentagon's in-house idea factory, the Defense Advanced Research Projects Agency (DARPA). The agency's specialty has been described as fostering disruptive innovations that begin as far-out ideas. Many of its ideas leave the drawing board and wind up in the equivalent of an electronic wastebasket. Other DARPA projects have had major impacts on defense technology in particular and on the wider world of information-age innovation in general. One of them, thirty years ago, was successful to the point of changing the way the world communicates. It began as Darpanet, a technology for moving large amounts of information in small electronic packages through dedicated networks. Darpanet was a primitive but workable version of what later evolved into the Internet. Few private-sector firms were willing to touch the idea at the time.

IBM famously turned down an offer to participate in the project, saying that it was impractical.

Darpanet was a small, inside-the-Pentagon project in the 1970s until it attracted the attention of computer buffs across the country. This was the breakthrough they were looking for: a digital alternative to slow-speed networks such as telephones and teletypes. Most of Darpanet's original terminals were located in universities and other research facilities populated by a new generation of computer users. What particularly attracted them was that Darpanet was a free service. In a short time, the experimental network grew so big that its operations were civilianized in the 1980s and transferred to the National Science Foundation.

DARPA's reputation as a far-out experimenter continues to this day. "Anytime you propose something that's clearly achievable, they say it's not a DARPA problem," says John Sherbeck, an engineer with M-Dot Aerospace, an Arizona start-up company that has helped produce a DARPA-sponsored gas turbine the size of a D-cell battery. DARPA likes to specialize in miniature technologies such as molecule-sized computers and six-inch spy planes, two of its more recent interests. One of the agency's far-out projects is a robotic surgical system that allows doctors to operate on a wounded soldier on the battlefield from a remote location. The robot, known in DARPA–speak as a trauma pod, carries out the surgeon's commands. The surgeon in turn receives a continual video feed from the robot while using long-distance surgical manipulators to perform the operation. The technology builds on the experience gained in robotic surgery currently practiced in many civilian hospitals where doctors perform surgery from a remote console.

Most of the Defense Department's current IT projects are designed to replace traditional military equipment with digital devices. In recent years, the Department of the Army has been working on a "future combat systems" project designed to supplement heavy tanks and other battlefield equipment with a more agile mix of manned and unmanned vehicles. Originally budgeted at $82 billion, the project's costs doubled, leading to "major concerns" about the project by the watchdog Congressional Budget Office.[21]

The Navy's recent focus has been on developing a new class of ships, operating close to shore and capable of providing gunfire and missile support for troops as far as 100 miles inland. The ships, known as the DD(X) series, will be electric-powered, bristling with high-tech gear, and manned by half the crew required for present-day destroyers. The original price tag for each of the first generation of DD(X) ships was $260 million. By 2007, this estimate had escalated to $375 million, leading Navy officials to order the prime contractor, Lockheed, to halt work on the project until a fixed-price contract could be negotiated.[22] Later that year, the cost overruns led to a congressional decision to cut funds for the project.[23]

The biggest increase in government IT spending in recent years has been in response to the 2001 terrorist attacks on New York and Washington. Most of these funds have been allocated to the Department of Homeland Security (DHS), a collection of twenty-two former federal agencies brought under one bureaucratic roof after the attacks. DHS soon had an annual budget of over $30 billion, which included $6 billion for IT goods and services.[24] DHS funds are allocated to a wide variety of security projects, from those managed by federal and state agencies on down to so-called first-responder units — primarily local police and fire departments.

Congress has never been offered a more tempting pork-barrel opportunity, with legislators lining up to make sure that their districts got their share. The Washington region has benefited heavily from the new homeland-security largesse. In 2004, Virginia's governor Mark R. Warner announced that new DHS funding would finance the hiring of 10,000 new workers across the state.

Interspersed with many useful projects, the DHS budget supports some that are questionable as anti-terrorism aids. One grant to Washington, D.C., for example, provided $300,000 to pay for a computerized car-towing system. City officials defended the outlay as an efficient way to clear the streets after a terrorist attack. This and similar outlays prompted a wave of congressional investigations. A government inspector general's survey of DHS funds found that of the half-billion dollars allocated to seaport security nationwide over a three-year period, less than $107 million had been spent.

Washington-area IT companies are major beneficiaries of anti-terrorist funds. Homeland Security's $10 billion U.S. Visit project, designed to track travelers as they enter and leave the country, is managed by a local prime contractor, Accenture Ltd., and supervised by the department's Bureau of Customs and Border Protection. The bureau oversees the daily comings and goings of over a million passengers, 50,000 trucks and containers, 355,000 vehicles, and 2,600 aircraft at border crossings.

The rush to secure DHS contracts extends to smaller companies, many with innovative applications of IT methods for dealing with terrorists. One example is the Harbinger Technologies Group in Annapolis, which developed a software program based on phonetics to match Arabic words with names on terrorist watch lists. Users type in the Arabic phonetically; the software generates every variant and matches it against a central database of suspects. If a variant turns up on a watch list, security officials take a closer took at the individual involved.

The search for IT answers to security problems has resulted in a new generation of technologically savvy products, some small enough to fit in a wallet. A new plastic identity card has been developed, drawing on the fast-growing science of biometrics. These smart cards are an upscale improvement on cards that allow access to an ATM machine or a building. They store and process all forms of print and visual data, a big technological step beyond standard magnetic-strip cards. These biometric versions have embedded computer chips that hold images of the cardholder's fingerprints, facial features and even eyeball characteristics.[25]

Biometrics is now a multibillion-dollar business with a bright future. In the Washington region, federal agencies are funding more than three dozen smart-card projects. The Defense Department has developed an Open Access Card for its 3.5 million employees. In 2005, the Homeland Security Department announced plans to issue 200,000 cards to police, fire, and emergency-response employees in the Washington area.

Newer research advances allow the cards to be scannable by multiple systems that had previously been technically incompatible — a requirement if they are to be useful across a spectrum of different organizations and locations here and abroad. Such flexibility is being tested by "biometric identifiers" to speed passengers through airports. Meanwhile, the State Department has begun issuing new passports with biometric capabilities. Each document's chip contains a digital record of all the information printed on the passport, including the holder's photograph, enhanced by facial-recognition technology. Each chip also has a built-in miniature antenna that uses radio waves to transmit the data to a machine reader at passport-control points.

The new cards have raised civil-liberties concerns. Groups representing travel-related businesses as well as privacy advocates say the high-tech chips may do more harm than good. "If you're walking around in Beirut, it would be well worth Al Queda's money to use one of these readers to pick out the Americans from the Swedes without any problem," says Barry Steinhardt, head of the American Civil Liberties Union's technology and liberty program.[26] Despite these criticisms, the State Department began to distribute the new passports to its diplomats in 2005 and to the general public a year later.

From smart cards to smart battleships, the IT industry and its products are transforming government operations, with particular impacts on Washington. In 1970, just before the influx of high-tech companies, the District of Columbia was the ninth largest city in the nation, with a population of over 700,000. Today, it has 200,000 fewer inhabitants, ranking it a pale twenty-fifth in size among U.S. cities, easily surpassed by Phoenix, San Diego, and San Jose. District residents represent only one in ten of the metropolitan area's inhabitants. While the population has been dwindling inside the city, the region as a whole has experienced steady growth, much of it the result of information-age industries.

Although the IT industry conducts its local business largely in the suburbs, its presence has had a transforming effect on the District of Columbia. The city is witnessing an urban renaissance, including a new prosperity reflected in a booming downtown business district that was largely a dead zone only a few years ago. In the process, Washington is becoming hip, smart, and sassy, reflecting its municipal slogan: "DC: the place to be."

Among other impacts of this change, the city has taken on a newly significant role as a financial center. Traditionally, Washington had been a fiscal outpost, no serious challenger to New York, Chicago, and other big money markets. A generation ago, its banks were largely local enterprises, servicing small accounts. The flagship bank was the Riggs National Bank, which boasted of being "the bank of presidents," having managed the accounts for twenty-one First Families over the years. Riggs loans helped finance the Mexican War and the purchase of Alaska. More recently, the bank handled financial arrangements for many foreign embassies in the city, an activity that became its undoing. In 2002 a scandal involving questionable financial dealings with the government of Chile led to Riggs's demise. Meanwhile, many of the nation's largest banks, long disdainful of the city as a place to do business, have moved in and set up local branches.

The city's new financial status now extends well beyond bank branches. By the year 2000, Washington was the site of the nation's third-largest business district, surpassed only by New York and Chicago, according to a *Washington Post* survey of national markets.[27] An early indicator of this shift was the arrival in the 1980s of the Carlyle Group, a venture-capital firm. By 2007, Carlyle had become one of the largest financial houses in the world, with outposts in fourteen countries and over $60 billion in investments under management — in corporate buyouts, real estate, venture capital, and specialty finance. From its downtown headquarters, the firm's diversified portfolio focuses heavily on leading-edge sectors such as IT and telecommunications. However, it is also an equal-opportunity enterprise, seeking out a range of investment projects that in recent years have included Dunkin' Donuts, Baskin-Robbins ice cream, Hertz rental cars, and Manor Care nursing homes.[28]

Among other talents, Carlyle officials know how to play the political game. Former government officials among the firm's advisers have included a U.S. president, secretary of state, secretary of defense, and chairman of the Securities and Exchange Commission, as well as a former British prime minister. Its reputation for fiscal astuteness suffered in the credit-market turmoil late in 2007. It had to lend $200 million to rescue Carlyle Capital, one of its divisions, from a potentially disastrous failure.[29] The firm suffered further losses along with other investment firms as a result of the severe recession that continued into 2008 and 2009.

Other Washington equity firms have done well by specializing in the local IT and defense sectors. Regional venture-financing deals overall reached $866 million by the middle of the decade, according to MoneyTree, a local tracker of venture firm activities. For the first time, Washington is a credible private-investment center, putting billions of dollars into play to start new companies, while helping others go public, merge, or expand.

Washington's financial sector is only one part of the District of Columbia's private economy that has benefited from the new concentration of IT firms in the area. Their presence has been a bonanza for a wide swath of local professionals — lawyers, lobbyists, think-tank members, economists, financial advisers, and political consultants, each on a self-appointed mission to guide the newcomers through the intricacies of the Washington bureaucracy. From humble beginnings in the middle of the last century, the process has taken on the dimensions of a high art in the new digital environment. Unlike the rest of the region's IT-based activities, these enterprises are located primarily in the District of Columbia. They tend to congregate in an area that stretches from downtown on up to Capitol Hill along what is known locally as the K Street Corridor, flanked by cookie-cutter office buildings.

What the new breed of local professionals offer IT companies is "a Washington presence," a seat at the political table where decisions are made about the industry's financial, legal, and technical interests. This service is particularly important for IT firms, because many are start-up companies, technologically savvy but often politically innocent, who need all the help they can get in navigating the federal government's bureaucratic maze.

The most prominent activity of this influence-peddling sector is old-fashioned lobbying, a word that is a throwback to the days when the practice involved buttonholing members of Congress and government officials in hallways. This simple technique, satirized over a century ago by Mark Twain in *The Gilded Age*, has undergone many refinements in recent years while expanding into a major local industry. PoliticalMoneyLine, a research group that monitors local lobbying, estimates that the sector earned $2.6 billion in 2006, a nearly 11 percent increase from the $2.4 billion it collected the year before.

Other studies of the lobbying process indicate that this is only the tip of the proverbial iceberg. Direct contributions of Washington-based groups to the two major political parties make the District the richest political source per capita of such donations of any part of the country, according to the nonpartisan Center for Public Integrity. Reporting on lax enforcement of lobbying rules, the Center estimated in 2005 that at least 14,000 disclosure documents dealing with political contributions, required under congressional legislation, were not filed during the previous five-year period. These included documents that should have come from 49 of the city's 50 largest lobbying firms, according to the study. In short, Washington lobbying, both on and off the record, is big business.

As government budgets climb, the lobbying business has expanded dramatically. In recent years, the number of registered lobbyists has more than doubled from 14,000 to over 32,000. This figure does not take account of a large cadre of unregistered lobbyists in a trade where the rules are often unclear and the penalties for bending them are usually slight.

The IT sector is, by and large, a newcomer to the lobbying game, which historically depended on heavy industry, agricultural, and financial clients. Beginning in the 1980s, IT firms signed up in droves. There were a few exceptions, most notably Microsoft, which for years had a small presence in the city's lobbying fraternity. As *Washington Post* columnist Michael Kinsley commented at the time: "The company was called arrogant. Who the hell do you think you are? ... Real American corporations hire lobbyists. They maintain big District of Columbia offices and throw lavish parties where Washington big shots socialize with one another at the stockholders' expense. It's the American way! You got a problem with that, buddy?"[30] Microsoft eventually decided that it did have a problem and took steps to expand its Washington presence.

Until fairly recently, Washington lobbying was a relatively sedate activity, operating out of lawyers' offices and trade associations. AT&T was famous for its quietly persuasive ways of dealing with Congress and the bureaucracy, particularly in the decades before it lost its government-blessed status as the nation's telephone monopoly. Farmers, the railroads, the steel industry, and other economic giants generally followed a similar pattern. The emphasis was on small shoe-leather operations: walking the corridors of power, arranging quiet conferences, and judiciously dispensing campaign contributions.

This pattern has changed dramatically. Many of the old customs remain, but the pace and intensity is different, propelled by the introduction of information-age technologies, from BlackBerry communicators to the multimedia Internet, that put everyone involved in instant touch with one another. In many ways, Washington lobbying has become an around-the-clock, digitally driven business.

Meanwhile, occupational distinctions within the new generation of influence peddlers are changing. The lawyers provide a good example. There are, by rough estimate, 80,000 practicing attorneys in the Washington region, whose firms take in about $4 billion in annual gross revenues. Most of them do routine legal work, from drafting wills to handling divorce cases. Traditionally, outright lobbying was a small part of their activities, but today it is a big-time activity within the local legal profession, dominated by several dozen large firms huddled along the K Street Corridor downtown. Old distinctions between lawyering and lobbying are increasingly blurred, if not erased. Lobbyists work for lawyers, lawyers work for lobbyists, and they both work for corporations and their trade associations.

The information-technology sector has become a major client for lawyer/lobbyist firms in recent years, given the industry's increasing involvement in legal and regulatory issues. The outsized example of this new alliance was the role of a major K Street firm, Wiley Rein & Fielding, in representing Research in Motion (RIM), the Canadian manufacturer of BlackBerry equipment, in a patent-infringement case. The 270-lawyer firm collected more than $200 million in fees from the case by the time it was settled in 2006, according to *American Lawyer* magazine.[31]

Whether they act through trade associations or with individual firms, lobbyists for IT firms are usually worth their hire. Hewlett-Packard, a formidable player in the industry, reportedly has doubled its budget for contract lobbyists in recent years, with the money spread among a number of projects. Several years ago one of the firm's major efforts was to support Republican-backed legislation in Congress that would allow it to bring back to the United States at a lower tax rate as much as $14 billion in profits from overseas subsidiaries. The measure passed and resulted in the firm's saving millions of dollars in taxes. As John D. Hassell, HP's director of government affairs, pointed out at the time: "We're trying to take advantage of the fact that Republicans control the House, the Senate, and the White House. There is an opportunity here for the business community to make its case and be successful."

Mr. Hassell's comment points up the general political orientation of the IT industry. Its tilt is firmly Republican. A 2004 survey conducted by *Washington Technology*, a local trade paper, indicated that 79 percent of the executives among the top one hundred federal IT contractors identified themselves as Republicans. They are slightly less partisan in political contributions to the two major parties, hedging their bets against the day when the political weather shifts, as it did with the Democratic victories in both houses of Congress in 2008. Although generally favoring the Republicans, the industry plays both sides of the political street: over $13 million in IT–sector contributions went to the GOP during the 2004 presidential election campaign, compared with $8.4 million distributed to Democratic groups. The run-up to the 2008 presidential elections provided another opportunity for the lobbying community to demonstrate its political muscle.[32]

The combination of traditional legal work and aggressive lobbying has transformed the big K Street firms into full-service operations for their corporate clients. It is a very profitable arrangement, as described in a 2005 survey of their activities by *Legal Times*, a trade paper that tracks the local profession. The survey identified "the Influence 50," the big downtown law-and-lobby outfits. The list was headed by Patton, Boggs, a firm that took in $65.8 million in gross lobbying revenues during 2004, up 13 percent from the previous year. The runners-up were Akin, Gump, Strauss, Hauer & Field ($64.2 million), Hogan & Hartson ($51.6 million), and DLA Piper Rudnick Gray Cary ($42.4 million).

Their activities are part of a thriving network of other lobby groups who supplement the lawyers' efforts. Chief among these are the trade associations. The IT sector is among the latecomers to this group. Until a decade ago, its trade-association efforts were segmented into individual subsectors of the industry, such as the Semiconductor Industries Association, the Electronic Industries Association, and the U. S. Telephone Association, each focused on its sponsors' individual problems.

More recently, IT companies have moved towards integrated industrywide coordination of their lobbying efforts, centering on issues that reflect the technological convergences within the industry, with the aim of presenting a common position before congressional committees and federal agency regulators. This coordination has helped lift the sector from relative obscurity within the Washington lobbying scene to a new level of influential prominence. By 2006, the sector's collective lobbying efforts ranked fifth among major industrial groups, behind the pharmaceutical, insurance, electric utilities, and trade associations.

Lobbying on information-technology issues has changed dramatically in recent years. It was once limited largely to serving companies directly involved in producing digital goods and services. This is no longer the case. As digitization has spread through the entire economy, the subject has become a make-or-break issue for almost everything American industry produces, from breakfast cereals to bicycles. This shift has led traditional goods-and-services industries to adopt a new concern with lobbying digital issues in Washington. The resulting expansion of their digital constituency to the whole economy has been a bonanza for lawyers and other lobbying outfits in the city.

A recent survey by *Wired* magazine of the forty most innovative American companies in applying digital technology to their own operations reflects this change. The results showed a surprisingly eclectic mix. Digital leaders such as Apple Computers, Amazon, and Yahoo were high on the list, but Microsoft ranked twenty-eighth, well behind Toyota, Federal Express, and Jetblue airlines.[33] This new mix of firms focused on IT issues further expands Washington's lobbying industry with a lucrative base for its information-technology activities.

As a lobbying group, the U.S. Chamber of Commerce is in a class by itself, with three million members, including all the big IT firms. Thirty years ago, the Chamber had two lobbyists — one for the House and one for the Senate. In recent years its public affairs staff has expanded to eighty employees, including sixteen full-time lobbyists. The Chamber's activities are supported by a large pot of money: its lobbying budget in 2007 was $53 million, according to the nonpartisan Center for Responsive Politics.[34]

Washington lobbyists as a group live well. A recent listing of trade association executives put Robert Glauber of the National Association of Securities Dealers in first place with a annual salary of $9.4 million. Among the top five in the rankings was Thomas Wheeler, head of the Cellular Telecommunications and Internet Association, who clocked in at $2.1 million. Another lobbying group with a major interest in digital developments is the Motion Picture Association of America, for years headed by the legendary Jack Valenti, a former White House aide, who ranked only sixteenth on the list with an annual salary of $1.3 million.

The Washington influence industry also includes a floating population of political consultants, who work independently or in alliances with law firms and trade associations. They bring assorted talents to the trade — media strategists, direct-mail coordinators, and opposition-research gurus, among other specialties — but they tend to focus on elections. They have set up their own professional group, the American Association of Political Consultants, whose activities include an annual dinner where its members' accomplishments are acknowledged with the "Pollie Awards," the industry's equivalent of Hollywood's Oscars. Prizes are given in 130 categories, including one for the year's best automated phone calls.

Less influential than the lawyers, lobbyists, and political consultants but at least as earnest is another group of political operators, the good-government organizations or, in Washington parlance, the goo-goos. They include such groups as the League of Women Voters and the Consumers Union, each with a long record of influencing progressive legislation, and the fly-by-night advocacy groups set up to lobby a particular issue.

The goo-goos were generally slow in getting involved in digital-age issues until the 1990s, when a quirky genius, Mitch Kapor, brought high-minded concerns about the information age to Washington. An activist who knew what he was talking about, Kapor embodied Silicon Valley attitudes: anticorporate, nonconformist, and vaguely whole-earthish. At one point he was a counselor at a mental hospital where, as he liked to tell friends, he performed the psychic equivalent of emptying bedpans. After spending time as a disc jockey and a stand-up comic, he founded Lotus, one of the most successful early computer software companies. The firm's best-known product, the Lotus 1–2–3 spreadsheet, added stylishness and user-friendliness to the early efforts of computer users to come to terms with the new technology.

Kapor left Lotus in the early nineties to set up the Electronic Frontier Foundation in Washington, a public-interest group devoted to monitoring civil liberties in the new computer-driven environment. He showed up at the right time to press his digital agenda on the new Clinton administration, with its much ballyhooed election mandate to build a national information highway.[35]

Kapor became, in the local phrase, a Washington Presence: a star witness at congressional hearings and a guru on digital issues much quoted in the media. In the process, he led a serious public discussion of the meaning of the new digitization for American life, with an emphasis on its role in expanding personal freedoms. His concerns were a distinctive cut above the bottom-line interests of other advocacy groups in town. The Economic Frontier Foundation effort has since faded, but its legacy lives on in the dozens of public-interest advocacy groups that focus on IT issues in their lobbying efforts.

What all Washington lobbyists share is the digitization of their operations, from sophisticated databases and automated mass mailings to multimedia BlackBerrys. They have not, however, given up on time-tested marketing practices. None of these is more venerable than the evening receptions sponsored by virtually every lobbying group, particularly during the weeks when Congress is in session. An old local proverb remains valid: to understand political Washington, follow the shrimp.

Typically huge stand-up buffets, these parties are serious business, the most efficient way for lobbying groups to press the flesh with large numbers of legislators and their assistants. "It's not necessarily about fun," says one Senate staffer. "Everybody who sponsors a reception has an agenda, whether you are dropping by to see someone receive an award or to hear someone's position on the Patriot Act or library funding."[36]

Dozens of these grip-and-grin events are held daily across the city, particularly on Tuesdays, Wednesdays, and Thursdays, the days most Hill legislators are likely to be in town. The receptions vary in style, depending on the lobby involved. Beer wholesalers sponsor an annual Octoberfest, featuring their products along with a pitch about the evils of allowing beer to be shipped through the mails, a practice they oppose fiercely in the courts and in Congress. The information-technology companies like to use receptions to introduce a new high-tech product or service. Other receptions are out-and-out fundraisers, a year-round necessity for most congressional offices.

At the same time, Congress is under increasing pressure to put limits on fundraisers and other lobbying activities. A generation ago, lobbying regulation was lightly regarded. A Reconstruction Finance Corporation officer once told a Senate committee that he would accept a 12-pound ham as a gift but not one that weighed 13 pounds.[37] The subject of political gift-giving was highlighted in the 1950s, when a high official in the Eisenhower administration accepted a fur coat intended for his wife from a lobbyist. The president tried unsuccessfully to defuse the issue by declaring that "a gift is not necessarily a bribe. One is evil; the other is a tangible expression of friendship." Despite this explanation, the fur-bearing aide was forced to resign.

A high point of sorts in regulating lobbying activities was reached in 2003 when Congress approved new lobbying regulations that included, among other details, the conditions under which lobbyists could deliver free food and beverages to congressional staffs. The limit was set at $50 per staffer per day. This quickly became known as the pizza standard, since the practice often involves take-out orders delivered to staffers working late in the nation's interests, with particular attention to those dealing with legislation affecting the donating lobbyist's interests. Neither the pizza rule nor any other congressional regulations has yet seriously deterred the creative ingenuity of the city's lobbyists in working around the restrictions.

This became clear after a flare-up in influence-peddling abuses in 2005 that centered on the activities of lobbyist Jack Abramoff and involved pay-offs and lavish gifts to members of Congress and their staffs. Abramoff went to jail, and Congress undertook another exercise in limiting lobbying activities. After long debates and backroom deals, it passed legislation in 2007 that put further restrictions on lobbyists, including limits on gifts, meals, and travel provided to legislators. It also forced the lawmakers to attach their names to special-interest provisions and pet projects they slip into bills at the request of lobbyists.

The impact of these changes is probably transitory. As Dan Danner, a senior vice president of the National Association of Independent Businesses, pointed out at the time: "Entertainment may slow down for a while, but then people will figure out new ways to accomplish the same things, and it will likely be business as usual for a few years, until the next scandal."

Behind all this political maneuvering are small signs that the IT sector's role in Washington is changing, as the headlong expansion that has marked its activities in recent years levels off.[38] One indicator is the increasing number of firms, including some of the biggest, who find it difficult to handle big government projects on their own. An outsized example of this occurred in March 2005 when Lockheed Martin and Boeing announced that they would merge their space rocket businesses where they were competing for contracts. Tighter federal budgets and growing costs made it more difficult for them to operate independently. The merger was the culmination of a two-year legal battle in which Lockheed lawyers accused Boeing of cheating to win government rocket launch contracts. The new joint arrangement helped eliminate competition in the lucrative rocket market that includes NASA, the defense agencies, the National Security Agency, and the National Oceanic and Atmosphere Administration.

Deals like the Lockheed-Boeing arrangements suggest that the Washington area is entering a new phase in its evolution as a digital-age center. It is beginning to establish its own identity in ways that distinguish it from other U.S. regions. It is not Silicon Valley East — it does not have the in-depth combination of research and manufacturing resources of its California rival. Nor is it just a regional phenomenon, based on the bureaucratic whimsies of its biggest customer, the federal government.[39]

The local sector's growth engine, congressional budgets, is still its main strength, with IT appropriations doubling in the past fifteen years. This trend continues to grow but at a somewhat slower pace. The government's big digital infrastructure systems are now basically in place. The main problem now is to fine-tune these systems, expanding and updating them to take account of technological advances. Significantly, the Office of Management and Budget, the White House's watchdog on fiscal spending, has set up a "management watch list" to monitor overall federal outlays in information goods and services, following a 2005 survey that identified deficiencies in almost half of the government's major IT operations.

This effort to tighten up IT operations reflects a shift away from the pell-mell government spending patterns of the past decade. Input, a Washington market-research firm, sees a small but steady slowdown in the pace of congressional IT funding in the coming years, while predicting a continued rise in overall expenditures to $93 billion by 2011. Clearly, it is still a robust business for the firms that have settled in the Washington area in recent years. Moreover, a large backlog of already appropriated federally funded projects is moving slowly through the bureaucratic pipeline, enough to keep Washington-area IT goods-and-services firms in business for a long time even if not another penny were available from Congress.[40]

The current received wisdom among industry analysts is that federal budgets for IT goods and services will remain a solid base for continuing regional growth in the sector but that there will be significant shifts in how and where the money is spent. Some adjustments are already taking place in the wake of the 2008 economic recession. Pressure has escalated to cut back on a number of big-ticket programs, such as the F/A-22 Raptor fighter jet being built by Lockheed Martin and other contractors.

Faced with the prospect of smaller federal contracts, local IT managers have been looking for expansion opportunities elsewhere. In particular they are searching out new private-sector opportunities. Local prospects for this development are not, for the present, on a scale to match commercial IT enterprises in California's Silicon Valley, Boston, and other big digital centers. Nevertheless, Washington-area IT firms have seen steady, profitable expansion in commercial sales in recent years. Their prospects appear strong in biotechnology, dealing with the functions of the human body in general and a better understanding of diseases in particular, in large part because of the region's strength as a medical research center. The sector came to public attention in the post–9/11 years for its role in one limited area, namely identity cards that rely on biometrics, detailed measurements of the human body. For all the hype associated with the plastic cards, the costs often outweigh the benefits. The concern over their possible Big Brotherish misuse, raised by privacy advocates, is another obstacle.

Beyond biometrics, biotechnology has an important longer-term attraction for the IT sector, with particular implications for the Washington area, in large part, because of the region's strength as a medical research center. The National Institutes of Health in Bethesda are world leaders in biotechnology research, stretching across a wide range of medical problems from cancer to genetic disorders. Other strong biotechnology centers are the new Howard Hughes Medical Institute research campuses in Loudoun and Montgomery counties, where hundreds of scientists work on biotech projects.[41]

Washington's commercial IT sector is beginning to mine these research centers for new product ideas. From small beginnings in the 1990s, the biotechnology sector has expanded dramatically. By 2005, biotech firms had surpassed traditional pharmaceutical companies nationally for the third straight year as the primary source for new medicines, according to a report by industry consultants Ernst & Young. "This is an independent self-sustaining industry that is growing at twice the rate of the pharmaceutical industry. It is here to stay," says Ernest & Young executive Scott Morrison.[42]

As they have done in other technology areas, the state governments of Virginia and Maryland are making aggressive efforts to lure biotech companies to the region, trading on the respective strengths of their local research resources. As part of their marketing strategies, they are also using financial incentives such as tax breaks and subsidies.

Overall, however, the Washington region lags in the high-stakes effort to attract new firms in this sector. It ranked seventh in biotech investments in 2005, behind New England, Silicon Valley, and the New York City area. California leads the pack, having spawned the first biotech company, Genentech, in 1976. Most of the firms attracted to the Washington region are young start-ups, but a few have established strong roots. One of these is Gaithersburg–based MedImmune, Inc., which began operations in 1988 and later blossomed into a billion-dollar enterprise, based largely on the development of a flu vaccine that can be administered by nasal spray rather than by a shot in the arm. In 2007 a British drug company, AstraZeneca, bought the firm for $15.6 billion.[43]

Biotechnology is a risky business, definitely not for the financially timid. Overall, the industry lost $6.4 billion in 2004, according to the Ernst & Young study cited above. The report projected that the industry could reach profitability by the end of the decade. This prospect is important enough to investors that the AMEX and NASDAQ exchanges each sponsor a Biotechnology Index that tracks hundreds of companies in the field.[44]

The biotech trade is similar in some ways to its older cousin — the pharmaceutical industry. Both try to earn a big profit with products that result from expensive research carried out over a period of years. The drug companies have, on balance, been successful by taking a conservative approach through a process of trial and error, often knowing little about the underlying causes of disease. More often than not, their solution still tends to be to prescribe a pill for what ails you.

Biotechnology takes a more fundamental approach, relying on detailed medical diagnoses, with treatments based on slicing and dicing genetic material. Much of the interest in biotech research is on curing cancers, using genetic strategies rather than useful but often toxic chemotherapy drugs. The Food & Drug Administration (FDA), the government's regulator of new biotechnology applications, plays a critical role in this sector.

GenVec, a Maryland company, had been working for years on a gene therapy to shrink tumors, a project involving expensive clinical tests. In 2004, the FDA suspended the firm's tests in three types of cancer, citing concerns that the proposed drug, TNFerade, might cause fatal blood clots. GenVec's stock price dropped by almost half within a day. After the company allayed the FDA's concerns, the agency allowed the tests to be resumed. One result was that GenVec shares rose over 80 percent from their earlier low.[45]

Despite this and other successes, investment in biotechnology breakthroughs is not for the faint of heart. As *Washington Post* business columnist Jerry Knight points out: "The homework is hard. You have to understand the cutting-edge science in developing drugs, chart the complex regulatory route that all new treatments must traverse and calculate the economic payoff from medical breakthroughs — if and when they occur."

Nanotechnology is the other gee-whiz technology attracting IT companies and potential investors in the Washington region. It is the science of designing, manipulating, and building things at atomic and molecular levels, tinkering with the basic building blocks of matter. Digital variations of old-fashioned microscopes allow scientists to "see" atoms and molecules for the first time, revealing (as one observer has noted) "landscapes as beautiful and complex as the ridges, troughs and valleys of a Peruvian mountainside, but all at the almost unimaginable nanometer scale."[46] (A nanometer is a billionth of a meter, roughly the length of ten hydrogen atoms.)

Further advances in nanotechnology will be paced by improvements in the capacity of transistors, the microscopic switches found in all computer chips. Moving beyond current integrated chip technology will require shrinking logistical, memory-chip technology circuits to the scale of a few nanometers.[47] More recently IBM and Intel announced progress in developing a 45-nanometer transistor so small that more than three hundred can fit on a red blood cell.

This science of the very small is getting big attention these days throughout the Washington IT sector. A National Nanotechnology Coordination Office has set up shop in Arlington to track the subject. Overall, American nanotechnology research groups lead the world, measured by the volume of their scientific reports and the number of patents issued.[48] The Washington area has emerged as a strong player in this development: both Maryland and Virginia are national contenders in the nanotech sweepstakes. The two states have joined in a collaborative project, the Chesapeake Nanotech Initiative, to promote the region as a scientific and industrial leader in the field. *Small Times*, an industry journal, has cited the University of Maryland's Center for Integrated Nanoscience and Engineering as the number one academic location in the nation for both nanotech education and nanotech research.[49]

The subject is also attracting a lot of public and private investment. Federal budgets had allocated $3.7 billion for nanotech research by this middle of the decade. Individual states are also investing heavily, at a rate of 40 cents for every federal dollar of investment in the new technology, according to a 2005 estimate by the White House's Council of Advisers on Science and Technology.[50] Private investors are following up with somewhat more cautious funding, with the hope of coming up with a nanotech version of the research breakthroughs that created Xerox and Microsoft. By 2007, a Smithsonian Institution study found that nearly 400 nanotechnology-based products were on the market, ranging from cosmetics to sports equipment.[51]

All this is a bet on what is, for the present, risky technology whose capabilities are only beginning to be understood. Enthusiasts see a nanotechnology future of cheaper solar cells and new forms of semiconductors, among other breakthroughs. They point to nanotech's potential for revolutionizing the way drugs are made and delivered, particularly in the fight against cancer, allowing doctors to target and kill individual cells while leaving healthy ones alone.[52]

Other observers are more cautious about the technology's future, to the point of warning about a financial "nanobubble." Their hesitations are in part the result of recent research on the possible environmental, health, and safety risks posed by nanoscale products.[53] A 2006 report by the prestigious National Research Council recommended closer monitoring of these potential dangers. At the same time, the Environmental Protection Agency took the first steps to regulate consumer items containing nanotechnology elements.[54]

Whatever the prospects for practical applications of nanotechnology and other advanced research, the IT sector in Washington will be an increasingly important player in their development. For the foreseeable future, the federal government will be its largest customer. The Washington region may not reach the iconic status of Silicon Valley, but it is clearly poised to be a strategic economic force in the changes taking place as the nation moves more deeply into the information age.

4

Digital Bureaucracy, Bit by Bit

In a survey of the Washington area's economic prospects at the turn of the century, the *Washington Post* declared that the city would never go out of business, thanks to an ever-expanding federal bureaucracy. The *Post*'s prediction about the town's prospects has been further bolstered by a newly vigorous private sector dominated by IT firms and the service industries that support them.

Although federal budgets have soared in recent years, Washington and its surrounding suburbs have moved beyond their long-standing dependence on government spending to compete in wider commercial markets. The region has become an information-age power in its own right, challenging older centers from Silicon Valley to Boston and beyond. Nevertheless, the local IT sector still relies heavily on government business. It is useful to examine how the federal bureaucracy has influenced the tone and pace of digital developments in the region and, by extension, in the nation and the world beyond.

The survey begins with the fact that the U.S. federal establishment is the largest man-made organizational structure on earth, overshadowing such institutions as Wal-Mart, the Catholic church, and McDonalds. The government's activities are fueled by mind-boggling budgets: the funding proposal sent by the White House to Congress for the 2009 fiscal year involved over $3.1 trillion. The *United States Government Manual*, a 700-page annual index of federal organizations, describes fifteen cabinet-level departments and sixty other major agencies before listing hundreds of boards, bureaus, and councils from the Rubber Producing Facilities Disposal Commission to the National Cemetery Administration.

It is government-by-accretion. Very few federal organizations are ever completely eliminated; instead they are reorganized or transformed into something else. It took almost a hundred years to close down the Civil

War Battle Monuments Commission. Every incoming administration ritually pledges to reduce the size of government. Inevitably it fails, thwarted by interest groups that have a stake in maintaining the status quo or revising it to accommodate their interests, usually at the taxpayers' expense. In 2005, the Bush administration created a "Sunset Commission," charged with identifying over-the-hill agencies for possible elimination. No one expects any quick results; the commission itself is not scheduled to go out of business until the year 2026.[1]

The transition now taking place in federal government operations has one common element — a pervasive reliance on digital operations. The result is the most far-reaching bureaucratic change in over two hundred years of the republic. Some examples:

- NASA scientists are planning an interplanetary Internet to keep in touch with the agency's operations throughout the solar system. One of the project's first experiments was carried out in February 2005 when a NASA Rover machine on Mars sent and received Internet-style messages from a European space agency satellite circling Mars. Plans are under way to expand the digital link to other planets, which will involve formidable problems. One is that the network's hubs are millions of miles apart; the round-trip transmission time between Earth and Mars is about forty minutes.[2]
- The Department of Agriculture digitally tracks farm animals across the nation as part of an effort to prevent mad-cow disease and other potential epidemics. The project, scheduled to be in full operation by 2010, involves hundreds of millions of animals.[3]
- The Department of Health and Human Services monitors bird migration patterns throughout the world at its 24-hour computer center. The project is part of a strategy to combat health hazards such as avian influenza and the West Nile virus. The agency receives digital input from over a hundred bird-watching organizations around the world, including the Australian Waders Study Group.[4]
- To limit damage from tornados, the National Severe Storms Laboratory digitally simulates storms on its computers with the aim of improving weather forecasters' chances of spotting a tornado before it touches ground. A typical simulation on the agency's computers involves about four billion arithmetic calculations per second.[5]
- In 2005, the Bush White House announced plans to create a national network of electronic health records. The network, funded jointly by

the federal government and the health-care industry, will link all doctors' offices, hospitals, pharmacies, clinical laboratories, nursing homes, and home-care agencies. Estimated start-up costs: $200 billion.[6] In 2009, the incoming Obama administration adopted the program as one of its priority legislative goals.

As noted earlier, the federal bureaucracy has been generally slow in catching on to the advantages of computerization. At first, the new machines were generally regarded as useful adjuncts to tried-and-true paper-shuffling routines. Historians may one day record that the defining challenge to this attitude came during the Watergate scandal in the early 1970s, in which the Nixon administration was implicated in what initially appeared as a third-rate burglary of the Democratic National Committee's offices in downtown Washington. The White House's attempts to cover up its involvement in the project included destroying paper records, while ignoring the fact that a silent, semiautonomous system of recording devices in the White House had been monitoring many incriminating conversations throughout the episode. The tapes of these conversations provided electronic evidence that led to the first impeachment of a U.S. president. Although the machines were primitive devices by today's standards, they served as a warning of the power of the new electronics.

Computerization in all its forms has since become a critical part of federal operations at all levels under the rubric of E–government—*E* for electronic. A large part of the bureaucracy's day-to-day digital contacts with citizens involve familiar transactions: filing a Social Security claim, paying taxes, or checking the visiting hours at a Smithsonian museum. A 2006 survey of government computer operations by the Pew Internet and American Life Project found that digital transactions had doubled in the early years of the new century. By rough estimate, over 80 percent of routine citizen contacts with Washington agencies are now handled as database transactions. The Taubman Center for Public Policy at Brown University has identified 254 Web sites operated by federal agencies that can be accessed through the government's basic site, FirstGov.gov.[7]

Old habits persist, however. Half the citizen respondents in the Pew survey cited above said they preferred telephone or in-person contacts with agencies to Web or e-mail transactions. By and large, however, they have accepted the new digital services. Federal Web sites received a 73.4 percent favorable rating in the 2006 American Consumer Satisfaction Index survey conducted by University of Michigan researchers. (Private sector scores were somewhat higher, ranging from 76 to 80 percent.) A particularly popular government site provides information about Social Security, Medicare, and other federal programs. Another site, *GLearn.gov*, has provided distance-learning training for more than a million federal employees in recent years.

At times, the bureaucracy has stumbled in its rush to digitize, in part because of the Topsy–like growth of incompatible digital information systems within the federal structure. Unlike other governments, the United States does not have the equivalent of a Ministry of Communications or of Information to plan and coordinate information-technology operations. By contrast, Japan has had a master plan for national computer-network development since the early 1970s.

France adopted a similar strategy in 1978 for what it calls *telematique*. The results have at times been less than efficient: in 1989, a computer error by the Paris police accused local citizens of murder, extortion, and organized prostitution instead of fining them for traffic violations. The city sent out 41,000 apologies. In 2000, the European Union approved a regional plan, known as the "Lisbon Strategy," to upgrade the region's economy through more efficient use of information-technology resources, with a target date of 2010 for its completion.[8]

Washington's transition to electronics-based government operations began modestly in the early 1950s with the purchase of a half-dozen room-sized computers. Further implementation was slow in the early years, in large part because many agencies resisted changing old paper-shuffling habits. As noted, these attitudes began to shift in 1966, when the Johnson administration issued a directive to all agencies "to explore and apply all possible means to use electronic computers to do a better job." It was the beginning of a major effort to digitize government operations, supported by the White House and steadily increasing congressional appropriations.

An important step in this direction was taken in 1972 with the creation of the National Technical Information Service, whose mandate is to centralize electronic access to government technical research. NTIS soon had a library of 800,000 reports, with 60,000 new ones added each year, most of them available to the public in digitized formats. The e–Government Act of 2002 gave computerized government operations permanent bureaucratic status.

The result was to spur all federal agencies to adopt a full range of electronic record-keeping techniques, replacing file cabinets and storage boxes. The Internal Revenue Service has computerized access to the tax records of all individual taxpayers and businesses. The Social Security Administration stores a digital copy of the employment records of every American who has had a job since the 1930s. The National Institutes of Health created a Medlars/Medline network, which electronically distributes the Institutes' own research as well as articles from the world's medical journals, making them available to doctors and hospitals here and abroad. Digital storage facilities, increasingly available online, have also helped cut back on paper reports. In 1992 the Census Bureau issued 1,035 reports; ten years later its reports numbered only 635, each available online.

These digital innovations have resulted in a new kind of bureaucracy. Although the federal workforce continues to grow, its patterns have shifted dramatically in recent decades. Hundreds of thousands of jobs, involving secretaries, file clerks, messengers, bookkeepers, and other predigital classifications have been eliminated. Titles that reflect the new complexities have replaced old job descriptions. No longer content with simple designations like Manager and Assistant Manager, the new list of titles, culled from a *Washington Post* survey, included such aberrations as Associate Deputy Assistant Secretary and Deputy Associate Deputy Administrator. Salaries in this new hierarchy have risen accordingly: another *Post* survey revealed that the average salary of senior National Institutes of Health officials was $198,000, higher than the compensation given to members of Congress or Supreme Court justices.[9]

Office practices have changed in federal bureaus, as they have in private industry. Corner offices, once the domain of the boss, with a perky secretary sitting just outside the door, are fading away slowly but inexorably. The downscale hierarchy of lesser offices along the wall is also disappearing in favor of large open spaces full of "work stations" in cubicles divided, checkerboard fashion, by low partitions. In one experiment, the General Services Administration, the government's arbiter of office practices, moved all its senior officials at a major district headquarters out of their boxy offices into an open-office plan in search of a new organizational dynamic. The experiment was pronounced a success. "The future is now," says the GSA's Barbara Hampton, an expert in the new science of knowledge management, which includes office planning among its subdivisions. "We're already seeing a reduction in assigned offices."[10]

Difficulties in recruiting technically qualified specialists for government jobs have led to changes in hiring incentives. Under new rules issued by the Office of Personnel Management in 2005, applicants for highly specialized federal jobs, particularly those requiring advanced digital skills, can collect up to $25,000 annually for four years as a recruitment bonus. Another plan offers skilled employees "retention bonuses" of up to 25 percent of their base pay to stay in their jobs.

With higher salaries and other bureaucratic changes, the ways of doing government business have changed. There is a new enthusiasm for long-distance Web conferencing — virtual meetings that range from video phone linkups to fancy multimedia presentations networked to locations around the country. Called "telework" in the new jargon, these long-distance transactions cut down on time, travel, and paperwork.[11]

Telework's origins date back a dozen years to experiments in telecommuting, in which government employees were linked to their offices by computer circuits from their homes or from suburban telework centers. Telecommuting became official federal doctrine in 2000, when Congress approved a law requiring all government bureaus to set up telecommuting arrangements. Several years later, Congress strengthened the law by levying a $5 million fine on agencies that fail to make adequate arrangements for employee telecommuting. After some bumbling starts, telecommuting and other electronic work arrangements have become standard practice in federal agencies. By 2007, there were fourteen government telecommuting centers sponsored by the General Services Administration in the Washington area alone.[12]

Telework also relies heavily on portable BlackBerrys and other mobile devices. Washington was named "the best city for teleworking" in a 2006 study conducted by Intel, a local survey group. The survey claimed that a government employee's teleworking one day a week would result in an annual savings per employee of $4,887 in transportation costs and $2,708 in time.[13]

A study by CDW Corp., an IT services provider, found that 44 percent of respondents who work in federal agencies have the option to engage in telework, compared to 15 percent of private-sector employees. Overall, the International Telework Association estimates that over 33 million workers across the country, in and out of government, now spend at least part of their work time linked to their offices electronically.

The White House Office of Management and Budget (OMB), whose mandate includes keeping a lid on government spending, handles the overall monitoring of these workplace changes. OMB's influence on the size and pattern of IT operations has grown dramatically in recent years. Its own internal monitoring unit oversees the annual federal budget for digital operations, which stood at over $60 billion in 2006, with prospects for expansion to over $90 billion by 2010. OMB officials have a reputation for being tough in their reviews of agency budget submissions. In 2005, the bureau put 600 federal IT projects — more than half of those it oversees — on a special "management watch list," citing weaknesses in areas such as management performance and security.[14]

Despite these monitoring efforts, mistakes are made and taxpayer dollars wasted. Promising new technologies are often put in place before they are fully tested. This was the case when an Internal Revenue Service computer network was installed in 1997 to extract money more efficiently from the nation's taxpayers. The project was so technically inept that it had to be junked, at a cost of $4 billion.[15] The IRS has since improved its digital capabilities with an upscale computer facility, to the point where over half of all individual taxpayers now file their returns electronically. Other government agencies have had their share of computer glitches. The Federal Bureau of Investigation was plagued for years by flaws in a $170 million high-tech "virtual case file" system, designed to help its agents and local police officials exchange information electronically.

To be fair, corporations and other private groups have their share of IT failures. A 2002 study of corporate IT performance by the Standish Group, a technology consultancy, found that 30 percent of all private-sector software projects are canceled. Nearly half of them came in over budget, and 60 percent were considered management failures by the firms that initiated them. Overall, federal computer planners may be doing better. In a mid-decade survey of electronic government performance around the world, the United States ranked second in the standings, topped only by Canada. The Canadians scored higher in part because they do a better job of polling their citizens to test the effectiveness of their government's digital efforts, according to the survey.[16]

The other White House agency with a big stake in IT operations is the General Services Administration (GSA), an unsung agency that is all but invisible to the general public. Despite its grey anonymity, GSA is a major federal player with particular responsibilities for moving the bureaucracy into the digital age. One of its tasks is to process government contracts for projects that have survived OMB's budgetary oversight and the congressional appropriations system. This makes the GSA a critical element in the strategies of IT firms that want to sell goods and services to the industry's largest customer.

The first task these companies face is to get themselves registered on the GSA's list of approved contractors. This entails a journey through the agency's acronymic wilderness, following such obscure signposts as ORCA, GWAC, ESRS and FPDS-NG. A successful passage is usually worth the effort. In March 2007, GSA awarded its largest contract ever, a project for modernizing the federal telephone network that will cost about $40 billion before it is completed. The winners, a group that included AT&T, Qwest, and Verizon, spent hundreds of millions of dollars and nearly four years putting together proposals for this most extensive overhaul of the government's telecommunications resources ever attempted, involving advanced linkages to 135 agencies. "That is as good a reason as any," says one contractor, "why I show up at GSA headquarters at 8:30 on many mornings to make sure that things are moving along."

Federal spending for information-technology goods and services has increased dramatically in recent years, in part as a response to the 9/11 terrorist attacks. In the first surge to upgrade the nation's ability to deal with similar future attacks, the government awarded more than $115 billion in IT contracts, spread over several years. In particular, the terrorist threat has strengthened the Defense Department's role as the government's leading consumer of IT goods and services. The Pentagon's fiscal 2009 IT budget request was $33 billion. Overall, the department's budget accounts for over one-third of federal IT spending.

As noted in the previous chapter, the Defense Department's interest in advanced digital operations dates back four decades to an experiment that eventually became the Internet, originally planned as a Cold War military project by the Defense Advanced Research Projects Agency (DARPA). Among the early pioneers looking at Internet-type communications was Paul Baran, a researcher at the Rand Corporation, an Air Force–supported think tank. His solution involved a technology then in its infancy — packet switching — in which messages are broken up into small, digitized packages and sent in random fashion along available networks, to be reassembled at their intended destination. Baran, in association with other researchers across the nation, invented what we now call the Internet.

This outcome was furthest from the minds of DARPA officials when they budgeted a million dollars in 1966 to build an experimental packet-data network. Several dozen IT companies submitted bids on the project. One of the hallowed bits of early Internet lore was IBM's rejection of the offer to bid on the project, claiming that such a network could never be built. IBM has long since resolved its doubts, making the Internet a centerpiece of its production and marketing strategies in recent years. DARPA's experiment, dubbed Darpanet, was soon up and running, linking military and civilian research labs across the country.

The project was a success in part because a group of young graduate students had developed software, known as TCP/IP, that became the common language understood by computers on the Internet. One student, Vinton Cerf, later played a key role in adapting the network for civilian uses. Another, Doug Engelbart, invented the computer mouse. Darpanet was split up in 1983 when the government decided to separate military and civilian packet-switching operations. At the time, Darpanet connected about 300 host computers. Ten years later, its civilian offshoot — the Internet — had over ten million linkups.

DARPA continues to play a major role in the Defense Department's attempts to harness digital technologies to its military mission. The subject has created its own vocabulary of catchwords — *cyberdeterrence, netwar, digital battlefield,* and *information warfare,* among others. The result has been the emergence of a new strategic doctrine that became enshrined in the Pentagon during the 1990s as RMA, the revolution in military affairs. Researchers at the Rand Corporation defined its basic premise in an influential 1995 report on RMA prospects:

> The information revolution implies the rise of a mode of warfare in which neither mass nor mobility will decide outcomes: instead the side that knows more, that can disperse the fog of war yet enshroud an adversary in it will enjoy decisive advantages. At a minimum, cyberwarfare represents an extension of the traditional importance of obtaining information in war: having superior command, control, communication and intelligence and trying to locate, read, surprise and deceive the enemy before he does the same to you.[17]

Digital resources were seen as the centerpiece in implementing the new doctrine, including the prospect of computerized war-forecasting. One of the systems tested was called, in classic Pentagonese, the Tactical Numerical Deterministic Model (TNDM), whose predictive powers were based on a mountain of digital data, said to be the largest combat database in the world. The system also benefited from the input of a range of experts that included computer programmers, mathematicians, weapons experts, and military historians. The project's mixed overall record led to taunts by old-school military planners, who, according to Pentagon lore, referred to their own system as BOGSAT, or "Bunch of Old Guys Sitting Around a Table."[18]

Despite growing interest in digital-age defense strategy during the 1990s, the military services adjusted slowly to the new RMA doctrine.

They also downgraded the doctrine's alleged revolutionary prospects with a new title: "the transformation in military affairs." The Pentagon's interest in the subject ballooned abruptly at the turn of the century with the 9/11 terrorist attacks and the invasions of Afghanistan and Iraq. A lot of old-style military doctrine went by the boards as the focus shifted to a ragtag terrorist enemy that did not subscribe to the tenets of conventional warfare. Reacting to the new challenge, one defense expert noted: "This is not going to be a war of bullets and airplanes alone. It will be one of information." Managing digital warfare moved from think-tank theory to practical reality.

In its search for ways to deal with a new kind of enemy, the Pentagon did not give up its search for big-ticket conventional solutions, as demonstrated by the Air Force's Joint Strike Fighter (JSF) project. The plane, touted as the aircraft of the future, has been a cooperative project of the United States and nine European partners, with an eventual price tag of over $250 billion. The JSF project has been bedeviled with problems including technical setbacks and big cost overruns. DOD planners supported the JSF as a critical element in a new style of digital warfare, with advanced fighter planes, tanks, and ships each playing a role in a vast electronic network for sharing information and passing targets from one to the other. As the London *Economist* noted in a survey of information-age warfare developments: "In this 'netcentric' way of fighting, software and data-handling move to the fore while steel armor and heavy engineering take a back seat."[19]

The Washington region's IT industries have benefited from this interest in applying digital solutions to new defense challenges. The richest rewards have gone to a handful of megagroups. A big winner has been SAIC (Science Applications International Corp.), whose specialty is developing and integrating military IT systems. By 2004 SAIC had annual revenues of $7.2 billion, two-thirds of which came from Defense Department contracts. Other big firms have also profited from this emphasis on electronic warfare. In 2005, Boeing won a $21 billion contract to manage development of a massive Army modernization program.

The common theme in identifying these big defense contractors has been their ability to develop new generations of digitally capable military hardware. Lockheed Martin has usually led the pack with an array of advanced products, including participation in the Joint Strike Fighter project and early-warning satellite networks for missile defense. Lockheed has also teamed up with General Dynamics to develop a new generation of naval craft that operate close to shore, a shift in the Navy's traditional "blue water" strategy of controlling vast ocean areas. The result will be an electronics-laden "littoral combat ship" (LCS) that can handle a range of coastal missions from intelligence surveillance to support of beach landings. At an estimated $250 million each, military planners considered the LCS a bargain compared to the billion-dollar price tags of aircraft carriers and cruisers.[20] As with many of its defense projects, Lockheed has been plagued with cost overruns in the LCS project, to the point where Defense officials cut back funding for the project in 2008.

George W. Bush set the tone for digital changes in military programs when he declared: "The real goal is to move beyond marginal improvements with new technologies and strategies, to use this window of opportunity to skip a generation of technology."[21] The results so far have been mixed, particularly since the escalation of the war on terrorism, in which the military services deal with an elusive enemy operating largely outside the range of the new technologies. The challenge has sent military planners and their contractor allies back to the drawing boards. One result has been abandonment or scaling back of many projects that sounded promising when they were first proposed in PowerPoint presentations but which later came up short.

One such resounding failure was the Total Information Awareness project, a Big Brotherish proposal to track down terrorists by combing through massive databases of personal information, from bank accounts to Internet Web sites, around the world. The project was abandoned not only as being technically over-the-top but also because civil rights groups objected to it as a threat to personal liberties.[22]

Another DARPA project involves unmanned robot land vehicles designed to search out the enemy in rugged territory. In recent years the agency sponsored a Grand Challenge race of driverless vehicles across 250 miles of western scrub and desert, ending up in Las Vegas — a more-than-symbolic destination since the winner of the race would collect a million-dollar prize. The cars navigated with the help of roof-mounted radar, laser range finders, video cameras, and high-tech shock-mounted computers. No vehicle made it to the finish line in the first race in 2004, and the project was sent back to the drawing boards.

The following year the contestants had better luck. The race was won by Stanley, a driverless car sponsored by Stanford University's Artificial Intelligence Laboratory. (It is a sign of the times that Stanley's design began as a digital video game.) The project was so successful that the Stanford experimenters began constructing a civilianized version of the car, which they planned to test by driving down California highways from San Francisco to Los Angeles in seven hours without a human at the wheel.[23]

Supported by a large annual budget, DARPA has recently taken a leading role in other promising research areas. It has been working hard on unmanned aerial vehicles (UAVs), sophisticated intelligence-gathering planes, as well as pilotless combat air vehicles being developed by Boeing, Northrop Grumman, and other military contractors. Drone planes are not a new idea; the Air Force flew supersonic drones over China beginning in the 1960s.

The technology has changed dramatically since then. Now a technician in a Humvee truck hundreds of miles from the target uses a computer mouse to point and click pixilated dials similar to the ones in the UAV's cockpit. The drones, small as a crow or big as a Cessna, are designed to search out enemy units; UAVs can stay in the air longer than any manned aircraft and can see a battlefield better, all without endangering a pilot. They are also cost-efficient: crashing a half-million-dollar UAV is a lot cheaper than losing a $55 million fighter.[24]

More recently, DARPA has focused on nanotechnology, digitized memory elements that measure less than a billionth of a meter, opening up the long-term prospect of automated battlefields with tiny bug-like machines swarming over the enemy. Another DARPA research area is solar-powered battlefield equipment. Fifteen research universities together with corporations and independent laboratories across the country have formed a consortium to study the prospect of using solar cells to power the increased load of electronic equipment soldiers carry into combat.

After the Defense Department, the next largest Washington agency dealing with IT goods and services is the Department of Homeland Security (DHS), created in 2002 to coordinate civilian efforts in fighting terrorism. The new boy on the federal block, it quickly became an awkward and sometimes bumbling adolescent, in part because it was created by combining twenty-two old-line agencies, each of which had something to do with security matters. One of the new agency's particular problems was that it inherited a large number of separate computer networks, many incompatible with one another. This lack of digital coordination within the agency has continued to be a stumbling block to effective operations.

Other problems have bedeviled homeland-security operations. One of them is the congressional tradition of logrolling, assuring that each member's district gets its share of federal largesse. The DHS budget is a prime logrolling target. From the agency's founding, homeland security funds have been doled out district by district, including remote rural areas foreign terrorists would have trouble finding. Colchester, Vermont (population 18,000), was allocated $58,000 for a vehicle capable of boring through concrete to rescue people. In 2005, New York City, which suffered the worst damage in the 9/11 attacks, received an average of $25 per person in DHS funds. Rural Wyoming's average was $61.[25] Washington, D.C., site of another 9/11 attack, has been the beneficiary of a mixed bag of antiterrorism aid, including money for bicycles for the mayor and his staff to be used as "emergency transportation."

Part of the problem has been the pressure to get new antiterrorist programs up and running quickly. A major victim of this haste has been the effort to install digitized airport screening devices, a project that was budgeted at $15 billion in the five years after the 9/11 events. Boeing and other big defense contractors received the bulk of the money under arrangements that involved loosened fiscal rules and tight congressionally imposed deadlines.

A *Washington Post* investigative survey in May 2005 reported that Boeing's contract, originally set at $508 million, had doubled in eighteen months to $1.2 billion. According to the *Post*, government auditors learned that Boeing's estimated profit on the contract in 2002–2003 was $82 million, a return of 210 percent on the firm's investment in the project. (It was a charge that Boeing officials denied.) Homeland Security's inspector general also found that the agency had given the company $44 million in award fees without evaluating the firm's performance. Similar failings occurred in other DHS projects. The watchdog Office of Management and Budget reported at one point that only four of the thirty-three homeland-security programs it examined were effective.

Smaller government agencies are also involved in digitizing their operations. They include the Department of State, which has traditionally resisted changes in its diplomatic routines. The department did not set up telegraph connections with its overseas posts for over twenty years after the invention of the Morse telegraph in the mid-nineteenth century. Its first concession to the new technology at the time was to hire a clerk whose duties were to pick up telegrams addressed to it at the Western Union office in downtown Washington.

The department continued to resist technological changes well into the last century. As early as 1984, Zbigniew Brzezinski, President Jimmy Carter's national security adviser, chided State for its antipathy to digital operations. Traditional diplomacy in the age of computers was a boondoggle, he told a *New York Times* interviewer: "Governments should conduct business the way international corporations do, with special representatives in modest offices utilizing telecommunications. The whole diplomatic system needs to be modernized so that it can operate with more rapidity instead of maintaining extraordinarily costly establishments and entertainments."[26]

Brzezinski's advice was largely ignored at the time, although the State Department made some modest attempts to introduce computerization into its operations. All this changed dramatically in 2001 with the appointment of Colin Powell as secretary of state. From his experience as a Pentagon general, Powell understood the value of digital operations in a bureaucracy. He ordered improvements in State's rickety communications system with the aim of giving every department employee, in Washington and at embassies abroad, desktop access to department data resources and to one another through the Internet's World Wide Web.

By 2009 State employees at home and abroad were connected to over 16,000 desktop computers. One of the curious outcomes of this change is that many of the new machines are being supplied by Lenova, a company based in the People's Republic of China, as a result of Lenova's $13 billion buyout of IBM's personal computer division in 2005.[27] Within a few years, Internet messaging had largely displaced traditional telecommunications traffic. The department created a new unit, the Office of eDiplomacy, to monitor the transition to digital e-mail communications among its Washington offices and with its overseas embassies.

Meanwhile, another large agency, the Department of Veterans Affairs (VA) has linked most of its facilities in a state-of-the art digital network. With a quarter-million employees and almost a thousand hospitals and clinics across the country, the VA serves 25 million living veterans. About 70 million citizens — a quarter of the nation's population — are eligible for its benefits and services.

Digitization has long been standard practice at the federal government's wide-ranging network of research groups. The biggest of them all, the National Institutes of Health, has twenty-seven centers and institutes and an annual budget of over $25 billion, a large share of which is allotted to medical research. NIH projects involve over 200,000 scientists, whose work accounts for about 10 percent of all printed literature worldwide dealing with biomedical research.

The National Institute of Standards and Technology (NIST) is less well known, but it is the world's leading expert in measuring things, from radio frequencies to atomic particles, in ways that have set standards for American scientific breakthroughs for over a century. The National Science Foundation, created after World War II, is responsible for overseeing basic research in science and technology, as well as for the maintenance of a string of research installations that include the American outpost at the South Pole. Other digitally based research operations are embedded in government agencies such as the Department of Energy, which at mid-decade had a $3 billion research budget focused on looking at alternatives to rapidly depleting oil and gas reserves.

NASA, the National Aeronautics and Space Administration, has a research agenda that extends beyond the solar system. Its plans include sending a computer-crammed spacecraft by 2010 to Alpha Centauri, the brightest star within the closest stellar system to earth. (Fans of *Star Trek*, the long-running television series, will recall that Alpha Centauri was where Zefram Cochrane headed after inventing warp drive on Earth.) The NASA spacecraft's voyage, a round trip of 25 trillion miles, will investigate whether Alpha Centauri has orbiting Earth–like planets.

Other big federal users of new digital technologies include the network of spy agencies that like to call themselves the intelligence community. The best known of these, the Central Intelligence Agency, has its headquarters in a high-security campus in Langley, Virginia. The CIA was an early adopter of computer facilities in the 1960s, with particular attention to the problem of sorting out and storing the thousands of reports it receives daily.

Although the Central Intelligence Agency is the most publicly prominent of the spy operations, its activities are put in the shade by the Pentagon's own cluster of intelligence agencies, whose combined budgets are reportedly five times greater than that of the CIA. The group includes the National Security Agency (NSA), which eavesdrops electronically on communications and information facilities around the world, from telephones to supercomputers. The intelligence agencies, along with the FBI, have a particular problem in protecting classified information stored in their electronic facilities. In 2007, the FBI acknowledged that 160 of its laptops had been stolen or were missing.

NSA's reputation for supersecrecy was tarnished a decade ago when information about one of its digital projects, code-named Echelon, began to surface. Echelon's purpose, according to press reports, was to monitor telephone and other communications traffic across the world in search of intelligence leads. The project reportedly involved coordination with intelligence services in Britain, Canada, Australia, and New Zealand. The data it collected was stored in computers located in massive underground bunkers at Fort George Meade in the Maryland suburbs.[28] Although NSA was routinely mum about whether Echelon, or something like it, even exists, civil liberties groups including the Electronic Privacy Information Center and the Free Congress Foundation criticized the project. More recently, the agency has been accused of illegal wiretapping of American citizens in connection with its monitoring of terrorist groups.

The problem with these intelligence resources is that they often stumble over each other in the competition to market their products to policy makers in the White House and government agencies. This became painfully obvious in the lead-up to the 2003 invasion of Iraq, based on misleading intelligence reports about the existence of weapons of mass destruction. This in turn led to a public investigation that culminated in a White House decision to reorganize its spy setup, resulting in the creation of the Department of Homeland Security. As noted, DHS's mandate is to coordinate the data-gathering activities of over a dozen civilian intelligence agencies along with their collective budgets, an estimated $40 billion in recent years. The results to date have been mixed. A major problem, as noted, has been integrating the IT networks of formerly separate agencies, many with incompatible technical standards, to enable them to communicate among themselves and with the networks of similar intelligence grids operated by cooperating governments abroad.

Although the White House makes the basic decisions in these bureaucratic operations, Congress has a major say in the process. With 435 elected representatives and a hundred senators, it is the collective voice of the people, however confused and often incomprehensible its activities. Among congressional challenges in recent years has been the pressure to come to terms with information-age realities, including giving up many of its good-old-boy ways of doing business. Capitol Hill is slowly being digitized, both in what it does and how it does it.

A more-than-symbolic turning point took place in 2001 when the House of Representatives allocated more than a half-million dollars to outfit its members and their staffs with handheld BlackBerry devices, giving them digital contact with their offices, as well as with colleagues, constituents, and a wide range of databases. The most complex of the congressional data services is in the Library of Congress, whose electronic traffic annually involves hundreds of millions of transactions within the Congress and with the public at large.

Congress got its first big taste of the impact of electronic operations on its activities in 1979 when it agreed to let a former Commerce Department official, Brian Lamb, set up television cameras to record its proceedings for transmission to cable-connected households. Lamb called his project C-SPAN. He persuaded House Speaker Thomas P. "Tip" O'Neill to allow him to place fixed cameras in the chamber, broadcasting continuously while the House was in session. O'Neill insisted that the transmissions focus on the official proceedings without editorial comment or editing. The service was later extended to the Senate. From the beginning, cable operators have funded C-SPAN, an arrangement in which the operators allotted a few pennies of each subscriber's monthly bill to meet C-SPAN's costs, currently about $40 million a year.

C-SPAN attracted little interest at first, as few cable systems carried its transmissions. Many members of Congress were initially unaware of the program's popularity or its impact back in their districts. They soon found out, making C-SPAN a newly visible factor in national politics. The result, as a *Washington Post* survey of the channel's impact pointed out, has provided Americans "the kind of access to Congress that used to be reserved for a small clique of Washington insiders."[29]

C-SPAN has had some unintended impacts on public understanding of Congress and its ways. One involves the legislators' practice of delivering speeches in an empty chamber after the day's regular business is done. Traditionally, the speeches were given primarily for later inclusion in the *Congressional Record*. Concerned about the influence these empty-hall orations could have on C-SPAN audiences, Speaker O'Neill ordered the cameras to start panning the chamber so that viewers would see that the speeches were being delivered to rows of empty seats. The decision prompted complaints from House members, but O'Neill's order stood.

By the turn of the century, C-SPAN transmissions were bringing Senate and House debates, in both their glory and dreariness, to over 85 million American homes. The legislators' initial doubts about having television cameras trained on their deliberations were trumped by the popularity of the service among millions of political junkies across the country. In recent years, C-SPAN has expanded to three 24-hour channels, with a fourth ready to start up if the Supreme Court ever agrees to allow its proceedings to be telecast. For the present, this prospect is remote, given the attitudes of several justices, one of whom, David H. Souter, has publicly announced that cameras will enter the court's chambers "over my dead body."[30] Meanwhile, C-SPAN has expanded its reach by making many of its offerings, including its popular *American Perspectives* program, available as podcasts, audio programs that can be downloaded at the listener's convenience.

In other areas, Congress has had a more difficult time making the transition to digital age realities. In order to understand the changes taking place, it set up an Office of Technology Assessment (OTA), designed to provide its members with background reports on emerging technologies. The OTA set high standards in its evaluations of new digital breakthroughs, with heavy input from both academic and industry sources. Its reports shied from offering solutions to a given technological problem, relying instead on describing the options Congress might consider in dealing with the technology under study.

The OTA was abolished in 1995, allegedly to save $22 million from the $2 billion spent each year on congressional operations. The move, championed by a group of conservative legislators, was reportedly pressed by lobbyists from information-technology industries whose interests were being affected by OTA research findings that clashed with their commercial interests. An effort to restore the OTA or some version of it was led by Rep. Rush Holt of New Jersey, a former research physicist, and other lawmakers interested in improving congressional understanding of how advanced technologies impinge on their legislative decisions.[31]

This move to provide Congress with an independent assessment of IT developments is overdue. In the new century, almost every piece of legislation brought before Congress has digital implications. One issue that has been debated for over a decade is whether consumer purchases made over the Internet, such as Amazon's remarkably successful book-selling operation, should be subjected to local sales taxes. With billions of dollars in annual sales at stake, Internet marketers oppose such levies, arguing that their transactions do not involve any specific jurisdiction. State and local governments respond that online sales are no different from those made in a local store. They complain that they are losing up to $15 billion in taxes annually as a result of tax-free Internet transactions and that the losses increase as Internet retail sales expand.[32] Congress has avoided decisions on the issue in recent years, voting to exempt Internet buyers from paying the tax while it tries to find a more or less satisfactory compromise.

Another set of digital issues facing Congress involves threats to civil liberties and privacy in the information age. Concerns of ordinary citizens in this area were highlighted in 2003 when the government, acting through the Federal Trade Commission, set up a do-not-call registry, designed to block telephone calls from telemarketers. The list grew to 62 million households within a year, sending a message to lawmakers that the American public wanted to put limits on electronic intrusions into their privacy.

Congressional concerns about privacy issues go well beyond curbing annoying phone calls. The House and Senate first approved privacy legislation involving electronic intrusion in 1974, aimed specifically at federal government practices. This has not ended the problem. At the turn of the century, a congressional investigation revealed that thirteen government agencies were secretly using technology to track the Internet habits of people visiting Web sites, including, in one case, providing the information to a private company. The practice was stopped, at least for a time.

A more serious example of government snooping was a Defense Department–sponsored proposal for an Information Awareness Office whose goal was to monitor cyberspace data in the interests of catching terrorists. The project would have touched every citizen's personal affairs, including tax documents, medical records, telephone calls, credit card transactions, and shopping mall security-camera videotapes, among other items. Data would be fed into what one critic called a "multi-googol-plexibyte database" that electronic robots would mine for alleged terrorist connections. In the wake of sharply negative public reactions, the proposal was withdrawn, but not before Congress and the White House saw what a highly charged political issue it was. More recently, the subject has resurfaced again in the form of debates on whether to authorize a national identity-card system based on digitized driver's licenses.

Meanwhile, Congress continues to adjust to other digital realities. One involves a political variation on the familiar America Online tag "you've got mail." For congressional staffs, the old letter-to-your-congressman is a fading memory, replaced by e-mail. A study by the Washington-based Congressional Management Foundation found that the annual rate of electronic messages sent to the House of Representatives topped 100 million by the turn of the century. Moreover, the study noted, the new electronic tide was overwhelming congressional staffs. Only 17 percent of House offices and 38 percent of Senate offices reported that they were able to answer all the e-mails they receive with a similar electronic response.[33]

Another sign of congressional involvement in digital matters is the Internet Caucus, a newcomer among dozens of special-interest groups on

Capitol Hill. One result is a new wave of lobbying centered on efforts by IT companies to assure that their products and practices are protected, or at least not ignored, in congressional legislation.[34] One of their tactics is to set up "technology fairs" on or near Capitol Hill to familiarize members of Congress and their staffers with their latest products and services. "The bottom line," says Charles Cantus, a technology industry lobbyist, "is that I've got 535 bosses on Capitol Hill and I need to bring all of them up to speed. I want them to be able to say 'I've seen that before.'"[35]

Digital politics is here to stay, including its role in the most basic of politicians' concerns — how to get elected and stay elected. The era of relying on local party organizations and volunteer workers ringing doorbells is fading. Radio and television advertising, the mainstay of most campaigns in recent decades, is also giving way to digital practices. Computerized databases that classify voters across a wide range of interests include even their food preferences. This slicing-and-dicing of voter habits leads down strange paths: one poll's results during the 2004 presidential campaign found that Mercury owners are more likely to vote Republican than owners of other cars. Overall, the new digital surveys have eliminated many traditional election practices. Computerized voter profiles are increasingly reliable indicators in helping candidates decide which households to phone, which doorbells to ring, and which voters to take to polling places on Election Day. Compiling digital lists of voters and their characteristics is now a growth industry, much of it based in the Washington area. One local firm has produced the SRDS Direct Marketing List Source, which has been called the bible of the direct marketing industry. In its initial offering, it listed hundreds of voter-profile categories, from "beer-bellied reactionary Republicans" to "Colorado-model liberals." Most Washington politicians, including the heads of the major parties, increasingly rely on voter profiles that have been cross-referenced with multiple lists of e-mail addresses collected from commercial mailers and other readily available sources. For the 2004 presidential election, one polling company, Washington-based Voter Contact Services, marketed a 155-million-person voter file culled from e-mail sources.

Meanwhile, the Internet has become a major channel for reaching voters in over 70 million American homes. The network's role as a political force was dramatically defined, somewhat improbably, by a former governor of Vermont, Howard Dean, in his primary campaign for the Democratic presidential nomination in 2004. A virtual unknown in national politics at the time, he raised tens of millions of dollars from small contributors, relying heavily on appeals issued through his Internet site. One of his successful moves was to invite his followers "to join me at lunch" in front of their computers on the same day that Dick Cheney, the Republican vice-presidential candidate, was holding a $2000-a-plate fundraising lunch. Online contributions from Dean's lunchtime supporters matched what Cheney took in from his fundraiser.

"The Internet isn't magic," Dean declared after his unsuccessful run for the presidency. "It's just a tool that can be used to do things differently. We treated it as a community, and we grew the community into something that has lasted long after the campaign ended. The Internet let us build that community in real time, on a massive scale."[36]

Web campaigning by both major parties has since become increasingly sophisticated, allowing candidates to identify specific demographic and geographic profiles, a practice known as microtargeting. In the 2004 Iowa presidential primary campaign, Democratic candidate John Kerry ran ads in the "help wanted" section of the *Des Moines Register*'s Web site. Kerry also sponsored ads in the *Washington Post*'s classified pages, where responders were asked to provide their ZIP code, gender, income level, and other personal information. The data were then used to target advertising to individual users, to the point where two readers viewing the same Web page from separate computers would see different ads.

Internet-based electioneering became a critical element in the run-up to the 2008 presidential campaign, with candidates in both major parties relying heavily on a Web presence.[37] As noted above, fundraising has become a newly important element in this strategy. Barack Obama, an early frontrunner for the Democratic nomination, raised over $7 million in Internet contributions, compared to Hillary Clinton's $4 million, in the first months of the campaign. Equally significant, Obama's Internet receipts consisted largely of small contributions, a newly important factor in campaign fund-raising efforts that have been dominated in recent years by appeals to big-time contributors.[38] In another development, members of Congress and other candidates have targeted handheld digital audio players in an effort to reach the millions of voters who own the devices. In 2005, House Democrats joined the podcast bandwagon, releasing free downloadable audio files of speeches, news conferences, and radio addresses on both their own Web site and on Apple's popular iTunes online music provider.

"This is the next generation of politics and we're using the data in ways we never have before," says Jim Nicholson, a former chairman of the

Republican National Committee. "We're trying to push the technology to the edge. Tip O'Neill used to say: 'All politics is local.' But now all politics is personal." Eddie Mahe, a Washington political consultant, adds: "It's kind of democracy at work. Historically, those same things have been said in every campaign. The difference is that they used to be said in a bar or at a corner coffee shop. But now, on the Internet, everyone has a megaphone."

In the 2008 presidential election campaign, all of the leading candidates announced their availability in Web presentations. Hillary Clinton followed up her Web appearance with a series of interactive video chats. Meanwhile, both major parties spent millions of dollars upgrading their databases in preparation for the election. They zeroed in on specific voter characteristics that can affect election choices, including (according to one pre-election survey) the alleged tendency of women cat owners to vote Democratic.

In the spring of 2007, eighteen months before the presidential election, representatives of over 700 organizations met at George Washington University to discuss the role of electronic communications in the campaign. One prospect, advanced by Scott Randall, president of BrandNames, suggested creating video games featuring individual candidates in the same way his firm makes them for other products. "Candidates are brands," he told the conferees, "and the power of video games, like a brand mascot, is to create an emotional connection with the brand."[39]

The 2004 presidential election campaign was a turning point in establishing the role of digital information in American politics. Post-election surveys indicated that 75 million Americans — 37 percent of the adult population and 61 percent of online citizens — said that they had used the Internet to discuss candidates, debate issues, and participate directly in the campaign by volunteering or by giving contributions to the candidates.

These facts were not lost on Democratic and Republican party leaders as they prepared for the 2008 presidential race. For the first time, Web sites played a critical role in their appeals to voters, displacing much of their previous reliance on television and radio advertising. Digital electioneering, particularly on the Internet, introduced a new level of two-way contact with voters. It was a particularly effective strategy in their fundraising efforts. "Any time you can reach one million donors with the click of a mouse, you redefine the way campaign financing is done in American politics," Philip Musser, a Republican political strategist, declared as the campaign got under way. Moreover, the information gathered by the two parties during the fundraising process fed a database that was valuable in making other appeals. For the first time party officials had accurate information on, for instance, how many Democratic–leaning Asian Americans making more than $30,000 a year lived in the Austin, Texas, television market.

Equally important in the new digitally driven environment was the Internet's enhanced role in establishing a vigorous political dialogue. In part this involved links between the national parties and their respective supporters. Most election analysts gave higher marks to Democratic campaign officials for the way in which they organized an Internet support system that recruited volunteer activists across the nation. They placed heavy emphasis on organizing small groups of supporters with shared interests. One such group, formed in Maryland, had as its common link that its members had lived in Singapore at one point.

Social-networking sites such as YouTube, Facebook, and MySpace played a critical role in setting the pace and tone of the new digital dialogue in the months leading up to the 2008 election. Although these sites were officially nonpartisan channels, there was little doubt that the political traffic they carried during the months of campaigning was heavily weighted in favor of Barack Obama and helped lead to his decisive victory.

One digital issue that is not yet resolved is the question of electronic voting. The subject first surfaced in the 2000 presidential campaign, which ended in a fierce controversy over alleged voting-place miscounts of paper ballots in Florida. Congress responded in 2002 with the Help America Vote Act, authorizing $3.86 billion to install electronic balloting systems that presumably would be more accurate. Many states began installing machines similar to bank ATMs to enable people to vote with the touch of a computer screen. The results were mixed. Critics of the system point out that there is no paper trail to verify the accuracy of computer-based voting. Others noted the problems of software malfunctions and electronic vote tampering. These criticisms led some states to require a paper record of every computer vote.

Another prospect is absentee voting via the Internet. Proponents claim that it would make the process easier for older voters, particularly those with disabilities that prevent them from getting to a polling place. Critics point out that online voting would create inequities because many Americans still do not have Internet access, particularly those in lower income groups. They cite census figures that indicate that fewer than half of African-American and Hispanic households are connected to the Internet.

Nevertheless, Internet voting is a live prospect down the electoral road. Michigan's Democratic Party organization used it in its 2004 primaries with considerable success. More than 28 percent of eligible voters, a high turnout for such an election, chose to vote via the Internet. Overall, the primary recorded the second highest number of voters ever, twice as many as the previous primary.[40]

The Manhattan Institute's William Eggers sees a further expansion of democracy in the new digital techniques: "Campaigns and elections have changed immeasurably. The Net has enabled candidates and issue groups to target and customize their pitches to voters at a fraction of the cost of mail, TV or radio. Anyone can get updates on legislation he or she cares about, and can participate in a moderated discussion with representatives or their staff. Nobody writes long thumb-sucking articles about 'The Death of the Voter' or 'The End of Responsive Government.'"[41]

The study of digital government has become a new academic discipline, with research institutes devoted to the subject in a dozen universities across the country. Scholarly journals have sprung up to track the subject, including the *Journal of E-Government*, published at the University of Southern California's School of Policy, Planning and Development. The subject has even spawned a three-volume *Encyclopedia of Digital Government*, produced by political scientists at Finland's University of Tampere.

In summary, digital government is big and growing. It is changing the ways in which the federal establishment operates; and, by extension, it is having a strong impact on how ordinary citizens view the government. "In this future," William Eggers points out, "people will find it hard to remember that things weren't always this way, that government used to be remote, unresponsive, slothful and static. They're used to government that promotes markets and choices, personalization and citizen participation in decision making. A government that is less burdensome, less costly, more transparent and infinitely more accountable. The end of Industrial Age government will come when a return to the old ways seems unimaginable."

What will be the eventual impact of digital government on American life in general and on Washington, D.C., as an information-age capital? The question was posed a quarter-century ago by Ithiel deSola Pool, an MIT political science professor, who warned that the free-speech traditions of the First Amendment may be subverted in the new digital environment: "In that future society, the norms that govern information and communications will be even more crucial than in the past.... The onus is on us to determine whether free societies in the twenty-first century will conduct electronic communication under the conditions of freedom established for the domain of print through centuries of struggle, or whether that great achievement will become lost in a confusion about the new technologies." This challenge has particular meaning for Washington's role in the new digital environment.

5

The Last Colony

Washington, D.C., is both a leader and a follower in the present transition to an information society. This ambivalence tells a lot about the town's future as it adapts to digital-age realities. In the process it is shucking much of its stodgy past for a newer, edgier role.

This shift is still a work-in-progress, but its overall direction is clear. The changes are reflected in a civic landscape that includes, among other amenities, a pedestrian-friendly downtown, demographic diversity, good restaurants, a lively arts scene, a new Major League baseball team, and a steady influx of brainy young people wired up with cell phones, Black-Berrys, and other digital artifacts. In these and many other ways, the city's new mood is upbeat.

In making this transition, Washington has had to overcome a long-time skepticism about its role in American life. In the nineteenth century, Charles Dickens, visiting the city, wondered why anyone would want to live there. Novelist Henry James found it a town absorbed in politics in its narrowest sense: "Washington talks about itself and almost nothing else." Columnist Russell Baker described the city in 1967 as Middletown-on-the-Potomac. Richard Rovere, writing in the *New Yorker,* posed the question "hick town or world capital?" and came down heavily on the former. "There is," he declared, "an altogether pervasive parochialism about the place." These dismissive attitudes have been reinforced by other powerful voices, including that of Hollywood moviemakers. From *Mr. Smith Goes to Washington* to *All the President's Men,* films have often portrayed the city as a sinkhole of cynicism and corruption.[1]

Unlike New York, San Francisco, or even Kalamazoo, there are no memorably friendly songs about the city. In 1940, Cole Porter wrote one for a musical, *Something for the Boys,* but it was dropped before the show opened on Broadway. In 1951, a group of local boosters offered a $1,000 prize for a song that would proclaim Washington's glories, a sort of municipal anthem. The contest was won by a Hollywood entertainer,

Jimmy Dodd, who said that his entry could be sung as "a ballad, a hymn, a march or even a Latin American tune."[2] The D.C. City Council recommended that it be adopted as the town's official song. It never caught on, in part because of such unlyrical passages as "God bless our White House, our Capitol, too; And keep ever flying the Red White and Blue."

Most politicians have distanced themselves from the city since its founding. "My zip code is 78701. That's Austin, Texas," presidential candidate George W. Bush declared in January 2000. "I'm not of the Washington scene."[3] His willingness to denigrate the city where he hoped to work reflected general attitudes in the American hinterland.

"The mere phrase 'inside the Beltway' makes people hyperventilate," says former *Washington Post* columnist Sally Quinn. "K Street, the symbolic home of the lobbyists, is anathema. 'The Hill' conjures up images of corrupt congressmen taking paper bags full of money. 'Georgetown' is the impenetrable bastion of the elitists.... Enter at your own risk, fail to turn your back on it when you leave and you turn into a pillar of salt."[4]

Why do candidates, from presidents on down, feel that they have to run against Washington? "Because it works," says former senator Bob Kerrey of Nebraska. "It's been going on since democracy began."[5]

Nevertheless, Washington is changing these days, a shift that marks the city's third transformation since its eighteenth-century origins. The first two involved wars—the Civil War and World War II. Today's environment puts the city and the region at the center of a technological revolution, the one wrought by digital breakthroughs and their spin-off effects on contemporary America. The change was confirmed in November 2008 with the election of Barack Obama as the first national leader to understand and act upon the implications of an emerging information-age society.

In many ways, Washington is setting the civic pace and direction of information-age developments. It is also a factor in another national trend: the new dominance of large metropolitan regions. These are the two dozen or so "metroplexes," anchored to a large city and surrounded by concentric bands of inner and outer suburbs.[6] Washington is one of the smallest of these regions, listed only twenty-fifth in the metroplex rankings, behind Charlotte, El Paso, and Fort Worth. By other measures, however, the District of Columbia and its surrounding area make up one of the country's largest metroplexes. In particular, the region is growing at a much faster pace than many larger ones. The Washington metroplex is currently home to over five million people, with the prospect of adding two million more in the next quarter-century, according to projections by the Metropolitan Washington Council of Governments. The Council itself reflects the region's complexity in its membership, which includes the District of Columbia, two states, and a dozen counties.

Geographically, Washington is a region that is expanding in a rough circle stretching out almost fifty miles beyond its hub city. The main street of the region is no longer a downtown avenue but an eight-lane beltway, a traffic-tangled artery that connects the suburbs. The result is a pattern that regional planners call selective deconcentration and the rest of us call urban sprawl. One in four newcomers to the region, for example, now settles in Northern Virginia's Loudoun County, 20 miles west of the city. Two decades ago, Loudoun was a rural backwater of small towns and farms. Its population jumped 41 percent in the first four years of the new century, the sharpest increase among the nation's large counties. This pattern is being repeated in other "outer counties" in the Washington region. Overall, these counties are growing at a faster pace than any metropolitan area outside the Sun Belt.

Economic expansion, based heavily on new IT industries, is only part of this pattern. Equally important is the region's changing demographics. The old mix of a numerically dominant white WASPish population and a large African-American minority is changing. A 2005 Census Bureau projection described the new mix as 56 percent non–Hispanic white, 25 percent black, 8 percent Asian, and 10 percent Hispanic. About one-third of new babies in the area have foreign-born mothers, mostly Hispanic, according to a 2005 report by the Center for Immigration Studies. Because it favors limits on immigration, the Center's birthrate estimates have been challenged, but there is little doubt that the region's new population mix reflects what some demographers characterize as the browning of America.

More recently, Washington and other major cities have witnessed another trend in regional growth. Known as edge cities, these are smaller "downtowns" located between suburban communities. Washington's most prominent edge city is Tysons Corner, a jumble of high-rise buildings and shopping plazas located just off the regional beltway in Northern Virginia in an area that was mostly open land forty years ago. Tysons is the second largest downtown in the region and the fifth largest retail center and fifteenth largest office market in the country. It has a daytime population of 100,000 workers, most of whom go home to nearby suburbs each evening. After four decades of office-building growth, local real-estate developers hope to give Tysons Corner a more settled urban look by adding thousands of apartments in the next few years.[7]

The Washington region's outward push affects how and where people work. The same Council of Governments survey on population growth cited above predicts that, in the coming years, the District of Columbia will lose 3 percent of its current jobs, while the inner suburbs gain 12 percent, and the outer suburbs 22 percent. The trends are not just statistics; they will have a huge impact on millions of people in the region.

For urbanologist Joel Kotkin this is the "new geography," defining the current transformation of American cities and their surrounding regions. In each case, the shift results in demographic and economic patterns that reflect information-age realities. Kotkin points out: "Workers in the information field ... represent the ascendant new middle class of the twenty-first century, earning roughly twice as much as other private sector workers. The information economy is likely to determine the locale of the elite pockets of wealth.... Wherever intelligence gathers, in small town or big city, in any geographic location, that is where wealth will accumulate."[8]

Kotkin's analysis has particular implications for Washington's future as an information-technology center. As noted, this trend accelerated during the dot-com-bubble recession at the turn of the century. While the rest of the nation was mired in an economic turndown, Washington gained more jobs than any other large metropolitan area. This was due in part to the rise in federal spending for digital goods and services after the 2001 terrorist attacks. Business growth, measured in jobs and output, has continued unabated ever since. A local economic development agency, the Greater Washington Initiative, reported in 2005 that in the previous year 77,000 jobs had been created in the region, more than twice the number in runner-up Atlanta. The capital area's economy churned out a record $313 billion in gross product that year, ranking fourth in the nation, according to the GWI report.

These changes have had a special impact on the region's center — the District of Columbia. Its evolution as an information-age city has followed the pattern of other leading IT centers, but with a twist. The most obvious difference is the city's role as the political hub of a continental nation whose principal business for over two centuries has been the production, storage, and distribution of information, the raw material of government operations. Moreover, as one local observer has noted, "It is the biggest company town in the world, and we own the company."

Other factors impinge on the District's new digital role. By constitutional fiat, it is squeezed into a ten-square-mile box. It will never grow bigger. Every weekday its population expands by half again as over a quarter-million commuters cross its borders. There is a smaller but significant daily outflow of District residents to suburban jobs. This heavy traffic has made Washington the third-worst gridlocked area in the country, after Los Angeles and San Francisco. In 2006 the region's average daily commute time was 33 minutes, second only to New York's 34 minutes among larger metropolitan areas.[9]

Other big cities have dealt with the added budgetary costs this daily migration creates by imposing a tax on commuters. Although the District government has proposed such a tax, it will never happen. The 1974 Home Rule Act passed by Congress specifically forbids the city from levying such a tax, a provision inserted by Virginia and Maryland congressional delegates, each aware that the tax was strongly opposed by their commuting constituents.[10]

For all its problems, from traffic gridlock on, the District of Columbia retains its uniqueness. The federal presence insures that it will never go the way of nearby Baltimore, where many manufacturing companies have disappeared, turning large parts of the city into a rust-belt wilderness. In particular, the District is a magnet town in ways that extend well beyond the business of politics, attracting young people over the years. The pattern has strong roots in the 1930s, when many professionals moved into the city, drawn by the challenges of the Roosevelt New Deal.

The trend continued through World War II and into the postwar decades, steadily reinforcing the city's image as a place to make one's professional mark. Washington's present attraction for newcomers extends well beyond the prospects of a federal job. It includes a wider mix of opportunities in research institutions, think tanks, universities, and private companies, all increasingly engaged in the city's transition as an information-age center. Washington attracts more of these young careerists every year. As noted earlier, it has a higher proportion of residents with graduate degrees than any other large American town.

Within this gentrification trend, however, lie paradoxes. One is that, overall, the District's population has not increased noticeably in recent years. In the early years of the twenty-first century, the city's population stood at about 550,000, with the prospect of declining further in the next decade, according to U.S. Census Bureau estimates. Anthony Williams, who was Washington's mayor at the time, declared this prediction "laughably wrong." He and other civic leaders challenged the Bureau's figures, leading to a recount that added 31,000 residents to the town's estimated population.[11]

"We need lots of different kinds of people in the city, including singles, childless couples, and empty nesters," says Alice Rivlin, director of the Brookings Institution's Greater Washington Research Program. "Upper-income people with no kids are a big help on the resource front. They pay taxes, and they don't use many services." Moreover, she adds, these affluent arrivals can help pay for housing subsidies and other services that benefit low-income residents.[12]

Some experts think that the city's population losses may not be a bad idea. Robert Lang, director of the Metropolitan Institute at Virginia Tech, says: "Washington may not be for everyone.... Smaller is better." Demographer William Frey sees the city's role as "a niche for professionals, a niche for young people and a niche for a certain elite."[13]

Meanwhile, Washington officials mounted a highly visible campaign to draw 100,000 new residents to the District. With the slogan "DC — it's the place to be," the city's planning office has sponsored meet-and-greet sessions with prospective residents, most of them young professionals attracted to urban amenities. The campaign has had some success, slightly reversing the city's downward population trend.[14]

Some unforeseen complications have arisen in meeting the campaign's original goal, beginning with the dramatic rise in local housing prices in recent years. The low-rent downtown boarding houses where many young careerists lived when they first arrived have disappeared, often refurbished as expensive apartments.[15] Meanwhile, median sale prices for single-family homes and townhouses rose 86 percent in the five years after 2000, higher than in any local jurisdiction except trendy Alexandria across the river. The number of houses in the District valued at $500,000 or more increased from 9,900 to 33,800 in the same five years, according to a D.C. Fiscal Policy Institute survey.[16] The rental market boomed, sending the vacancy rate in 2006 to a rock-bottom 2 percent, and has remained relatively steady since then, despite the economic recession at the end of the decade.

The District government has also encouraged home ownership by offering financial incentives, including a $5,000 income-tax credit for first-time home buyers and low-interest loans for down payments or closing costs. Nevertheless, the shortage of affordable housing is real, driving many potential town dwellers to the suburbs, forcing them to give up the urban amenities they had hoped for. Revitalizing the city and, in particular, reclaiming its large slum areas pose special problems for urban planners.

Washington has a unique historical status that militates against the kind of bulldozing demolition that has drained the center-city vitality of other American towns in recent decades. The District of Columbia has forty officially designated historic districts, including 23,000 landmark structures, according to the city's Historic Preservation Office.[17] Enough damage has already been done to the city by inept planning to send up warning flags about megaprojects designed to upgrade older neighborhoods.[18]

The fact is that expansion of any kind within the District is complicated. The town's architectural character is defined not only by Pierre L'Enfant's original plan but also by later decisions, particularly one generally restricting building heights to 130 feet. Real estate developers have argued in recent years for an easement of this restriction. "Density is critical. We're running out of land. We need to build up," says Christopher Leinberger, a land-use expert at the Brookings Institution. Leinberger has argued for raising the height limit in ways that could take pressure off development in and around historic districts. The alternative, he says, is that the city will run out of land for housing and commercial uses in a decade or so.[19]

Building-height restrictions, however, have been a factor in making Washington an essentially livable city. In 2006, the city government developed a master plan for civic development that emphasized the need to preserve the town's unique qualities as envisioned by L'Enfant two centuries ago while allowing for modern improvements.[20]

Washington has always had a floating population of short-term residents, but it also boasts a solid permanent core. According to the 2000 census, almost one-third of its citizens were born in the city, including a slight majority of its African American residents. Richard Nixon's comment that "everybody here is from someplace else" is slowly losing currency. Part of his complaint was that Democrats dominated the city's population. Today, Republicans make up less than 10 percent of the District's registered voters, with almost no hope among GOP leaders that the ratio will improve very soon.[21]

Meanwhile, significant changes are taking place in the city's African American community. After two centuries of being concentrated largely within Washington itself, less than 40 percent of the region's blacks now live in the District. Most of the rest have migrated to the middle-class suburbs in recent years. An adjoining county, Prince George's in Maryland, boasts the most affluent, best-educated black community in the nation.

Overall, Washington and its surrounding counties are economically well off, although they are not particularly a haven for the very rich. The region has its share of affluent residents, many of them attracted by federal largesse, but the general pattern is more complex. For a long time, the list of the area's wealthiest inhabitants was dominated by the Mars family, which made its money not from government contracts but from Mars candy bars and other sweets. In a listing of "the most expensive ZIP codes" compiled by DataQuick Information Systems, a California consultancy, District of Columbia neighborhoods run well behind such moneyed enclaves as Beverly Hills, Purchase, New York, and Boston's Beacon Hill.[22] However, the Washington metropolitan area has led the nation in the number of wealthy census tracts it contains.[23]

The Washington region also differs from other parts of the country in being a center for well-to-do African Americans. One of the most prominent, the local entrepreneur Robert Johnson, won the cable network franchise for the District of Columbia in the early 1980s with a $15,000 bank loan. By the time he sold his business, Black Entertainment Television, to a larger cable operator, the firm was worth $3 billion.[24]

Overall, the income of District residents has risen faster than that of residents in any of the fifty states, according to some estimates. Per capita personal income in the city was $54,985 in 2005, up 7.5 percent from the previous year. (Nationally, income-per-person had risen 4.6 percent.) The city's problem is the growing disparity in income distribution among its residents.[25] Former mayor Anthony Williams has summarized this situation in earthy terms: "The bell curve of incomes in Washington looks like a bosom. There's a mound of rich people, a mound of poor people and a gap where the middle class should be."[26]

The District's economic prospects are rooted strongly in changes in its municipal politics in recent decades. Although created as an independent city as part of the 1789 constitutional compromise, the town was essentially a congressional fiefdom for over two centuries, with some exceptions. In 1820, District voters were given the right to choose a mayor and council. Congress ended this arrangement in 1874 and replaced it with a White House–appointed commission that ran the city for almost a century. By the 1960s, a Free DC movement emerged, led by a firebrand young activist, Marion Barry, which sought equal political status with the rest of the country. Its mantra was: "DC — the last colony."

As a result, a series of steps restored some rights to the town's citizens. This led to a Home Rule Charter, passed by Congress in 1973, which provided for an elected mayor and city council. The charter's benefits did not, however, extend to giving Washingtonians voting representation in Congress, an issue that is still a sore spot in the District and beyond. International groups such as the Organization of American States and the Organization for Security and Cooperation in Europe criticize the U.S. government for treating District residents as second-class citizens.[27] In 2007, a bipartisan congressional proposal to give a House seat to the District while adding another seat for Republican-leaning Utah was debated and then dropped without coming to a vote.

The 1973 home-rule decision was an important turning point for Washington in its dual role as a viable metropolis and the seat of national government. However, the transition to limited self-government has been difficult at times. The first mayor, Walter Washington, was a distinguished black leader who brought personal dignity and managerial competence to the job. The second mayor, Marion Barry, almost ended the self-government experiment as a result of his administration's general incompetence. Over the course of three terms, eleven of his top officials were convicted of corruption; Barry himself wound up in jail on drug charges.[28] The city government was put into a form of receivership that included strict budgetary oversight by a congressionally appointed board.

For all the changes that have taken place in the city in recent decades, none was more important than the home-rule decision, giving the city a platform for playing a positive part in the region's new role as an advanced information-age center. After the Marion Barry debacle, a new generation of black leaders has taken over. The two mayors who succeeded Barry — Sharon Pratt Kelly and Anthony Williams — made major contributions to restoring the town to civic respectability. The current mayor, Adrian Fenty, represents the new generation of African American professionals who have emerged since the civil-rights revolution.[29]

Despite this new leadership, problems remain. Congress has generally underfunded the District government's annual financial subsidy. This subsidy derives from the federal government's control of about one-third of the city's land, which is not included on the tax rolls. In 2003, congressional payments to the District government amounted to $6.44 cents per inhabitant.[30] New Jersey, by contrast, received 62 cents per capita. More recently, the city's new prosperity has brought a rise in local tax receipts, triggered by a strong real estate market and the economic fallout from new information-technology enterprises in the region. By 2005 the City Council found itself in the unfamiliar position of dealing with a $1.2 billion reserve fund and a surplus of $300 million. Standard & Poor's and Fitch Ratings, two national credit-rating agencies, gave the city government an A rating, restoring the grade for the first time in several decades.

These events reflect a new confidence not only in the District government but in the wider city itself. In large part, they underscore the progress Washington has made in transforming itself from a slow-moving federal enclave into the hub of a vibrant region.

Among other changes, this progress is apparent in the way the city government has upgraded its digital infrastructure in recent years, beginning with a rush in the 1990s with the decision to wire up the District with fiber-optic networks. Nine telecommunications firms (including Bell Atlantic, the local phone company at the time) were given permission to install competitive fiber cable networks capable of handling vast amounts of voice, print, and visual messages simultaneously. It was, as one observer noted, a digital gold rush. Meanwhile, another technology, wireless cell phones, was being introduced on a large scale. The overall result is that the District of Columbia has one of the most sophisticated digital infrastructures of any city in the country.[31]

These changes have transformed the city government's previously primitive digital capabilities. When an able administrator, Suzanne Peck, took over as the District's chief technology officer in the late 1990s, she inherited a communications infrastructure that included thousands of antique rotary-dial telephones, dozens of communications networks that didn't "talk" to each other, and an e-mail system with a capacity of only two hundred messages a day.

In short order, she carried out a sweeping reform of the District government's communications assets. It was reportedly the largest municipal information-technology project in the nation at the time. A high-tech communications center was set up on the grounds of St. Elizabeth's Hospital in Anacostia to coordinate police, fire, 911, and nonemergency public-safety calls. The city government's Web site was upgraded to 120,000 pages of information in seven languages for local residents, businesses, and visitors.[32] The result of these improvements, according to the London *Economist,* is that the District "has become a model practitioner of e-government."[33]

In another innovative move, the District government turned to satellite technology to improve its operations. Under contracts with private firms, satellites track municipal operations, including the locations of every school bus and garbage truck during the day, as an aid in assuring that they are deployed efficiently. Satellite technology is also used to track one of the city's great resources — its trees. The high-flying satellites keep a running census of the trees and help identify those that are diseased or otherwise in trouble.[34]

The most visible signs of the city's resurgence can be found on its downtown streets. Washington has a thriving central district for the first time in decades. Until the 1940s, downtown DC was a pleasant mix of fashionable department stores, hotels, theaters, and "movie palaces." The Fox cinema on F Street boasted an enormous Wurlitzer organ and a fifty-piece symphony orchestra that rose from the pit at the start of the lavish stage shows that preceded each evening's movie. On Ninth Street, the Gayety Theater billed itself as "the acme of theater perfection" when Katherine Hepburn appeared there in *Much Ado About Nothing*. Over in Lafayette Square, touring companies gave performances in a 1700-seat opera house.

There was a serious flaw in this pattern, however. The downtown area and its attractions were effectively segregated by race: African Americans were not welcome. It was a highly visible example of the city's underlying tensions that erupted in the spring of 1968 in a massive race riot in which large sections of the central city were torched. In the aftermath of the riots, the downtown district fell on hard times. Its old attractions were cut back or shut down. White Washingtonians retreated to outlying shopping malls and entertainment facilities. Tourists avoided the area. Cheap outlet shops replaced old-line department stores; the movie theaters disappeared. As soon as commuting office workers went home each day, the city's core was abandoned to deserted streets and to crime.

Slowly, then ever more rapidly, the city center's fortunes began to improve. The change had begun improbably a decade earlier as a result of a Labor Department study on office space for federal workers. It was an unlikely forum for introducing proposals to renew downtown Washington. Instead of focusing on office-space problems, the group turned its attention to upgrading Pennsylvania Avenue, the southern boundary of the city's business district and a street that played a key role in Pierre L'Enfant's original plan for the capital city. Because it connected Capitol Hill and the White House, L'Enfant saw the avenue as a symbol reflecting both the separation of constitutional powers and the fundamental unity of the new American government. This vision was soon forgotten in the muddy realities of the new town.

Among the instigators of the project to upgrade Pennsylvania Avenue in the early 1960s were Secretary of Labor Arthur Goldberg and his assistant, Daniel Patrick Moynihan, a young Harvard scholar then in his first government job. The committee's final report, overseen by Moynihan, described the avenue as "a scene of desolation," consisting of decaying buildings and tawdry streetscapes. Goldberg left his Cabinet job soon after, but Moynihan stayed on to pursue a varied government career that included service as a White House assistant, Labor Department official, ambassador to India and, finally, senator from New York. Throughout his years in Washington, he never abandoned his mission of returning Pennsylvania Avenue to L'Enfant's vision of its role as the main street of the republic. He was aided in his campaign by support from Jacqueline Kennedy and an imaginative Chicago architect, Nathaniel Owings.[35]

Moynihan and his colleagues were also instrumental in finding new uses for some of the city's historic downtown structures like the Old Patent Office (now housing two Smithsonian museums), the Old Post Office, and the Pension Building, now the National Building Museum. In protecting these buildings from the wrecking ball, Moynihan and other civic activists assured that the downtown district will continue to have architecturally important reminders of the city's past. The result is a refreshing variation from the cookie-cutter architecture of many present-day urban centers across the nation.

Largely as a result of Moynihan's persistent lobbying, Congress created the Pennsylvania Avenue Development Corporation in 1972, charged with the overall redevelopment of the street. It was a big step towards the revitalization of downtown Washington. Pennsylvania Avenue became the southern base for a vibrant city center by giving it a strong lower boundary and transforming nondescript blocks of shoddy stores and decaying buildings into the grand avenue envisioned two centuries earlier by Pierre L'Enfant. There were some setbacks to the project: Moynihan and his associates could not prevent the construction of a new FBI headquarters, a concrete eyesore located halfway between the Capitol and the White House.

A half-century after Daniel Moynihan first proposed a revitalized Pennsylvania Avenue, downtown Washington is booming, in large part because of a successful collaboration between the District government and private interests. One result has been to boost the city's image as a business center. The city government now boasts that the District is the third largest office market in the country, with more than $70 billion in investment since the turn of the century.[36] One program, bureaucratically labeled tax-increment financing, encourages retail shops to locate in the new office buildings. A private group, the Downtown DC Business Improvement Initiative, has sponsored a special program for sprucing up the area's street vendors, from hot-dog stands to tourist-souvenir carts.[37]

The result is a newly vibrant city center, combining corporate business, retail shopping, and entertainment facilities. Important additions in recent years have been the Verizon Center, a multipurpose sports facility, as well as the upscale Gallery Place mall, with trendy shops and a fourteen-screen cinema complex that has helped revive the tradition of downtown movie-going. Live theater has also made a comeback with the addition of an enlarged Shakespeare Theater and the smaller avant-garde Woolly Mammoth Theater. Another important addition is a six-block-long convention center, opened in 2003 and designed to handle three million visitors a year.

In addition to convention-goers, tourists are returning to the city after a sharp drop-off following the 9/11 terrorist events. By and large, that loss has been reversed. In 2006, over fifteen million visitors came to the city, adding over $5 billion to the local economy.[38] In recent years Washington has been the fourth most popular tourist destination in the nation, nudging ahead of San Francisco but still trailing Orlando, Las Vegas, and New York.

Traditional visitor trails from the Capitol to the White House have expanded in recent years to include new attractions. One is a tour of sites associated with Washington's reputation as an international espionage center, which once included a Chinese restaurant where a secret meeting between American and Soviet go-betweens took place that helped defuse the 1962 Cuban nuclear missile crisis. This fascination with spies also explains the success of the commercially operated International Spy Museum, opened in 2002 on Pennsylvania Avenue. Its popularity threatens to outpace that of some of the Smithsonian Institution's museums and art galleries.

Most important, people are returning to live in downtown Washington for the first time in many decades. The trend began in the 1990s when a few urban pioneers moved into rehabilitated lofts and old office buildings. The trickle of newcomers has become a flood in recent years. This in-migration is happening throughout the downtown district, but its primary focus has been the newly named Penn Quarter bordering on Pennsylvania Avenue. By the middle of the decade, thousands of apartment units were under construction as part of over $3 billion of private investment in the area. Penn Quarter now contains amenities that would have been unthinkable a decade earlier, including grocery stores, dry-cleaning shops, restaurants, theaters, and a community association where residents debate neighborhood issues.[39]

Penn Quarter got a significant boost in 2001 when city officials made an attractive offer to the Freedom Forum to move its Newseum into the District from Arlington. A media museum, the Newseum is a showplace for displaying American media achievements. The city offered a prime piece of Penn Quarter real estate across from the National Gallery and accelerated the usual building-permit timetable to close the deal in six months. The museum building, which also includes retail stores, offices, condominiums, and a restaurant, opened in 2008.[40]

More recently, the building boom has extended to the northern borders of the downtown district. One project, on the site of an old wax museum, involves a $133 million mix of 600 apartments, retail stores, a Starbucks café, and other amenities. A public-private development coalition is promoting another large tract of real estate near Union Station, as a center for media, technology, and the arts. Known as NoMa (for "north of Massachusetts Avenue"), the project upgrades a large area that had been a civic eyesore for decades, abandoned to weeds and parking lots.[41]

The downtown area's new housing is both trendy and expensive. It is also a highly visible part of the District government's overall strategy of attracting a new generation of young professionals to the center city. City officials and private developers have cooperated in helping upgrade other close-in neighborhoods. Leading the list of revitalized areas is the "14th Street corridor," north of the downtown district. In the early decades of the last century, it was a mixed neighborhood of Victorian-style mansions, with middle-class housing on the grid streets and lower-income housing on the side streets. It also contained a retail area, including an "auto row" that was the place to buy a car in the city. All this ended in 1968, when racial rioting sparked by the assassination of Martin Luther King Jr. devastated the area, an event that including killings, looting, burned-out buildings, and other destruction. For years after the riots, the area was a place to be avoided.

More recently, 14th Street Northwest and other main streets north of the downtown center have undergone a slow, steady renaissance.[42] The changes include trendy shops, restaurants, coffee bars, and renovated lofts attracting young careerists seeking urban amenities. The neighborhood's prospects have been raised by the addition of new cultural attractions, including theaters and art galleries, giving Washington an "off-Broadway" district for the first time. In 2005, one theater, the Studio, upgraded and expanded its operations to three stages, located on a block that once featured an automobile showroom.

Another area undergoing an urban rebirth is Mount Pleasant, further north on 14th Street. Its rehabilitation includes the restoration of one of the city's finest old movie palaces, the 2,500-seat Tivoli, which had been slated for the wrecking ball after being trashed in the 1968 riots. Upgraded housing, shopping centers, and offices are also transforming Mount Pleasant. The refurbished Tivoli has become home base for the GALA Hispanic Theater, one of the city's major drama groups.

The one business sector that has not been heavily involved in the District's revitalization is information technology. At the turn of the century, it accounted for less than 1 percent of the District of Columbia's job base, according to a survey by economist Stephen Fuller of George Mason University.[43] Efforts by the District government and local private business-development groups to attract IT industries have been generally unavailing: the region's IT growth continues to take place almost entirely in the suburbs. The sector's impact on the District's new growth has been largely indirect, in particular through the role played by the city's white-collar workers, including lawyers, lobbyists, and government officials who support IT firms in the Washington suburbs and beyond.

There are many factors driving the city's changing image, but none is more important than the influx of educated young careerists from all parts of the nation. As noted, their motivation in past years focused on the prospects for jobs in the federal bureaucracy. This remains a formidable attraction, particularly as the government adjusts its hiring patterns to include more highly paid professional jobs requiring advanced digital skills. In general, however, today's newcomers are not so heavily tuned in to the traditional pattern of a federal career, involving a slow climb up the bureaucratic ladder. Increasingly their focus is on the local private sector and its digital-age jobs, from computer engineers to nanotechnology biologists.[44]

There is an underside to this shift, one often hidden by the glare of the other changes taking place in the city. It involves, first and foremost, the stubborn effects of Washington's past, the legacy of a city split down the middle by race. This division was enforced in modern times by a "code of ethics" promoted by the Washington Real Estate Board, which declared that "no property in a white section should ever be sold, rented, advertised or offered to colored people." Curiously, the code also included similar restrictions on dealing with "Persians and Syrians." These housing covenants were not declared illegal until 1948.[45]

In many ways, the divisions created by these covenants persist. The genteel catchphrases for this are "east of the park" and "west of the park," the park being Rock Creek Park, historically the verdant dividing line between the two racial and economic halves of the city. A generation ago, historian Constance McLaughlin Green made a more realistic distinction between the "capital city" of the public imagination and the "secret city" inhabited by an African American majority population, a group that was largely ignored by west-of-the-park whites.[46]

This division has been diluted in fits and starts in modern times, but it remains a stubborn fact of Washington civic life. Many former black residents of rundown slum neighborhoods have moved up the economic ladder, allowing them in many cases to migrate to middle-class neighborhoods in the suburbs. The formerly solid black presence east of the park has also been changed by a new influx of Hispanic and Asian families, many of them recent immigrants. This pattern has been further modified by the gentrified takeover of formerly African American neighborhoods by young white careerists. At one level, this trend reflects a net improvement in the quality of the city's housing stock, along with better neighborhood amenities in once rundown districts. The downside to this otherwise healthy trend is that the new influx of gentrifying families means that many lower- and middle-income residents are being pushed out of housing they could otherwise afford.[42]

This two-way housing migration tends to widen the economic gap between the newcomers and older, mainly black residents. A mid-decade survey by the DC Fiscal Policy Institute reported that income of the top two-fifths of Washington households was thirty-one times higher than that earned on average by the lowest fifth. More recently, incomes among the city's richest households grew 38 percent, while those of the poorest rose just 3 percent. The overall result is a divided city where the rich and poor populations are expanding but the middle class is not. The District's economic vitality in recent years has generated thousands of jobs, but suburban commuters have filled a large share of them.[48]

Urban renewal in the District has a mixed history, including a decision a half-century ago that involved government agencies and private developers. Their plan was to bulldoze a large part of the city's Southwest quadrant, then a ragtag neighborhood of row-house slums, and replace it with garden apartments, broad streets, leafy parks, new schools, and a large theater complex, along with a revitalized waterfront along the Potomac.

This "new Southwest" was hailed at the time as an example of smart urban planning. However, the project had a dark underside as hundreds of black families were pushed out to make way for the upscale improvements. Some of these families retreated to public housing; others had to make do with slum apartments as bad as or worse than what they left behind.[49] More recently, the District government, working with private developers, has drawn up a master plan for redeveloping the area, correcting some of the mistakes made four decades ago.[50]

This pattern has been repeated since, on a somewhat smaller scale, as lower-income neighborhoods become gentrified.[51] According to SOME — So Others May Eat, a Catholic social services agency, the result is that Washington has the smallest stock of affordable housing of any large city in the country, with the added factor that the remaining affordable units are disappearing at an alarming rate, as affluent newcomers bid up the price of inner-city housing. SOME also points out that, although 40 percent of the city's homeless are employed, they cannot find low-rent housing.[52]

The number of affordable housing units in the city has dropped by nearly 12,000 in recent years, according to a D.C. Fiscal Policy Institute analysis of Census Bureau statistics. At the same time, median rents jumped 9 percent, median house values soared 32 percent, and almost 30,000 new housing units were in the pipeline, most of them in the higher-priced range. *Washington Post* economics columnist Steven Pearlstein sees these trends as threatening economic growth in the city and region: "Unless we can figure out some way to increase the supply of housing and begin moderating the cost, Washington is in real danger of pricing itself out of the market for new jobs, forcing companies and even government agencies to channel their growth somewhere else."[53]

Another *Post* writer, Colbert King, points out that the city's boosters, whom he calls the economic-development hucksters, ignore the lack of decent housing and other unfulfilled needs of lower-income citizens. Despite the boosters' happy talk, King sees a city in danger, centered on the collapse of black families.[54] He puts a human face on the problem by describing a series of incidents that occurred within a few days:

- Two funerals took place, one for a 14-year old girl killed at four o'clock in the morning by a stray bullet, another for a 17-year-old boy shot to death inside Ballou Senior high school.

- A 14-year-old boy, stopped by a traffic cop on a local street for not wearing a seat belt, had a .380 semiautomatic handgun in his pocket and a Mac-10 submachine gun in the pouch of his sweatshirt, both fully loaded.
- Four children, including a three-month old baby, were found in an apartment alone, with an empty refrigerator, a bowl of raw chicken parts, and a can of beans that had been pried open so that a child's hand could fit inside.

The District, King argues, may be luring well-heeled apartment dwellers, but "it is in danger of losing a large portion of something more precious and irreplaceable than the new faces and tax dollars flooding our town: our next generation." These losses include the collapsed state of family life among lower-income residents that he says is the Great Unmentionable.

The evidence is stark. About 60 percent of babies in the city are born to unmarried mothers. A single parent heads most black families. At mid-decade, the city had the highest AIDS rate per thousand in the country, roughly ten times the national average. African American women account for over 90 percent of all women infected with HIV/AIDS in the city. As a 2005 *Washington Post* editorial noted: "If the District was a country, it would rank 11th in the world in HIV prevalence, between Mozambique and Tanzania.[55]

For years, Washington led the nation's big towns in the annual rate of local homicides — twice that of Los Angeles and more than six times New York City's. The District's annual rate has since dropped to under two hundred incidents in recent years, but it remains one of the most deadly cities in the country, with a homicide rate as high as 35 incidents per 100,000 residents. By comparison, Boston, which is about the same size as the District, had an equivalent rate of ten homicides. Although the situation has improved more recently, the shorthand description of the town as the "murder capital of the nation" has been harder to shake.

The city's greatest running scandal is its public school system. A half-century after the District's schools were desegregated, they have been overwhelmed by failure. In some perverse ways, the system may have been better managed and, overall, more effective under the old two-tiered racial setup, with its demeaning labels: "First Division" for white students and "Second Division" for black students. This segregation had mixed effects. One "colored" high school, Dunbar, played a significant role in training many of the black leaders of the civil rights movement, sending them off to Harvard and other elite universities. Racial lines were drawn tighter in the 1950s when school desegregation led to the "white flight" of families who decamped to the suburbs in search of good schools for their children. A variation on this migration is being repeated today as more affluent black families leave the city for the same reason.

The story of Washington's continuing schooling crisis is told partly in statistics and other public records. In 2005, a typical year, the city led the nation's states in spending, over $11,000 per public school pupil, according to *Education Week*, a public-education trade paper.[56] It does not follow that the extra funds — twice that of Utah's annual per-pupil spending — have led to quality education. A quarter of the system's teachers were not properly credentialed in recent years. Half had never gotten a license in the subjects they taught; many in the other half had expired licenses. The problem involves more than professional skills: under the Bush administration's No Child Left Behind law, the city stood to lose important federal funds if its teacher corps was not fully certified. The deadline passed with little evidence of a significant improvement in the accreditation rate.[57]

The results of this mismanagement are disheartening. Again, the evidence is in the statistics. In 2007, nearly 36 percent of District residents, a total of 170,000 persons, were functionally illiterate, according to a survey by the city's State Education Agency.[58]

In 2006, the U.S. Department of Education, which dispenses federal subsidies to school districts, designated the District schools as a "high risk" recipient of such grants, a distinction no other school system in the continental United States had earned. Among the failures charged to Washington's schools is their inability to make adequate use of new educational tools, particularly those involving computers. Following a six-year attempt to install a $25 million computer system, the *Washington Post* declared the project "an obvious flop."

Perhaps the most telling example of the local school situation was embedded in a 2005 study of the per-student cost of insuring security within public school buildings. According to a survey of such costs by major urban school systems, the District's annual per-student outlay ($280) was twice that of Atlanta, the next-highest spender on school security in the country.[59]

Local school officials defend the system, pointing to individual improvements in dropout rates and daily attendance. Nevertheless, about a third of the system's students drop out before they finish twelve years.

In 2007, the installation of a new mayor, Adrian Fenty, led to a showdown battle between City Hall and the school board over who should have primary responsibility for running the school system. After a bruising bureaucratic battle, overall control of the system was transferred to the mayor's office.

This decision may improve matters, particularly if the city deals with its basic racial patterns and their economic overtones in a more deliberate way. Such an approach would include more attention to Washington's new demographic mix, which has Latino and Asian families softening the old hard lines of de facto segregation. Another challenge is that of meeting the needs of younger professional couples, both whites and minorities, who have moved into the city in recent years. For most of these parents, the alternatives to largely dysfunctional public schools is to enroll their children in one of the District's expensive private schools or move to the suburbs.[60]

Encouraging signs of change could translate into a swifter pace of overall economic and social improvements for the District. The alternative is a continuation of the mix of fractious racial, economic, and social forces that have held the city back for so long. The prospects for improvement include a more vibrant demographic pattern, and, above all, a new sense of the city's place as the hub of a metropolitan region that is emerging as a leader in a new kind of information-based society.

A new inwardness and sense of foreboding created by worldwide terrorism poses a new threat to these hopes. It has already had its effect on the look and feel of the city. As Jurek Martin, a columnist for London's *Financial Times*, has observed about the town's post–9/11 atmosphere: "The charm of Washington used to be its sense of accessibility, but this is now being compromised by the new focus on security." Increasingly, he adds, Washington is taking on the look of a permanent armed camp: "The road separating the White House and Lafayette Park has been turned into a secure but Stalinist concrete pedestrian walkway. The ultimate irony is that just as the long-derided and neglected citizens of Washington have got their act together, federal security considerations are rendering it less than 'that shining city on a hill' it was and should be."[61]

One hopes that Washington can overcome the forces that hold it back in the new age. There are reasons to believe that this can happen. As writer Alfred Kazin points out:

> Washington is the most visible sign of America's continuity and relative consistency as a political system. Society in America, as all our literature says, is

always in flux, often in eruption, tense with race and class conflicts. Our big cities present the greatest wealth in the world, the most daring architecture, side by side with beggary, open degradation, homelessness. But Washington presents on the surface, for official purposes, a show of national stability that is warranted enough when you consider the revolution and counterrevolutions that have yanked so many nation-states from their roots.[62]

The ultimate tribute to Washington's pull on the American imagination may have been expressed some years back by *New York Times* reporter Tom Wicker. Recalling his first visit to the city as an eleven-year-old with his parents after an all-night train ride from North Carolina, he wrote: "I remember coming out of Union Station the next morning in brilliant sunshine and looking across the great plaza to the Capitol: fierce choking patriotism blazed in my breast. I thought the dome against the sky was the most beautiful sight I had ever seen, and I still do."[63]

6
Hip DC

Washington is changing in the new century almost in spite of itself. Many of its encrusted patterns remain, but the city is no longer focused so intently on bureaucratic routines or on four-year presidential cycles, its version of Nature's circadian rhythms. Newer, more fluid forces are in play: the town is shucking old habits that clash with digital-age realities.

These changes are part of a larger national pattern, as digital production, storage, and distribution of information take their place as America's primary business. While reflecting this general shift, Washington adds its own special twists as it makes the transition from its traditional status as a government town to the more complex pattern reshaping the city and its surrounding region.

A new demographic reality constitutes a critical factor in this change, namely a generation of savvy young professionals impatient with the practices that defined Washington in the past. The old order, based on a shifting pattern of money and political clout, is still alive and well. Its membership is broadly identified in a local publication, *The Social List of Washington, D.C.* Known as the Green Book from its traditional cover, it is a 400-page annual listing of the town's movers and shakers, compiled by an anonymous selection committee.

There will always be a floating elite in Washington. The current group is centered, as in the past, on the White House, the Congress, and the major federal agencies, together with the city's network of power brokers in corporations, lobbying firms, trade associations, and other interest groups. Now men and women not listed in the Green Book challenge their influence. These are the professionals linked to the town's evolution as a digital-age center. Overall, they are a different breed: highly educated, sassy, and uninterested in the old ways of doing things.

As a group they cut across the racial, economic, and cultural lines that historically defined American professional elites. In Washington the roots of this change trace back to the 1930s and the extraordinary group of (mostly) men who joined the new Roosevelt administration under the banner of the New Deal. Dubbed the Brains Trust, they helped define an expansive new role for the federal government and, by extension, American politics. Among other achievements, they provided the ideological force behind social and economic reforms that included the Social Security system, the forty-hour workweek, urban slum clearance, and the electrification of rural America.

The New Deal's brain trusters were young, brash, and self-confident. Moreover, they brought a new demographic mix to the process: the brightest of them were often Jewish or Irish from northeastern cities, groups that had played limited roles in previous administrations. (Blacks, Asians, and other minorities were still conspicuously missing.) They moved into boardinghouses in Georgetown, ate and drank at Billy Martin's new post–Prohibition tavern on Wisconsin Avenue, and rode the streetcar downtown to their government jobs.

The current crop of professionals are the latter-day successors to the New Deal's young rebels, making Washington one of the hottest "brain gain" metropolitan areas in the nation. At the turn of the century, the Census Bureau ranked the city fourth (behind San Francisco, Los Angeles, and Atlanta) in attracting young professionals. "Cities and metros are more focused on this indicator than just about any other indicator these days," says Bruce Katz of the Brookings Institution's Center on Urban and Metropolitan Policy. "The places that can capture larger and larger shares of these educated people can grow and prosper."[1]

The result is a fierce competition among U.S. cities to attract digitally savvy young careerists. "In a Darwinian fight for survival, American cities are scheming to steal each other's young," the *Washington Post* declared in a survey of the new migration. "They want ambitious young people with graduate degrees in such fields as genome science, bioinformatics and entrepreneurial management."[2] This pattern differs from the regional migrations that took place during the Rust Belt's decline and the Sun Belt's growth in the 1970s and 1980s. A new generation is voting with its feet to live in foul-weather havens up North where the work is smart and the culture cool. As demographer William Frey notes, they seek a different environment in what he calls "ideaopolises."

Washington has been a particular beneficiary of this change. Big cities are no longer automatic destination points for the new generation. New York and Chicago did not make the list in a 2003 Brookings Institution survey of fifty cities with the highest percentage of residents with college degrees. Washington was first in the ranking, followed by Atlanta and San Francisco.

As in other digital-age centers, young Washington professionals are among the most restless demographic groups in the country: three quarters of them changed residence in the last five years of the twentieth century, according to the Census Bureau's most recent decennial count. Tens of thousands of single college graduates migrated to the region during the 1990s, but the same number moved out. More recently, however, they are moving in and staying. This pattern appears to be holding in the new century, reinforcing the steady shift to what some urban planners call the region's thought-based economy.

About half the jobs available to the newcomers are in management, professional, and related occupations, compared with a third in other major cities. Washington city officials estimate that two-thirds of the town's economic growth through 2010 will be in these job categories, with a large share filled by young professionals.[3]

Meanwhile, the newcomers are changing the face of the town. They tend to live in refurbished row houses and converted condos in Columbia Heights and a half-dozen other formerly seedy neighborhoods, attracted by the short commute to work, upscale restaurants, art galleries, theaters, and other amenities. The result is a new kind of gentrification that adds to Washington's trendy image. As noted in the previous chapter, this is part of a pattern that includes large dollops of private investment, a massive downtown building boom, and a more competent city government, among other signs of a town redefining itself.

The new dot-com generation originated in California, and specifically Silicon Valley, south of San Francisco. Beginning in the 1960s, a group of start-up IT companies moved into a new industrial park near Stanford University in Palo Alto. It was the beginning of the valley's mythical early days of late-night coding, libertarian politics, take-out pizza, and the first generation of digital-age professionals. The staffs of these firms divided roughly between "ponytails" and "suits," the former representing the long-haired, blue-jeaned computer nerds and the latter the more sartorially proper front-office managers. Together they played a strong role in creating the digital lifestyles that are changing American society.

The young professionals now moving into the Washington area are the demographic descendents of these California pioneers. They represent a somewhat different mix of talents from those that marked the early Silicon Valley group. Pony-tailed techies are still well represented in the new flow of professionals into the capital region. But the migration also reflects other aspects of Washington's interests, including a wide range of what might be called social science professionals — economists, political scientists, sociologists, public-opinion analysts, and the like. The bond uniting them is their stake in the region's digital transformation, following the steady buildup of an information-technology private sector. Professional opportunities made available by the parallel expansion of job opportunities in think tanks, universities, and government research facilities also attract these young professionals.

Overall, the newcomers bring a vibrant mix to Washington and its surrounding region. Demographically, they are more diverse, with the traditional cohort of Northern European whites now sharing professional ranks with blacks, Latinos, Asians, and other previously underrepresented groups. For the first time gays are becoming a larger, more identifiable part of the pattern. The biggest change is the presence of more women among the area's new digital professionals, reflecting broader national trends. Traditionally locked into lower clerical jobs, women have pushed the famous "glass ceiling" upward, advancing to higher levels of responsibility in government and private sectors.

These trends have had a special impact on job patterns in the Washington region. The District ranks ahead of all fifty states in women's median wages, with Maryland a close second and Virginia eighth, according to a study by the D.C.-based Institute for Women's Policy Research. "The federal government is relatively good for women because equal employment opportunity laws are very strict," Amy Caiazza, the study's director notes. A downside to the Institute's findings is the salary gap between white women and women of color in the District. According to the survey, white women's median salary was $55,200 compared to $33,700 for black women. Although working women in Washington had the highest median salaries in the nation overall, the city also had more women living in poverty than did their counterparts in forty-seven states, according to the study.[4]

These economic shifts have had a particular impact on the lifestyles of the city's young professionals. It includes the emergence of more two-income couples able to afford the higher costs of living in town. Typically, these newcomers are childless, postponing the day when they have to decide whether or not to move to suburbs that offer more capacious housing and better schools for their children.

As noted, the area's political jurisdictions compete with one another to attract young professionals. The most visible of these efforts has been the District government's campaign to persuade them that, in the words of one of the campaign's marketers, Washington is "hip, happening, the hot place to be." For the Brookings Institution's Bruce Katz, the irony of the city's recruiting effort is that it took so long for the municipal bureaucracy to get around to it. Setting its goal at 100,000 new residents, with an emphasis on young professionals, the campaign has focused heavily on the advantages of city life. The campaign's early messages were targeted at childless couples and gays. "That is the low-hanging fruit," says Valerie Sumner, one of the campaign's managers. "It's a market we felt could happen quickly." Although the goal of 100,000 new residents is still a distant reality, there has been a steady rise in the number of young professionals who choose to live in the city.

It is useful to take a closer look at this group. In many ways, what is happening in Washington and its surrounding region reflects national trends. But Washington is unique in its impact on the rest of American society, politically and socially. Overall, the city is a test bed for both the shape and speed at which these changes take place. The significant trendsetters, young professionals, are often difficult to pin down, given their demographic and cultural diversity. They tend to be oblivious to or disdainful of long-standing social conventions and patterns that previously defined differences within American society. By many measures, they no longer fit the old mold.

One way to identify them is by the information-age artifacts they rely on in their public and private lives. *By their gadgets ye shall know them.* They are wired up — or, increasingly, "wirelessed" up — to digital devices that link them to their friends and professional colleagues. In part, this pattern involves traditional computers, from wall-sized models to desktop machines. Increasingly, however, they are following the national trend that emphasizes smaller portable devices.[5] By the middle of the decade, notebook-style laptops accounted for almost a third of all personal computer sales in the country, with the prospect that they will outnumber the larger machines in a few years.[6] International Data Corp., a major industry consultant, estimates that men and women who rely on cell phones, laptops, and other mobile devices on the job will account for over 70 percent of the workforce by the end of the decade. Meanwhile, mobile-phone companies compete to market smaller, more versatile products. In 2006, Motorola began selling a cell phone that was only nine millimeters thick.

Increasingly, this downsizing extends to a wider range of devices, including updated versions of such old standbys as wristwatches and pocketknives. In recent years Victorinox, the company that markets Swiss Army knives in the United States, has developed a profitable market in knives that provide digital services in addition to their traditional functions of clipping and cutting. The firm's Swiss Memory model stores up to 512 megabytes of memory and can be plugged into a computer's USB port. It also includes a wire crimper and cutter intended for repairing digital gadgets. In another version, the knife blade and other accessories can be detached so that the data storage device can clear airport security. The response to these digitized knives has been "phenomenal" in Washington and other U.S. markets, according to Suzanne Rechner, president of Victorinox's American subsidiary: "Our problem is keeping up with demand."[7]

Another familiar item, the wristwatch, is being digitized. They are latter-day versions of the fictional Dick Tracy two-way wrist radio worn by the comic-strip detective back in the 1930s. The new versions include exotic features, from telephones to personal organizers. Microsoft has marketed a "smart watch" that uses an FM radio signal to bring news, sports results, stock prices, and other data to the watch's face. LAKS, an Austrian firm, has taken the ultimate step with a watch that has a built-in flash memory and a standard USB connector in its strap, enabling it to be plugged into a computer. The firm's overall sales doubled as a result.[8]

Digitized pocketknives and watches still play a minor role among the portable devices used by Washington's young professionals, who are more likely to carry BlackBerrys. A quintessential example of a product fitted to their digital needs, BlackBerrys emerged in the late 1990s, after ten years of research and testing by Research in Motion (RIM), a Canadian startup that had been looking for a breakthrough in mobile communications. The first idea was to market it as a red device, the StrawBerry, because its little keys looked like strawberry seeds. According to company lore, one of RIM's founders, Mike Larides, wanted it to look more serious. It needed to be black — a BlackBerry.[9]

The result was a marketing triumph, with a particular impact on how Washington does business. BlackBerrys were an improvement on earlier handheld devices such as Palm Pilots, which only kept track of addresses and appointments. BlackBerrys added the decisive improvement: sending and receiving e-mail messages. They quickly became a high-tech alternative to cell phones, which had already had a strong impact on Washington's digital habits. The BlackBerry's new role in the city's political life was confirmed in 2001 when the House of Representatives appropriated $5 million to equip its members and their staffs with BlackBerrys.

Statistics on the BlackBerry's geographic distribution are not readily available, but it is a safe bet that Washington and its suburbs contain an outsized proportion of them. Striking evidence of the BlackBerry's role in federal government operations emerged in 2005 when the Department of Justice filed a legal brief in a patent dispute involving BlackBerrys, asking the court to delay a proposed shutdown of the devices on the grounds that doing so would limit the efficiency of federal officials in carrying out their duties. More recently, the BlackBerry's role as the all-purpose portable communicator was threatened by a new generation of hand-held devices, including Apple's iPhone, introduced in 2007.

BlackBerrys and other portable services have to be connected to electronic networks. The most basic of these is the plain-vanilla telephone landline system, which began as a wire-based service and is now being transformed by wireless technologies, most notably cell phones. The other network critical to the new digitization is the Internet, which depends heavily on utility-company circuits, both wired and wireless, to deliver its information.

The Washington region is a hotbed of these electronic services. This is particularly true of the federal city itself, where the combination of limited geographical size and the focus on information-based activities makes it one of the most wired-up urban areas in the world. At another level, the city plays a special role in defining the pace and direction of information-age developments on a national scale. This turns on the fact that large parts of the new infrastructure are publicly regulated services in such areas as technical standards, rate structures, and legal status. By setting the rules on these matters, Washington bureaucrats, from Congress on down, have defined the legal and regulatory boundaries for the digital transformation of America.

All this is happening at a time when the current status and future direction of the country's communications resources are in splendid disarray, beginning with the telephone system. Until the 1980s, the system was largely the domain of one company, the American Telephone and Telegraph Co. (AT&T), which had a congressionally mandated monopoly based on its promise to wire the entire country in a single integrated network. The promise was fulfilled, and AT&T prospered, with annual revenues by the 1970s greater than the gross national products of two-thirds of the world's nations. Once upon a time, only a few decades ago, its network was focused primarily on providing what phone-company people called POTS — plain old telephone service. It did this both efficiently and imperially. Comedienne Lilly Tomlin became famous for a telephone-operator skit that tweaked AT&T's corporate nose by telling her imaginary customers: "We're the phone company. We can do no wrong. We serve everyone from kings and presidents down to the scum of the earth."

Times have changed. AT&T's total dominance was effectively ended as a result of the government's 1982 decision to break up its monopoly. The company became a diminished player in a telecommunications sector being transformed by new technical and economic realities. In 2005 the firm's assets were taken over by SBC Communications in a blockbuster $16 billion deal. The transaction had an ironic twist in that SBC's phone operations were originally one of the regional parts of AT&T's nationwide network. Later, AT&T roared back with an $85 billion takeover of Bell-South, another former segment of the AT&T monopoly. The result, the *Washington Post* declared, was "a new corporate giant that will stand astride the telecommunications industry like none other."[10] At the time AT&T had a market capitalization of $225 billion, four times greater than Verizon, its leading competitor.

These corporate deals are outsized examples of the transformation occurring in the American communications sector. At the core of this shift is the digital revolution: any form of information — voice, video, or print — can be transmitted digitally over wire lines or by wireless circuits in mix-and-match combinations. Bits and bytes don't distinguish between a teenager's phone sessions, an Internet video, or a weather report from a NASA station on Mars. This new flexibility has transformed what was once a stable, cautious communications sector. Old-line phone companies have felt the major impact of the shift and been turned into multi-media businesses competing with cable-TV firms, satellite networkers, Internet providers, and media outlets such as newspapers and television stations. Meanwhile, phone companies are still the primary suppliers of communications circuits in the country, the backbone infrastructure of the American information age.

In Washington, this means Verizon Communications. Its local presence is special because of the city's unique communications requirements, in particular those involving the government. Federal offices in downtown Washington have long been "hard wired" with special tamper-proof cable circuits designed to shield sensitive government voice and data traffic.

They are part of a local grid that has given the city the most sophisticated communications facilities on earth.

Verizon is a major player in this process. It is no longer your father's phone company. In common with its corporate counterparts across the country, the firm's challenge in recent years has been to reinvent itself to provide a new generation of advanced services in Washington and the other regions where it operates. It has been an expensive undertaking: Verizon spent $13.5 billion in 2005 upgrading its nationwide facilities. It then went on a buying spree that included the $8.5 billion purchase of MCI Corp., the maverick firm that helped establish the Washington area as a major telecommunications-services center a generation ago. The deal gave Verizon control over MCI's Internet backbone network as well as access to its lucrative government and corporate clients.

The range of Verizon's services has expanded steadily in recent years, but the company pays special attention to the biggest change of all — wireless telephones. The first commercial cell phone call was made in October 1983 between a phone company official in Chicago and Alexander Graham Bell's grandson in Berlin. Since then, the technology has exploded into a $600 billion global industry as cell phones began to outnumber wired instruments in many regions. By the middle of the decade, more than two-thirds of Americans owned a cell phone, according to the Yankee Group, a Boston consultancy. The rest of the world is not far behind: a survey by the London-based telecom consultancy Mobile World estimated global cell phone ownership at 3.5 billion persons, equivalent to almost half the world's population.[11]

In the United States, one outcome of this shift is a steady decline in the number of wire-line calls. Verizon lost a million wire-line customers nationally in one three-month period in 2006. At the same time, it picked up 1.8 million wireless customers.[12] The tiny cell phones are everywhere, particularly in crowded metropolitan areas. Within the District of Columbia, cell phone density reached 72 percent of the population, putting the city in third place nationally, slightly behind Atlanta and Detroit.[13]

In their competitive search for new customers, cell phone companies have begun targeting children. In 2005 Sprint Corp. joined with the Walt Disney organization to market an instrument decked out in vivid colors such as Bubblegum, with a backpack hook and a Mommy and Daddy button for one-touch dialing. Disney also launched a special mobile phone service designed to allow parents to keep a tight rein on their kids' phone usage, including tracking voice minutes, text messaging, and downloadable content. Within a few years, nearly half of American young people eleven to sixteen years old had cell phones.[14]

In the Washington area, Verizon found itself in stiff competition locally for a wide variety of telecommunications services, both wired and wireless. Comcast, the area's largest cable company, offered what it called a triple-play bundle of television, broadband, and telephone services over its high-speed cable lines. New competition also came from Internet providers, including AOL, aiming to expand their customers' Internet habits from desktop computers to cell phones.

At the same time, a new group of companies introduced telephone service on the Internet, using a technology known as VOIP — Voice Over Internet Protocol. Start-up firm Skype took the lead; its software allowed users to make free calls to other Skype-using telephones and very cheap calls to other phones. From small beginnings in the late 1990s, Skype's customer base had expanded to over 100 million subscribers worldwide by 2006.[15] All of this spelled trouble for Verizon and other conventional phone service providers. In September 2005, eBay, the leading online auction house, bought Skype for $2.5 billion in hopes of tightening its grip over the Internet auction market. A Skype button was added to eBay's Web pages, allowing buyers easy, cost-free access to potential sellers. This and other innovations attracted millions of new Skype subscribers worldwide.[16]

These incursions into the traditional telephone business were expanded with the 2006 announcement by America Online that that it would offer users of its instant-messaging service a free phone number that would permit them to call from regular phones while they are online, typically using headsets or microphones attached to their computers. It was a new twist on services that allow calls between regular phones and PCs. These online challenges to traditional telephony led the London *Economist* to predict that the result would be the "slow death of the trillion-dollar wired telephone market."[17]

These developments may be trumped by a new kind of phone introduced by Apple in 2007. Dubbed the iPhone, it was one of the most sophisticated of a new generation of "smart phones" marketed by equipment firms in recent years.[18] Apple's iPhone is a mobile phone and Internet communicator packed into a thin (11.6-millimeter) handheld device. It was the first phone to offer "visual voicemail" to save users from the hassle of listening to all their messages before getting to the important ones. "It is the Internet in your pocket, a revolutionary product that changes everything," Apple's founder Steve Jobs declared. Within a few months of its introduction, iPhone triggered a new, wide-ranging round of competitive offerings by other companies.[19]

Some industry analysts predict that iPhone and other smart phones signal the beginning of the end for wired-telephone companies in the Washington region and elsewhere. The obituary may be premature, however. By 2009, old-line phone companies, including Verizon, had reacted vigorously to the cellular challenge, primarily by joining in the competition. Verizon has an advanced cellular network that provides ultra-fast wireless Internet access in Washington and thirty-two other regions across the country, supplying voice, print, and video services to owners of cell phones and other handheld devices. The company has also increased the capacity of its existing wire network with fiber-optic circuits, providing multimedia links to home computers, telephones, and television sets via a single high-speed circuit it calls FIOS.

This shift to integrated digital services has changed the telecommunications sector in the Washington region. "We're not a telephone company any more," laments one veteran phone company executive. "We're a communications and entertainment company." Her nostalgia underlines the fact that old habits of staying in touch are being transformed. One example is the marketing tug-of-war between Verizon and its cable-company competitors in the Washington area. In 2005 Verizon went into the cable business with an initial installation in the Northern Virginia suburb of Herndon as part of a billion-dollar nationwide bet that multimedia cable services would keep the company profitable as its traditional telephone business declines.

Meanwhile, Comcast, the largest cable company in the Washington region, began to market its own telephone service to customers, using VOIP technology. Infonetics, a communications consulting firm, has estimated that cable companies and other VOIP providers will attract 24 million subscribers nationally in the next few years. One result of the new competition has been a scramble among service providers to expand their range of services. In 2007, Cingular began offering mobile-phone services to children under twelve years old after marketing surveys indicated that cell phones were their first choice on holiday wish lists.[20]

Verizon and other telecom companies anticipate the day when customers regard digital devices the way they now think of their watches — one device for leisure time to wear with jeans, one for work, and another for nights on the town. Finland's Nokia Corp., one of the world's largest cell phone suppliers, has a futurology department that is investigating the possibilities of an undershirt made of special materials that can convert body heat into electricity to power mobile devices, eliminating the need for frequent battery charges. DoCoMo, a Japanese telecom firm, is betting on a digital chip embedded in its handsets that allows users to make retail purchases from funds stored on the chip.

Whatever innovations finally catch on, they will be linked to the new generation of all-purpose broadband networks developed by Verizon, Comcast, Cox Communications Cable, and other Washington–area providers. Almost two-thirds of all American homes already have such capabilities, and there is a rush in the communications industry to close the gap. In Washington, Verizon has a special program for marketing high-speed connections in new housing projects throughout the region. The extra fees involved are often built into monthly homeowner-association dues.[21]

The result of this increased availability of electronic circuits is to introduce new kinds of digital practices. None has caught on faster than blogging, the catchall word describing the spread of personal Web sites. (Blog is short for "Web log.") Within ten years, there were over thirty million Americans with blog sites on the Internet.[22] Many of the sites are seldom used, but a startling number of them are active around the clock. The Washington area is a major center for blogs of all kind. Some are social and informational, from ontapDC, which provides a directory of happy hours and other social events around town, to viennesewaltz, which supplies information about waltz lessons and fancy-dress balls in the area.[23]

This being Washington, many of the area's blogs focus on politics, sporting such names as InstaPundit, Leanleft, and Carpetbaggerreport. Political blogging came into its own during the 2004 presidential election, when bloggers were given press-gallery accreditation at the Democratic and Republican national conventions for the first time. Since then, the practice has became so widespread in Washington that a leading local Web site sponsors a listing of the hundred best political blogs in the area. Blogging has also spread to Capitol Hill, where legislators have launched blog sites in an effort to sidestep the mainstream media by taking their messages directly to the public.

Political blogging has gotten unfavorable reviews in some quarters, but Barbara O'Brien, a Washington blog watcher, disagrees. "For so long," she says, "our political discussion has been packaged from the top down. The great thing about the blogosphere is that it's a big conversation. We write, people connect, other people connect to the comments — it's like a vast salon."[24]

If anything, her comments underestimate blogging's impact in Washington and across the country. A study by the Pew Internet & American Life Project confirms that blogging is primarily a young person's game. Teenagers and young adults account for 40 percent of bloggers, compared with 9 percent for GenX–ers and the same percentage for 51- to 59-year-olds.[25] "I think people want to dismiss blog readers as unemployed people in their basement. Apparently not," says Glenn Reynolds, one of the sponsors of the conservative blog InstaPundit.

Blogging has reached a point where it has spawned its own version of Hollywood's Oscars. It is the Bloggie awards, involving dozens of categories including ones for the best African and Middle Eastern blogs. In 2006, more than 100 blogs were selected as finalists for the best in Weblog publishing. Instead of being chosen by anonymous committees as in Hollywood's pattern, voting is open to the public.

In Washington and elsewhere, blogging has lost some of its original antiestablishment innocence by linking up with commercial interests. Advertisers have taken notice of the growing readership and influence of these Internet postings, spending upwards of $200 million a year on blog marketing, according to Forrester Research, a Boston consultancy. Among other practices, companies are seeking greater exposure on blog sites, courting blog writers with public relations effort and inviting them to blog on their corporate sites. In 2005, America Online bought Weblog, the publisher of eighty-five freelance sites, as part of an effort to increase advertising revenues from bloggers.[26] AOL also allowed bloggers to integrate their own Web sites on AIM, its instant-messaging service, free of charge. At the same time, Yahoo and Google, two major search services, announced plans to make it easier for blog audiences to search millions of Web sites.[27]

Meanwhile, the Internet is being expanded beyond its original role as a limited data storage-and-delivery resource to a new level that emphasizes social networking. It explains the rise of such interactive Web sites as Blogger.com, Wikipedia.com, and MySpace.com, all of which have experienced spectacular growth in recent years. Blogger.com, owned by Google, has attracted over fifteen million users in a typical month. "The growth in blogging reminds us that the Internet is fulfilling its original promise about participation," says Gary Arlen, a Washington–based communications analyst. "This medium empowers users in such a way that they can do what they want and be heard."

More recently, blogging in Washington and elsewhere has been challenged by YouTube.com and other Web sites that encourage users to "broadcast yourself" by posting short print messages and video clips on the Internet.[28] From a standing start in 2005, the YouTube site soon attracted six million visitors a day. Its offerings are an eclectic mix of subjects, from political commentaries to advice on how to act on a blind date.

YouTube, along with similar services, played an important role in the run-up to the 2008 presidential and congressional elections. All of the major candidates became the focus of praise and criticism on the new electronic networks. Joe Trippi, an advisor to Democratic candidates, suggests that this kind of Internet discussion helps them create a sense of community among their supporters, encouraging them to engage in two-way dialogue on election issues.[29] Just as John F. Kennedy mastered television as a medium for taking his message to the public, Trippi points out, Barack Obama has transformed the art of political communication by his use of Web sites during his election campaign and in his reorganization of the White House communications operation after he took office.

As with print blogs, YouTube's large and growing audience has also attracted the attention of advertisers. "Marketers are already interested in how to invest in it," according to Lucian James of Agenda Inc., a marketing firm. "It comes at a perfect time when brands are looking beyond the thirty-second commercial and are looking for new ways to connect to their audience." Blogs and other populist Internet channels increasingly set the pace and lifestyles of Washington's young professionals. From the central city to the outer suburbs, they were among the first adopters of the Internet-as-socializer. Along with other changes, this has influenced the ways in which young professionals get together, particularly in coffee houses and other social centers. Increasingly, the relevant technology is Wi-Fi, acronymic shorthand for a wideband network that began by enabling laptops to get wireless access to the Internet and beyond. At the turn of the century, an anonymous marketing genius in the Starbucks organization saw Wi-Fi networking as a way of attracting customers to the firm's stores by letting them send e-mails from their laptops while sipping their lattes. It was a convenient way of keeping in touch, and besides, it was free.[30]

Wi-Fi has since spread beyond coffeehouses in Washington and other cities to wider applications in ways that pose an economic threat to telephone companies and other network providers. The threat became a reality in 2005 when the Philadelphia city government decided to provide Wi-Fi access stations (known as "hot spots") throughout the entire city, despite the strong opposition of Verizon, the local phone company. Mindful of these political implications, Washington–area governments were slow to pick up on Wi-Fi services. By 2006, however, private groups had installed experimental Wi-Fi services on the Mall and in the Dupont Circle district in downtown Washington.[31] Across the Potomac, Alexandria officials began offering free Wi-Fi access in its downtown historic district, the first local government to sponsor al fresco Web surfing at no charge. From its modest beginnings as a coffeehouse promotional gimmick, Wi-Fi installations have expanded rapidly.

Wi-Fi is only one of the networks in the Washington area that are bypassing older communications networks. Another is small neighborhood "listservs," Web–based electronic bulletin boards that allow users to post messages on local activities and issues in neighborhoods such as Cleveland Park, Dupont Circle, and Chevy Chase. The Dupont site's creator, Ed Grimm, sees the service as a community bulletin board. "We wanted someplace where we could explore issues, post notices, and let people know what's going on in Dupont Circle on a regular basis. It's a place where people can feel comfortable to go and just express themselves and talk about the Circle." The messages are not screened, but the Dupont site warns users coyly but firmly that "overtly commercial content and offensive sandbox behavior will not be tolerated."[32] From small beginnings, listservs have blossomed in other neighborhoods throughout the Washington region.

Of all the services offered over the Internet, none has more appeal for Washingtonians than the Google search engine. Created by two graduate students in a California garage in 1998, Google's success is based on one big idea: search pages are ranked according to how many pages are linked to them. A half-dozen years after it began operations, the firm's computer bank had stored over three trillion pages of searchable material, with the number of queries exceeding two hundred million in a typical day.

Spurred by their corporate slogan "Do no evil," Sergey Brin and Larry Page, Google's founders, rose from graduate-student poverty to fourth place on the annual list of global billionaires by 2005. At $11 billion each, they ranked just behind two other digital pioneers, Microsoft's Bill Gates and Apple's Steve Jobs. Google's success has been powered by its willingness to challenge older digital folkways and practices. In 2005, the company blithely offered to build a wireless telephone network for the city of San Francisco in exchange for allowing easy access to Google resources.

Google's services are free. The engine driving the company's economic growth, as well as that of its competitors, has been its ability to sell advertising on the pages searched by millions of computer buffs around the world.[33] Google succeeds in generating advertising revenue because their ads can be carefully targeted to specific audience groups, unlike most other media channels. Advertisers on Google pages pay only when individual users click on their ads. This reduces the scatter-shot approach of most media advertising by focusing on what the ad industry calls "eyeballs," in this case Internet surfers looking for the kind of specific information Google provides.

Google's advertising prowess is causing dramatic changes within the U.S. mass media sector. By 2005, Google was selling $6 billion worth of online ads, more than double the rate of the previous year, putting it in direct competition with newspaper chains, magazine publishers, and television networks. More recently, Google and other online advertising outlets have faced competition from mobile-phone operators that are selling ads on their networks.[34]

Meanwhile, Wi-Fi and other wireless devices have loosened young Washingtonians' reliance on older information and entertainment channels. Beginning with the original Walkman portable cassette player in 1979, music has become a mobile commodity. The Walkman is now a museum piece, displaced by a new generation of smaller music providers. Apple Computers sold over thirty million of the first generation of its hand-held iPod music players. Podcasting became the rage, with its promise of allowing individuals to produce their own writings, songs, videos, and photos and upload them onto a Web site for anyone who wants to sample them.

More recently, podcasting capabilities have expanded to a range of competing products, including Apple's Nano, which weighs two ounces and provides multimedia access, in addition to storing addresses and appointments, a world clock, and a stopwatch. Google and AOL retaliated by rolling out a service that lets Internet users search and play back thousands of video clips. Ever-smarter software promises to expand these capabilities, allowing users to cull vast digital storehouses of news, real estate listings, traffic reports, and other data resources. Apple's iPhone, with its powerful multimedia capabilities, adds a strong competitive dimension to this mix.[35]

Among other outcomes, these new electronic outlets threaten older entertainment providers in Washington. Television and cable networks are scrambling to come to terms with the new competition.[36] Radio stations are losing listeners and ad revenues to the new generation of portable music-playing devices and satellite-delivered radio services, subscribed to by listeners looking for a wider variety of commercial-free programs. Local record stores have been hit hard by the new digital downloading of songs, with sales plunging at traditional music stores. In 2006, Apple's iTunes Music Store crossed the marketing goal made famous by McDonald's hamburgers with more than one billion downloads of songs.[37] In 2005, in a more-than-symbolic gesture to the new trend, Warner Music, a major record company, announced the debut of a new rock group in every digital format *except* compact discs.

These digital offerings are helping change Washington's longtime reputation as a dull patch in the national landscape, a town that closed down every evening when the last bureaucrat left the office. This reputation was symbolized for decades by a city ordinance that permitted the sale of alcoholic drinks to customers only if they were seated at a table. The regulation has since been abolished, replaced by a new wave of trendy attitudes and practices. Washington is becoming, improbably, a funky party town.

Local observers of this shift date the change from the 1980 opening of the 9:30 Club, a late-night bistro whose inaugural attraction was the Lounge Lizards, a post-punk jazz band. Thirty years later, the club still flourishes, having won national Nightclub of the Year honors four times in surveys by *Pollstar*, the industry's trade journal.[38] Its success has spawned dozens of similar nightspots in the city, including Ibiza, a capacious club located in a former warehouse. Opened in July 2007, Ibiza accommodates three thousand patrons.[39] The city also boasts its own version of New York's East Village in Adams Morgan, a stretch of five downtown blocks favored by late-night revelers.

These changes translate into a new cultural mobility, set in motion by the town's changing demographics. "This is an international center with a diversity of audiences," Douglas Wheeler, president of the Washington Performing Arts Society, points out. "We have a high income base and a high education base that can support a huge volume of arts activity." The Washington area has consistently ranked first among the top twenty-five metropolitan regions in percentage of adults who buy hardcover books, according to Scarborough Research, a consumer-survey firm. Predictably, political books rank first among local readers, but poetry is second.[40] Local readers are also heavy patrons of online booksellers such as Amazon.com, with its hundreds of thousands of titles. Audiences in the Washington region on average watch less entertainment television than people in every other top-ten market except San Francisco.

The biggest shift in the city's cultural life involves the oldest of human relationships — that between men and women. For two centuries, Washington was a man's town, run by men for men. With some notable exceptions, women followed a symbolic step behind. This pattern has been dramatically reshaped in recent decades, driven by a new mix of political, economic, and cultural factors. The outcome still falls short of full gender equality, yet new patterns of social mobility have opened increasing opportunities for women.

This demographic change is particularly apparent in the gains women have made in professional fields, particularly those associated with new digital practices. The evidence is found, among other places, in statistics buried in U.S. Department of Education surveys of higher education trends. In 2005, 133 American women graduated from college for every 100 men. By the end of the decade, the ratio is projected to be 142 to 100. This gap is particularly striking in the case of African American women graduates, who will outnumber their male counterparts two to one in a few years. Another measure of the new gender gap in education is that of women's performance in professional studies: at mid-decade, women earned 57 percent of master's degrees, half of all law degrees, and a rapidly rising 44 percent of medical degrees.[41]

The impact of these trends extends beyond the workplace, to the changing forms of the traditional mating dance. As noted earlier, a *Men's Health* magazine survey proclaimed Washington the sexiest city in the nation, based on its expanding population of single, college-educated men and women. The survey also reported that the city ranked second among metropolitan areas in the number of Cialis, Levitra, and Viagra prescriptions dispensed per capita.

Forbes magazine, in a 2005 survey rating the region's overall social patterns, listed the D.C.-Baltimore area as the second best locality in the country for single men and women, based on such factors as economic prospects, cultural attractions, and "coolness." A *Wired* magazine story on the "the best geek cities" in the country recently listed Washington among the top ten for mating activities. "Washington isn't just a policy-wonk utopia" the magazine noted. "It's also the ultimate place for a coder looking for love. There are more postings from the nation's capital on Geek 2 Geek, an online dating service for nerds, than from any other city we surveyed."[42]

Although many traditional boy-meets-girl practices are alive and well in the Washington area, they are being overtaken by digital-age variations. In 2005 the *New Yorker* satirized the trend in a cartoon of a young couple who had just met. "I can't wait," he tells her, "to see what you're like online." The Internet has in fact become a meeting place of choice. Com-

Score Networks, which monitors consumer behavior on the Net, notes that forty million Americans visited at least one dating site in a typical month, accounting for 27 percent of all Internet users.[43]

Online services have become more sophisticated in recent years, providing Web searchers with detailed information about a potential partner, from a photograph down to such practical details as his or her credit history. "It's never really a blind date anymore," says one client of the many Washington dating services on the Web.[44] Meetroduction, a Chicago–based service, helps pinpoint the search by offering information on potential partners who live in or near the searcher's neighborhood. For young adults who have not been lucky in their search for electronic partners, some psychologists have identified the problem as SNAD — Social Networking Anxiety Disorder.

Meanwhile many young adults still rely on more traditional dating strategies. A typical one is It's Just Lunch, a Washington enterprise that markets its service to busy upscale professionals by setting up introductory mid-day encounters. "It's like hiring a personal assistant to handle your dating life," the firm's ads promise.

Washington has an outsized number of the 18,000 coffeehouses that have sprung up across the land in recent years. It is an industry that sponsors its own lobbying organization — the Specialty Coffee Association of America. The new digitally friendly coffeehouses like Starbucks and Caribou, filled with customers toting laptops, cell phones, and other gadgets, encourage social networking across the room or across town.[45]

Internet surfing for a date is just one indicator of the changing tribal customs that mark the full emergence of Washington's Creative Class, with its mobility and its smarts. In the process, its members are a force in shaping the town's third civic transformation since its founding over two centuries ago.

7
Arts and Ideas: The New Meld

The new generation of digitally savvy professionals in Washington is a transforming factor in the city's political and economic life. They have softened the town's reputation as a stuffy bureaucratic enclave. The persistent image was that of a city that could not compete culturally with brassy New York, laid-back Los Angeles, upbeat Atlanta and Houston, or older world capitals such as London, Paris, and Rome.

It is useful to look at the factors that are challenging these perceptions of Washington's cultural identity. The subject is not only relevant to this survey of digital-age changes but may even be the most dynamic element in defining the town's new pace and tone.

Recent studies by regional-development economists make this point as they examine urban patterns in the information age. They see critical connections between economic development and the diverse cultural and demographic patterns emerging in high-tech centers such as Silicon Valley, Boston, and Dallas. Conversely, they argue, it is the lack of strong cultural resources that has led to the migration of talented professionals from Cleveland, Detroit, and other industrial-age cities.

Toronto University's Richard Florida puts Washington high on the list of cities fitting the new pattern. He ranks the city first among metropolitan areas of one million or more population in its openness to what he calls the Creative Class — young, educated, highly motivated professionals. Moving beyond the usual agenda of dry economic models, Florida and his colleagues give cultural factors high visibility in their analysis of the region's current transition to an information-age environment.[1] To this mix of technology and talent, they add a third "T" — tolerance. It is the Creative Class's strong acceptance of ethnic and lifestyle differences that strongly influences economic growth and social transformation in information-age cities.

These trends are hard to pin down statistically, but they are a critical force in Washington's changing identity. In making this shift, the city has had to overcome a legacy of scorn for its provincialism, a theme fostered largely by out-of-town cultural mandarins. The late theatrical producer, Joseph Papp, scoffed, "Washington is so goddam boring.... What can you do there? Washington reminds me of Russia." Architectural critic Peter Blake called it "a city almost devoid of culture." Former Washingtonian Frank Rich, a *New York Times* columnist, includes in his litany of Washington's cultural failures the assertion that its restaurants can't even compete with those in Las Vegas. Meanwhile, beyond the Beltway and the Hudson River, the tendency is to disparage both New York and Washington. Making a comparison between the two, says Texas writer Joe Bob Briggs, is like asking who has the best disco in Guatemala.

Increasingly, the critics are being proved wrong about Washington's alleged provincialism. They ignore the reality that, in recent decades, the city has undergone a major cultural transformation powered by information-age changes, in particular the presence of its larger and more affluent professional class. Nevertheless, the image of a middlebrow town persists. The Washingtonian response to this attitude tends to be statistical. How can you disparage a city and a region that has the largest library on earth, a dozen world-class museums, a lively arts community, impressive research centers, a wide array of colleges and universities, et cetera, et cetera, et cetera. Yet critics continue to see a city that doesn't pull its weight culturally.

Washington's evolution as a center of the arts and sciences has a long, uneven history. Pierre L'Enfant saw the new city as a cultural force, reflecting his Enlightenment views of a democratic society. Among his plans for a monumental central mall, parks, and other public places, he visualized the town's main street, Pennsylvania Avenue, lined with gardens and theaters, along with "rooms of assemblies, academies, and all such sorts of places as may be attractive to the learned and afford diversion to the idle."[1] This idealistic vision was quickly overtaken by the realities of the city's evolution as a political oasis, a place useful in its way but no cultural challenge to New York, Philadelphia, Charleston, or Boston.

For decades after its founding, Washington was a backwater where pigs ran loose and hillocks of mud overturned carriages on the streets. One nineteenth-century visitor described it as "the most ill-conditioned city on the continent, a dead city, with no trade, ... kept alive only by the money of the government employees." A few examples challenged this image of a cultural wilderness. One was the 1835 opening of the National Theater on Pennsylvania Avenue, an enterprise that still flourishes despite five fires, a bankruptcy, and a four-year period (1948–52) when an actors' boycott forced it to close down until black citizens were admitted to its performances. The major exception to Washington's early provincialism was the Library of Congress. From small beginnings, it has evolved to its present-day status as the greatest library in the world, with a collection of over 100 million items, including vast holdings of audio recordings, films, photographs, maps, manuscripts, and other archival resources.

Apart from this great library, Washington's cultural credentials were weak during its first seventy-five years. The turning point was the Civil War. Under siege, the city became a national capital in fact, and a new set of civic leaders took over when the conflict ended. For the first time, Washington attracted a stable, prosperous elite willing to cast its lot with the town's future, including the upgrading of its cultural resources. The postwar years saw the creation of many private arts and scientific groups within the city, including the National Geographic Society, the Cosmos Club, and the National Academy of Science, among others. These activities laid the groundwork for the founding of federally funded scientific facilities such as the Naval Observatory, the U.S. Coast & Geodetic Survey, and the National Bureau of Standards. Overall, it was a heady period of organized cultural and academic uplift, much of it sponsored and maintained by the city's elite.

This new emphasis on the arts and sciences involved many individuals, but none epitomized the period better than Alice Pike Barney. Born into a wealthy Cincinnati family, she married a prosperous businessman in 1874 and moved with him to Washington a decade later. A talented artist, she was appalled by what she regarded as the city's provincialism. "What is Washington life, after all?" she declared shortly after she arrived. "Small talk and lots to eat, an infinite series of teas and dinners…. Art? There is none."[2] For over forty years, Barney used her personal connections, money, and formidable talents to upgrade the town's cultural resources. She was a painter in her own right whose works are still in the collections of the Smithsonian American Art Museum. She was also a playwright and a theatrical producer who, among other projects, bullied the government into sponsoring the outdoor Sylvan Theater on the mall, the first federally funded theater in the nation. Until 2001, the building housing her atelier, Studio House on Sheridan Circle, was a museum maintained by the Smithsonian Institution.

Alice Barney was also an early activist in the women's suffrage movement. For decades, in the words of one of her biographers, "she whirled through Washington's cultural scene planning theatricals, painting pictures, opening exhibitions in New York, Boston, Paris, and London, importing avant-garde artists such as modern dancer Ruth St. Denis to enliven a charity event and providing exotic evenings of entertainment at Studio House."[3]

Barney had a special impact on the Washington arts scene, but other forces were also at work. These included an outpouring of private philanthropy that gave the city a formidable collection of cultural institutions. The process began in 1829 with a bequest from an enigmatic Englishman, James Smithson, who never set foot in America. His money helped fund what became the Smithsonian Institution, which currently oversees more than two dozen museums and other educational organizations in and around Washington.

Smithson's generosity was followed by that of other philanthropists, resulting in the Corcoran Gallery, the Folger Shakespeare Library, the Freer Gallery of Asian art, and the Phillips Collection, the first modern-art museum in the nation. Cultural philanthropy reached its high-water mark with the construction of the National Gallery of Art in the 1940s, a project that benefited from the energy and money of philanthropist Paul Mellon. He was determined that Washington should have an art museum that would equal or surpass the Louvre in Paris and the National Gallery in London. Overall, Mellon gave the Washington gallery $208 million, along with 900 works of art.[4]

Private philanthropy has continued to play a critical role in establishing Washington's cultural credentials in recent times, but the larger factor has been the slow, hesitant involvement of the federal government in the process. The idea of public funding of the arts was a will-o'-the-wisp hope for over a century after the city's founding. In 1910, Congress created a federal Fine Arts Commission but limited its charter largely to deciding where statues and other monuments should be located in the city. Attitudes on government-subsidized arts began to change in the 1930s, following a congressional decision to allocate 1 percent of the construction cost of large new public buildings to murals, sculptures, and other the decorative arts. The idea, originally proposed by a local banker, Edward Bruce, resulted in a Section of Painting and Sculpture to monitor the program, improbably located in the Treasury Department.[5]

An important shift in public involvement in cultural programs occurred in the 1930s, when many artists were unemployed as the result of the economic depression. To give them jobs, a federally funded Public

Works of Art program was created, among other projects. The District of Columbia was a beneficiary of one particularly controversial project. Among the local works commissioned under the program were murals by Ben Shahn, a left-wing artist, and a series of paintings by Boardman Robinson and Maurice Sterne in federal office buildings. From the start, religious groups roundly attacked these works for their displays of nudity and other alleged improprieties. A militant mural in a new War Department building was first curtained off and then painted over.

Despite these incidents, federal support for the arts became a permanent feature on the Washington scene. Such funding is now largely the province of the National Endowment for the Arts, a perennial congressional whipping boy for some of its grant-making decisions. Among its more questionable projects in recent years has been support for "performance artists" in California whose activities included handing out ten-dollar bills to street vagrants. Despite congressional attacks, the arts endowment program continues to thrive. The District government has also become involved in arts funding, with a program that dispenses about $20 million annually.

The larger development in recent decades has been the emergence of a lively commercial arts-and-entertainment sector in the city, one that increasingly competes with New York and other cultural centers. Its origins are a mixed bag, but one of the critical elements was the arrival in town of Patrick Hayes, a genial Irishman from New York who came looking for a job in the early 1940s. He was hired to manage the local National Symphony, a musical group that, at the time, was little better than an oompah German band. From this perch, he moved on to establish the Hayes Concert Bureau and the Washington Performing Arts Society (WPAS). Decades later, at a ceremony honoring him, violinist Isaac Stern summed up Hayes's impact on the local arts scene: "He took a moribund little town and made it a capital."[6]

Among other accomplishments, Patrick Hayes helped break the tradition of segregated audiences in the city. This included arranging a concert performance by baritone Todd Duncan, who had created the original role of Porgy in George Gershwin's *Porgy and Bess*. He later chose Duncan to be the first chairman of WPAS. Hayes also sponsored contralto Marian Anderson's inaugural appearance in Constitution Hall, helping erase the indignity she had suffered in 1939 when the Daughters of the American Revolution refused to let her sing in the hall because she was black. By the turn of the century, Hayes and other local arts impresarios had put Washington firmly on the national performing arts map.

Arena Stage, which set up shop as the city's first professional resident acting group in 1950, played a special role in this transition. From small beginnings in a renovated downtown movie house, Arena moved to an abandoned brewery in the Foggy Bottom district, and thence to its present home, a handsome facility in the District's Southwest area. Its initial distinction was the introduction of theater-in-the-round productions, an innovation at the time. Within a decade Arena emerged as one of the leading regional theaters in the country. One of the group's early original productions, *The Great White Hope* starring a young James Earl Jones, moved on to great success on Broadway and across the nation.

The election of John F. Kennedy in 1960 gave a special boost to the effort to establish a strong performing arts sector in Washington. The president's wife, Jacqueline, a knowledgeable patron of the arts, took on her First Lady role with the clear intention of promoting American artists. Her efforts famously included a series of White House cultural evenings featuring a wide range of performers, from jazz trumpeter Louis Armstrong to cellist Pablo Casals. It was the beginning of a tradition that, for the Kennedys, ended with the president's assassination in November 1963.

That tragic turn had unexpected consequences for Washington's cultural prospects. It involved long-standing plans to create a national performing-arts center in the city, in part to make up for the lack of theaters capable of handling major attractions. During its infrequent visits to the city, New York's Metropolitan Opera performed in the Capital movie theater downtown where, as one observer noted at the time, "If the stagehands are speedy, set-changing takes forty-five minutes."[7] Congress gave the idea of a national performing-arts center an initial push in 1958 when it passed a bill authorizing the center's construction, including a $650,000 appropriation to buy an eight-acre site in the Foggy Bottom district along the Potomac. Curiously, the lawmakers' motivation for the project hinged largely on the need for the president to entertain foreign dignitaries.

The cultural-center proposal languished for several years. After the Kennedy assassination, there were numerous suggestions that the center be dedicated to his memory. The idea's realization was largely the work of the chairman of the committee charged with planning the John F. Kennedy Center for the Performing Arts. He was Roger L. Stevens, a New York financier who had once headed a syndicate that bought the Empire State Building. He was also a theater buff who had produced a long string of successful Broadway productions, including *West Side Story*. His talent at managing both money and the arts was a major factor in creating the Kennedy Center.[8]

The new center, opened in 1971, provided the first adequate performing space for the National Symphony, led by a series of distinguished conductors that included Mstislav Rostropovich. It has become the home of the Washington Opera and the Washington Ballet, both of which had previously performed in cramped auditoriums around town. The Kennedy Center also provides a striking performance space for hundreds of other American and foreign artistic groups, from the New York City Ballet to the Royal Shakespeare Company. One of the center's unique features is the Millennium Stage, a performing area located in the Grand Foyer, a space large enough to contain the Washington Monument lying on its side, with 75 feet to spare. The Stage has mounted over 3,000 free performances by acting, musical, and dance groups since it was inaugurated in 1997.[9]

Inevitably, the Kennedy Center has been criticized by those who claim that its managers pander to middlebrow tastes. In part, this stems from the center's role as a tourist attraction, supervised by the National Park Service. It is also the home of the longest-running production in American theater history, a knockabout mystery play, *Shear Madness*, with no pretensions as great drama. (Its script, including the identity of the murderer, changes with every performance.) In fact no other performing-arts center in the world has taken on such a wide range of productions over the years, from standard fare to edgy drama, including a famous (and artistically unsuccessful) operatic characterization of a president, *Nixon in China*. Other over-the-edge performances have included a 1984 American Ballet Theater premiere of choreographer David Gordon's ode to a folding chair, an event, as one critic noted, "that echoed with booing boos, hearty applause and a deliciously sassy creative hum."

The debate about Washington's impact on the national cultural scene continues, kept alive by the town's detractors across the country. Meanwhile, the city and its surrounding region have been the beneficiaries of a lively new arts community that embraces theater, graphic arts, music and the dance. The trend includes an emphasis on offbeat presentations. Local theater companies offer a varied menu from standard classics to campy in-your-face rock shows like the Landless Theater's *Carrie Potter at the Half-Blood Prom*.[10]

By 2006, Washington hosted a Capital Fringe Festival, including over a hundred off-the-wall events in twenty downtown locations, from conventional theaters to alternative spaces in galleries, lobbies, and vacant storefronts.[11] One group, the Washington Improv Theater, has performed on sidewalks in the Adams-Morgan district, the town's version of Greenwich Village.[12] Catscratch Theater anticipated the festival with a combination of movement performance and guerilla theater, mounting its productions on the platforms of Metro subway stops, moving both the actors and the audience from one station to the next as the evening progressed.[13]

Another avant-garde group, Synetic Theater, has offered local theatergoers an adaptation of *Hamlet* in a 90-minute movement-based version without dialogue. The performance collected three major prizes in the annual Helen Hayes Awards competition, Washington's version of New York's Tony Awards. The Synetic players followed up their *Hamlet* success with a voiceless *Macbeth* in 2007.[14] A few months later, another group, the Washington Shakespeare Company, pushed the limits of Shakespearean interpretation further with actors performing *Macbeth* in the buff. The results, according to the *Washington Post* review of the performance, were naked but not exciting.

Commenting on Washington's countercultural activities, local critic Nelson Pressley points out: "The result is an eclectic mix of productions, most produced on a shoestring, populated by now-you-see-it, now-you-don't groups with names ranging from Meat & Potatoes to Taffety Pink.... A restaurant will do, or a nook tucked away in a funky gallery, or a nightclub with a makeshift stage: any hole in the wall just big enough for actors and audience to get together."

For the first time, distinctive arts districts are emerging in the city. The revival of Penn Quarter, the downtown district north of Pennsylvania Avenue, includes new art galleries, bookstores, and theater companies. Woolly Mammoth, an avant-garde theater group that had operated for years in cramped quarters in uptown Mount Pleasant, moved into a sparkling new space in Penn Quarter in 2006. A major boost to downtown theatergoing took place at the same time with the decision of the Shakespeare Theater, a mainstay of the city's theater scene for over half a century, to become part of a new $75 million Harman Center for the Arts in Penn Quarter.

Meanwhile, a local version of New York's Off-Broadway theaters is emerging just outside the downtown area, along a stretch of 14th Street that had been burned out in the 1968 race riots following the assassination of Martin Luther King.[15] Its anchor, Studio Theater, had moved into an abandoned warehouse in the early 1970s with a repertory of experimental plays. In recent years, it has been expanded into a three-theater complex accompanied by acting studios. More recently, Washington's Off-Broadway has migrated east to the new H Street complex in the city's Northeast quadrant, which includes a three-theater complex, dance studios, and other cultural amenities, all housed in a renovated seventy-year-old movie theater. The H Street complex has been the home of the African Continuum Theater, specializing in black themes, with occasional forays into interpretations of plays from other traditions. In 2005, the company mounted *Kingdom*, an adaptation of Shakespeare's *Richard III* set in an apartment above a barbeque take-out store.

This new minority presence in the local arts scene marked the end of a long period when such ethnic offerings were effectively walled off from the rest of the city's cultural life. Until recently, African-American arts activity was located largely along U Street, north of the central district. It was Washington's Black Broadway, a center for the movement in the arts and letters known as the New Negro Renaissance in the early decades of the last century. Washington artists played a significant role in the movement, including Duke Ellington and poet Langston Hughes. U Street's Howard Theater, built in 1910, is the oldest legitimate African-American playhouse in the nation, predating the more famous Apollo Theater in Harlem by a decade.[16]

The greater visibility of black artists and audiences in recent decades has since been extended to other minorities. The rapidly growing Hispanic community has expanded its cultural presence with the inauguration of a major arts complex in Columbia Heights in what was an abandoned movie palace, the Tivoli. The recent $37 million refurbishing of the property includes a separate theater for the experimental GALA Hispanic Theater. For the first time, the area's expanding Latino community has a commercial drama facility that serves as a cultural outreach to the rest of the community.

Whether these efforts will result in a full-blown artistic renaissance centered in Washington remains to be seen. What is clear, for the present, is that the city is no longer a cultural outpost. A *Washingtonian* magazine survey of the local scene at mid-decade provided statistical support of the new trend. It reported that arts-and-entertainment projects totaling more than $800 million were underway or about to start throughout the city and its surrounding suburbs. By the magazine's count, the Washington area was home to 85 professional theater companies, which drew 2.2 million local residents, four times as many as fill the seats at FedEx

Field each year for Washington Redskins football games. The result, the survey pointed out, is that the city is "becoming an alternative to Broadway instead of a test run for it."[17]

An important element in this new mix is Washington's expansion beyond the more genteel arts that dominated the local scene for most of its history. It is a change that reflects population trends taking place in the region. The city and its suburbs are serving up a rich new demographic stew these days. It includes young white college graduates, candidates for the Creative Class, flying into Dulles airport on their way to their first jobs along Northern Virginia's research corridor. It also includes the newest Latino immigrants, documented or not, stepping from a Trailways bus downtown, ready to take any kind of a job. The hopes that each brings will help define Washington's evolution as a digital-age region in the coming decades.

The area's most significant demographic change does not involve new arrivals. It is the slow, often hesitant erosion of the racial barriers separating the African-American community from the rest of the city. As noted earlier it is a pattern that stretches back to Washington's origins, involving physical separation by neighborhoods.

Many factors maintained this divide, but a few stand out. One was a federal government decision early in the last century that effectively barred blacks from advancement in the Civil Service, a critical barrier to African-American upward mobility and economic progress in the region. Another defining event was the wholesale migration of white families in the 1950s to the suburbs, the so-called white flight, which had the effect of tightening segregation patterns in large areas of the city. The problem of what to do with dispossessed low-income black families was largely ignored. More recently, the stepped-up migration of newly affluent black families to formerly all-white suburbs has helped ease the situation.

As noted earlier, these changes have been influenced in recent years by the arrival of migrants from all corners of the world. The Washington area has become the seventh largest urban gateway for foreigners in the country. Overall, the new arrivals made up nearly half of population growth in the Washington region in the 1990s.[18] In the early years of the new century, almost one in five workers in the area was born abroad, according to a Center for Immigration Studies survey. The comparable figure three decades earlier was one in twenty-two.

Washington's immigrants tend to be different than newcomers in other parts of the country. Overall, among the ten leading U. S. metropolitan areas with large immigrant inflows the capital region has the highest percentage of foreign-born residents who speak English well and have the lowest poverty rate. Only about 10 percent of Washington's new arrivals are officially rated as poor. Another critical factor is that the region's newcomers come to stay—and to work. A 2004 study of immigration trends sponsored in part by Harvard's Kennedy School of Government indicated that the chief motivation cited by 84 percent of the new wave of immigrants was the opportunity to get ahead.

These attitudes reflect the fact that the region's newcomers are better educated than their counterparts in other metropolitan areas and therefore more likely to fit into the capital region's new high-tech information economy.[19] According to a Census Bureau analysis of 233 counties, three Washington-area jurisdictions rank among the top five counties in the percentage of adults holding bachelor degrees.

This new demographic mix in the Washington area also involves the African-American community. It is still the largest nonwhite ethnic group in the region. Statistical projections of racial trends are notoriously unstable, but there are enough indicators now to suggest that both African Americans and Northern European whites—the two racial pillars in Washington's past—are giving way to the new wave of migrants, part of a national trend that has resulted in a higher proportion of foreign-born residents than at any time since the 1930s.

These changes raise important issues about American cultural identity in general and their impact on the Washington region in particular. The subject has been given public prominence by historian Samuel Huntington in an influential 2004 book, *Who Are We? The Challenges to American National Identity.* Huntington asks:

> Would America be the America it has been (and, in some measure still is today) if it had been settled in the seventeenth and eighteenth centuries not by British Protestants but by French, Spanish, or Portuguese Catholics? The answer is no.... Only in the mid-twentieth century did Americans begin to think of themselves as a multiracial multiethnic society. This is, I submit, not a very pleasing but highly realistic portrayal of American identity, free of moralism or hysteria.[20]

Other observers have vigorously challenged Huntington's thesis. The debate about changing racial and cultural patterns will continue, as will the flow of immigrants into the country. A Census Bureau study released in 2003 underscored the situation statistically when it identified Hispanics as the nation's largest minority group at 37 million, outnumbering

African Americans for the first time. In the period covered by the Bureau's survey, the Latino population grew by almost 5 percent, compared to 1.5 percent for blacks, and 0.3 per cent for the white, non–Hispanic population. "It is a turning point in the nation's history," says Roberto Suro, director of the Washington-based Pew Hispanic Center. "If you consider how much of this nation's history is wrapped up in the interplay between black and white, this serves as an official announcement that we as Americans cannot think of race in that way any more."

This demographic shift has particular significance for the Washington area, given its role as a special magnet for overseas migrants. As noted, the largest local intake, about 40 percent, is from Latin America and the Caribbean. In many ways, this Latino impact mirrors that of other new migrant groups, with some important twists. One of these involves simple demographic arithmetic: about a third of the babies born in the area in the new century have Hispanic roots. This suggests a scenario in which Latinos may become the area's largest ethnic group, perhaps even the majority, in a relatively short time. Given the generally higher birth rates among other newly arrived migrants and within the African-American community, this leads to the prospect that white residents from Northern European stock may soon be a distinct statistical minority in the Washington region.

These demographic projections have are all kinds of implications, but the one that is relevant to this survey is their impact on the Washington region's evolution as an information-age enclave. As the new arrivals are, on balance, better educated on arrival than earlier immigrants, they are also emerging as an active political force. Nationally, in the 2008 presidential elections, these groups proved to be a decisive voting bloc in assuring Barack Obama's victory.

The local Latino community, in particular, is emerging as a strong cultural force. Hispanic Heritage Month in September is now a prominent annual event across the region, supported by politicians appealing to the growing pool of Latino voters and by merchants seeking a share of the community's $700 billion annual spending power.

Another demographic group that has become more visible in recent years is the gay and lesbian community. For generations, its members were a largely invisible factor in the region's population mix. In the 1960s, they began to assert themselves as a group to the point where, by 1977, a leading local gay leader declared that Washington was the gay capital of the nation. Among other projects, gays successfully campaigned to force the city government to drop most of its discriminatory regulations. Many observers credited their collective voting power for Marion Barry's first upset victory in the District's 1978 mayoral election. "Probably no city in America has seen a greater transformation from total repressiveness to openness," local gay leader Frank Kameny declared at the time.

Since then Washington's gay community has been fully outed. A Gay Pride parade each year draws tens of thousands of participants and onlookers to the Mall where, among other events, the Atlantic States Gay Rodeo Association offers rides on a mechanical bull. Gays and lesbians are a small but increasingly visible element in the city's new Creative Class mix with its open-ended attitudes, showing willingness to welcome newcomers on their own terms and talents.

Supporting these demographic trends is the large and growing presence of research resources in the Washington area, sponsored by government, academic, and commercial organizations. This combination tends to be occupationally incestuous, as young professionals move easily between the three sectors. Collectively, they work in the largest conglomeration of research facilities in the country, from the massive National Institutes of Health (NIH) complex in Bethesda to the latest downtown think tank. NIH alone would qualify Washington as a research powerhouse, given its $25 billion-plus annual budgets. No one has put a price tag on the region's combined public and private annual research activities, but $75 billion would probably be on the low side.

Washington's emergence as a major research center is largely a modern development. Its roots, however, stretch back 150 years, beginning with the first government sponsorship of such scientific groups as the National Bureau of Standards and the Coast and Geodetic Survey. Large-scale government-sponsored research was stimulated by the creation in 1976 of the White House Office of Science and Technology Policy, whose director is known unofficially as the President's Science Advisor. The post-war years saw a steady increase in federally funded science and technology research, from the large-scale activities of the Defense Department's Advanced Research Projects Agency (ARPA) on down to hundreds of smaller projects managed by little-known outfits such as the National Geospatial Intelligence Agency.

Meanwhile, another specialized Washington research activity, public-policy think tanks, came into its own. The pioneer was the Brookings Institution, founded in 1927 with a self-anointed mission to be the "capstone to the educational arch of the country," including the task of tutoring the nation's political leaders on big issues.[21] Today, there are an estimated 125 private think tanks in the Washington area, each cultivating its own piece of policy turf. During the Watergate scandals in the early 1970s, think-tank involvement in political issues led to an aborted Nixon administration proposal to carry out a break-in of the Brookings offices to seize allegedly incriminating files regarding illegal White House activities.

Expansion in the size and influence of higher-education resources in the region in recent decades gave another boost to Washington's credentials as an information-age center. Local academic growth was part of the overall surge in the numbers and influence of American universities after World War II. Previously, Washington had played a relatively modest role as a center for higher education.

The city's founders, including George Washington, had held high hopes for establishing a national university in the new capital. Washington himself mentioned the project in his last address to Congress and also in his will. His most forceful statement was a letter to the newly appointed Commissioners of the District of Columbia asking them to do "something handsome" by way of endowing a local university. The commissioners did not act on his suggestion, but Congress issued charters to two schools — the Jesuit-run Georgetown College and Columbian College, sponsored by a committee of Baptist ministers. The schools, now Georgetown and George Washington universities, have constituted distinguished assets in the region's educational resources ever since. Howard University, founded after the Civil War, is a leader among the country's historically black colleges and universities.

For most of its history, though, Washington has been outshone academically. From the beginning, government agencies relied heavily on imported leadership talent, originally drawn from Eastern colleges. More recently, academic migrants from schools in the Middle West and the West Coast have dominated. But this pattern is changing; universities in the Washington region are now formidable suppliers of professional talent to both government and private enterprises in the area.[22] A turn-of-the-century survey found 285,000 students enrolled in over fifty higher-learning institutions in the city and surrounding suburbs. Universities and colleges are the biggest private job providers in the District of Columbia, accounting for five of the twenty top employers in recent years.[23] No one blinked several years ago when Stephen Trachtenberg, then president of George Washington University, was chosen to head the city's Board of Trade.

State-supported universities in Maryland and Virginia play an important role in the region's new information-technology culture. Maryland has invested heavily in IT–related research at its schools, particularly at the flagship University of Maryland, a nationally recognized leader in nanotechnology research, among other digital disciplines. In recent years, Virginia has appropriated over $200 million to expand scientific research facilities at its public universities. One of these, George Mason University, has emerged as a leader in this effort. Founded in 1957 as a branch of the University of Virginia, the school has since expanded to over 30,000 students on several campuses in Northern Virginia.[24] It has also become a research magnet for IT companies in the region, including an unusual program that allows them to share campus research facilities with the school's faculty.

Private higher education also plays a special role in the region's growth as a research center. Johns Hopkins University, with its main campus in Baltimore, has major research facilities in the Washington region. Its Applied Physics Laboratories in the Maryland suburbs is a national scientific power. One of its recent projects is supervision of a $720 million NASA program to photograph the surface of Mars, a digital undertaking that will fill 15,000 compact discs by the time it is completed. This and similar research efforts have boosted the school's already formidable reputation as an academic powerhouse.[25]

Beyond their role as research resources for the local IT sector, colleges and universities in the region are restructuring themselves to prepare students for life in the new digital environment. "They come to us now more wired up than any previous generation," says one local educator, referring to the cell phones, laptops, and personal Web sites that are now standard trappings of undergraduate life. The students' digital involvement with Washington-area universities begins before they ever show up. The Internet now serves as their primary guide in selecting which school to attend. Judy Hingle of the National Association of College Admission Counselors points out: "It has changed from the Internet being a supplement to being a first source. For a great majority of students, this is going to be their first impression. This is going to be their handshake."[26]

Some local educators deplore the new electronics. Most don't. "All faculty want students to take more responsibility for their own learning," says Randy Bass, director of Georgetown University's Center for New Designs in Learning and Scholarship. "Tools such as Weblogs provide an ideal environment to foster that.... What blogs ... provide is a flexible and accessible space for students to play with ideas, turn them in the light, expand them through dialog with each other, and make them their own."[27]

Georgetown and other local schools are experimenting with other ways to use digital technology. American University's Kogod School of Business has distributed BlackBerry phones and HotSpot wireless broadband Internet service to its students with the aim of creating a more realistic business environment for their studies.

Another academic area undergoing rapid change in the Washington area is distance learning, in which the link between teacher and student is an electronic circuit. Once a minor factor in American education, emphasizing mail-order studies, distance learning has boomed in recent years, thanks largely to the Internet's ability to provide universal access to course materials.[28]

A recent study funded by the Alfred P. Sloan Foundation found that almost two million students across the nation were enrolled in such courses, which the foundation defined as having 80 percent of course materials delivered online.[29] At the same time the National Center for Educational Statistics projects that online enrolment was growing at a rate ten times that of campus-based schools.[30]

Distance learning is thriving as an alternative to traditional educational practices in the Washington region. Among other local schools, Georgetown University has digitally expanded its national outreach. It is a member of an online network, JesuitNet, which links twenty-eight Jesuit colleges and universities across the country in a collaborative effort to consolidate expenses and share coursework. Beginning with a half-dozen courses, the network has been expanded to over forty degree programs.

Meanwhile, there is a seamy side to the new enthusiasm for online education. It involves electronic diploma mills focused on bottom-line profits rather than scholarship. The largest of the online schools, the University of Phoenix, with 300,000 students, has been severely criticized in recent years for the low quality of its curriculum offerings.[31] "There are now more fake online MBA programs in the United States than real ones," says Vicky Phillips, CEO of GetEducated, a Web site that evaluates online degree programs.

For-profit higher education has a strong and growing base in the Washington area. One of the largest of the local operations is Laureate Education Inc., which has developed a significant niche in running career-oriented schools here and abroad, using a combination of online and campus programs. By the middle of the decade, Laureate had enlisted over

100,000 students in university-level programs, including a hotel management school in China.[32]

A local for-profit school, Strayer University, enrolls over 20,000 students in 35 locations in the Washington area and across the nation. The school's courses are heavily weighted toward business administration, accounting, and information technology, taught in classrooms and on Web sites. The ten Strayer centers in Washington and its suburbs are the largest grantor of MBA degrees in the region. Within the region, the average Strayer student is 34 years old, with over 70 percent of its students coming from minority groups.

Another major for-profit educational group in the Washington region is Kaplan University, a wholly owned and highly profitable educational subsidiary of the Washington Post Co. Originally focused on preparing high-school students for college-entrance exams, the Kaplan group has expanded in recent years to provide a full schedule of advanced courses for corporations and individuals. It does this in cooperation with sixty colleges nationwide, involving over 40,000 students in classrooms and in online offerings. One of its subsidiaries, Concord Law School, founded in 1998, claims to be the first institution in the country to offer a professionally recognized law degree online. Kaplan has signaled a move into international education, with plans for developing a for-profit private venture in Great Britain.

Old-line universities in the Washington area originally shied away from distance learning, but their attitudes have changed as they see both educational value and expanded revenues in the effort. Their interest increased after the Massachusetts Institute of Technology announced in 2001 that it would begin to post the contents of some of its courses on the Web. Within a short time 1.5 million independent learners were logging on to the school's "OpenCourseware" site each month. In 2007 MIT expanded its online offerings to include all of its 1,800 courses.[33]

Washington's evolution as a twenty-first century educational and cultural center remains a work in progress. The political capital on the Potomac is challenging New York and Boston for the primary title as the nation's intellectual hub. A 2005 *New York Times* survey of the city's prospects grudgingly admitted that "Washington has become the beneficiary of a gradual intellectual migration. As industry-financed think tanks grow and finance a culture of policy analysts and serious thinkers with ideological differences, more intellectuals have been drawn to a city previously considered a backwater of shallow politicians and colorless government bureaucrats.... Washington has, in a sense, matured. Intellectuals still reside in New York, Boston and Washington (and hop the shuttle easily among the three), but in a highly charged political environment, there has been a move away from academic ideas toward ones generated in the real world, or at least real government."[34]

In short, Washington's cultural and educational resources, with their ability to attract a digitally savvy Creative Class, are clearly a vital force in the city's current transition.

8
Washington's Digital Future

Washington's transition to a digital era is winding up after a quarter-century of technological change, economic growth, and an increasingly complex social environment. The most pervasive of these changes may be demographic, given a shifting population mix that includes a new wave of computer-savvy young professionals. They are the successors to the postwar baby boomers, the first of whom reached the age of sixty in 2007. The Census Bureau, with its penchant for statistical precision, notes that the boomers currently arrive at this milestone at the rate of 330 every hour.

The new professionals are hard to pin down in terms of charts, statistics, and other conventional measures. What is clear is their special impact on U.S society in general and on the Washington region in particular. Among large metropolitan areas, Washington is probably the most affected by their presence. They bring computer-honed expertise as well as different cultural attitudes to the region's major enterprises — the old federal bureaucracy and the new IT–oriented companies that have migrated to the area.

Though subject to ups and downs, this trend is permanent, rooted in the steadily expanding digital changes. Contrary to President Bill Clinton's 1992 claim that the era of big government was over, federal budgets increase every year, with a special emphasis on funding information-age resources. As noted earlier, Robert Huggins Associates, a British consultancy, places the Washington area near the top of its ranking of global IT centers, along with Silicon Valley, Dallas-Fort Worth, Boston, Singapore, and Osaka. The federal city is holding its own in this league despite the emergence of new regional challengers at home and abroad.

The Washington region is well situated to deal with these changes. Witness, for example, its role in the new wave of research breakthroughs, most notably in nanotechnology and biotechnology, which are becoming everyday parts of the area's digital structure. Their influence goes well beyond technical capabilities: each also introduces social, economic, and ethical factors requiring political decisions that directly involve Washington. The debate on human cloning presents a case in point, where a scientific breakthrough, based on advanced digital techniques, generates a public-policy issue that reverberates from the halls of Congress to backwoods fundamentalist chapels.

Obvious perils face anyone attempting to forecast the general impact, much less the particulars, of these developments on Washington and its surrounding region. Predictions are a fragile commodity, as they are with other large social shifts. In the 1950s, IBM executives estimated that the global market for their newfangled computers would amount to roughly fifty machines. Not only were they wrong about the impact of computer technology, they could not have imagined that, a half-century later, the company would sell off its small-computer business to a firm in the People's Republic of China.

Judgments on current IT breakthroughs often require decisions that cannot wait. MIT political scientist Ithiel Pool has pointed out that if human history were measured on a twenty-four-hour cycle, the computer age began at three seconds to midnight. The time allotted for adapting political and social policies and practices to new digital realities is steadily shrinking. In the nineteenth century, forty years separated the introduction of the telegraph and that of the telephone. This gap shrank progressively to thirty years for radio, twenty years for television, fifteen years for the computer, and ten years for Internet technology. More recently the time for considering the impact of digital breakthroughs is often measured in months.

Moreover, new technologies increase the rate of change not so much by shortening the time involved as by expanding the affected areas — political, economic and cultural. Technologies no longer emerge in a steady linear fashion. We deal today with converging trends that require quick decisions, leaving considerably less margin for error. The results too often are faulty judgments and waste. The turnover in obsolescent digital equipment is staggering: as noted earlier, the federal government disposes of over ten thousand older computers each week. This process is particularly difficult in a competitive economy where big industries need to protect their current products against a flood of upstart innovations, often forcing them to rush promising products to market before working out all the technical bugs.

The first generation of American information-age events (roughly 1950–1980) benefited from the ideas of a remarkable group of academics, many working in the Boston area. Collectively, they have had a strong impact on Washington's role in the new age, beginning, early on, with MIT professor Vannevar Bush, an important contributor to the new science of computers. As White House science adviser during World War II, Bush saw the need to establish a major bureaucratic role for advanced technologies in national policy. In his remarkable paper, "Science — The Endless Frontier," written after the war, he made the case for what became known as Big Science, with a particular emphasis on the importance of government involvement at the policy level, particularly in encouraging advanced research. His efforts, as we have seen, led in part to the creation of the National Science Foundation and the postwar expansion of federal investment in research. The long-term impact of his recommendations was to establish Washington's central role in planning and implementing the shift to a new digitally driven environment.

Bush's academic colleagues in Cambridge helped advance this change by defining the ideological underpinnings of the emerging information age. Harvard political scientist Karl Deutsch was one of the first to explore the social implications of computers in his 1963 groundbreaking study, *The Nerves of Government*.[1] He saw digital organization of information as a vital political factor in the new age, potentially more important than traditional forces such as the police or the military. The rising flood of computerized data was pushing us towards the limits of human capacity to cope. The solution, he suggested, was "intelligence amplification" through advanced technologies that would permit a wider sharing of the facts we need to survive and thrive.

Canadian communications scholar, Marshall McLuhan, who popularized the concept of an information-driven global village, picked up this theme, with evangelical overtones.[2] In a high rhetorical moment, he declared, "The computer is by all odds the most extraordinary of all technological clothing ever devised by man, since it is the extension of our central nervous system. Beside it the wheel is a mere hula hoop."

At about the same time, Harvard sociologist Daniel Bell gave this prospect a name. He called it the postindustrial age and declared that its major activity would be the creation, storage, and distribution of information. Computer-savvy professionals would replace industrial-era entrepreneurs as the preeminent social and economic class. Across town, MIT political science professor Ithiel deSola Pool probed the emerging role of a new communications technology known as packet switching in creating a universal information network. Although he didn't know it at the time, he was describing today's Internet, the crowded digital highway that has introduced billions of people around the globe to the information age. Populist advocates of the new information order echoed these early academic probings, with particular attention to the economic benefits it promised. Among the dozens of self-appointed seers, one of the most prominent was economist George Gilder, whose populist writings and lectures dominated the field in the 1990s. Gilder rode the wave of a new digital enthusiasm that gripped audiences across the country, including the 60,000 disciples who paid $300 a year for his newsletter. His work, he declared, was nothing less than a campaign powered by faith: "What does faith have to do with it, my critics will ask? This, after all, is a technology of facts and physics, not visions and passions. The answer is that only faith enables us to make this kind of leap."[3] The Gilder message lost much of its luster when his overly optimistic economic projections for the new age were deflated in the dot-com recession at the turn of the century.

Official Washington was often reluctant to embrace the digital faith in the early years of computerization. Overall, the federal bureaucracy was slow to give up its familiar paper-shuffling habits for the unproved benefits of the new technologies, with some notable exceptions. The Defense Department and the intelligence agencies were enthusiastic converts to computerization by the 1960s, helped by ample budgets to invest in computers and other digital products.

Most other government agencies adopted a wait-and-see attitude. Moreover, there was no strong pressure from the top to apply the new techniques. A June 1966 executive order in the Lyndon Johnson administration encouraging computerization within federal agencies was not seriously implemented. A 1976 White House committee headed by Vice President Nelson Rockefeller made the first attempt to define a workable policy approach to the new digital realities. The group recommended that "the United States set as a goal the development of a coordinated National Information Policy." The committee's report was quickly consigned to the bureaucratic limbo reserved for well-intentioned projects that are ahead of their time.[4]

Meanwhile, the federal bureaucracy was moving slowly into a digital-age environment. A Comptroller-General's 1977 report to Congress noted over ten thousand computers in offices throughout the government. But progress towards efficient computerization remained erratic. A 1984 presidential commission on waste in the federal government, headed by business executive Peter Grace, documented a record of obsolescence, incompatibility, and duplication of computer systems within the bureaucratic structure. The commission described as "woefully inadequate" the level of digital resources available to federal managers.[5]

Despite these shortcomings, computerization slowly became the new norm for government operations, particularly after the introduction of desktop machines in the early 1980s. At the same time, Congress began to recognize the need for laws to deal with the new digital realities. After years of piecemeal approaches, a major attempt was made to develop comprehensive legislation on the subject. The effort extended over a dozen years, resulting in the Telecommunications Act of 1996. The legislation defined, in 180 pages of small print, the first national consensus on the pace and direction of the information age. Large economic interests were at stake, ranging from such corporate giants as AT&T and IBM on down to small startup firms looking for a niche in the new digital order.

The 1996 telecommunications law was one of the most intensely lobbied pieces of legislation ever debated by the U.S. Congress. It was full of compromises, most of them designed to favor the interests of one segment of the new digital economy over another. These attempts to balance competing interests soon fell apart, mainly because ongoing research breakthroughs were constantly upgrading the capabilities of computers and other new devices. Previous legislation had regulated voice, print, and video services separately. The new digital networks could handle these basic services as a common set of electronic impulses on a single transmission line. Many of the carefully crafted compromises in the 1996 law were soon overtaken by this reality.

While corporate lawyers argued over the arcane details of the legislation, other events were trumping their efforts. The most important of these was the rapid growth of the Internet, expanding from a service used by small groups of computer buffs into a populist medium. A major achievement of the legislation was what it did not do: it did not put regulatory restrictions on the Internet, a decision that made obsolete many of the carefully crafted regulations in the new law. By the turn of the twenty-first century, over half of American homes had an Internet connection, as did most businesses and public services. For the first time, the information age was more than a cliché: its effects began to touch everyone.

This change affected the entire country, but its impact was felt with special force in Washington. As we have seen throughout this survey, thousands of information-technology firms moved into the region, motivated by expanding opportunities for their goods and services in federal budgets. The result was to reshape the way government does business. Slowly and steadily, a new kind of bureaucracy was emerging, different from anything that had preceded it.

What to call this new way of governance? An influential Rand Corporation report in 1991 proposed "cyberocracy" to describe what was happening. The phrase was quickly dropped because of its vaguely Orwellian overtones. The Manhattan Institute's William Eggers, with tongue-in-cheek, suggested "Government 2.0." Most commentators finally settled on the more neutral term, "e-government," pointing up the bureaucracy's new reliance on electronic resources.

These activities now extend from the government's most advanced research activities to the prosaic operations of the Postal Service, the one part of the federal structure that touches most Americans as it delivers mail to 150 million addresses across the country on an average weekday. The image of the friendly Norman Rockwell postman delivering Valentine cards and letters from Grandma faded as the service shifted to digital operations. Computerization has reached down to the 38,000 retail post offices, including thousands that have eliminated clerks and waiting lines by becoming totally automated. First-class mail volume steadily eroded as people increasingly paid bills online and sent e-mails rather than write letters. Faced with stiff competition from United Parcel Service and Federal Express for package delivery, the Postal Service created a digitized Click-N-Ship service that prints the postage at home and then schedules a free pickup.[6]

The Postal Service's experience with digital operations is an outsized example of the Internet's role in reordering American life in general and government operations in particular. Nicholas Negroponte of MIT's Media Lab has described the Web's impact as "10.5 on the Richter scale of social change." For Microsoft's Bill Gates, the Net promised a golden era of what he calls friction-free capitalism. Novelist William Gibson, who coined the word "cyberspace," saw the Internet as "the great anarchic event that defies conventional commercial exploitation."

Many explanations account for the Net's newly pervasive role in American culture but none more so than the decision, made a generation ago, to allow it to expand and grow in its own way, with minimal government oversight. Despite attempts to regulate it, the network is still managed by a private group, the California-based Internet Corporation for Assigned Names and Numbers, (ICANN), whose main job is to oversee the Internet's operational performance. In 2006, ICANN found itself dealing with a controversy about sex. The issue before the group was whether to authorize a new Web domain dedicated to explicit pornographic traffic. Proponents argued that the new domain (.xxx) would make it easier to control access to so-called adult material by young people. Opponents claimed that the site would simply help them go directly to pornographic Web pages. ICANN's directors rejected the proposal in a nine-to-five vote.[7]

The most serious threats to the Internet's independence have been the attempts by foreign governments to set up regulatory barriers to open network access. In 2006, the State Department set up an "Internet freedom task force" specifically to deal with these threats.[8] Overseas efforts to limit the Internet's impact can be attributed to the network's uniquely American origins, outreach, and influence. From its beginnings as a small Defense Department project, the network expanded as groups of computer buffs across the country adopted it as a way of keeping in touch with each other. The network grew rapidly after 1989 when Tim Berners-Lee, a British high-energy physicist, developed the technology for the World Wide Web, vastly simplifying access to Internet sites. As one Net watcher noted at the time, "The World Wide Web almost single-handedly transformed the Net from a members-only sandbox into a gigantic crossroads with strip malls and nouveau info-publishers."[9]

Combined with the growing popularity of small personal computers, the Internet has made a unique imprint on U.S. information patterns. By the year 2000, Americans dominated the Net both in its use and in its content. Most households had an Internet connection. All but 6 percent of the most visited Web sites originated in the United States. An American aura pervades the entire grid: "The Internet is profoundly disrespectful of tradition, established order, and hierarchy, and that is very American," says foreign policy analyst Fareed Zakaria.

This point was dramatically affirmed in the 2008 presidential election. The Obama campaign transformed the art of political communications, by putting digital resources at the center of its strategy. Its success reshaped the political landscape in ways that will be studied, and emulated, for years to come. It focused on the Internet as an organizing tool, bypassing to a large extent the traditional campaign reliance on television, radio, and print appeals. By the end of the campaign, Obama organizers had amassed an electronic database of ten million potential voters. Moreover, it was a two-way link: not only a transmitter of the campaign's messages but also a feedback channel for measuring voter attitudes and actions. Not the least benefit of this two-way flow was its value in raising money: the Internet was the critical channel through which over three million voters contributed funds for the Obama campaign.

It was a new kind of politics. As Democratic strategist Peter Daou pointed out after the Obama victory: "Once you have people connected through a network, you can't disconnect. It's like unbreaking an egg. People all across the country have formed these groups to support Obama. They've worked together for a successful purpose. You don't let go of that easily." His point has since been taken seriously by Democratic and Republican strategists who, in the months after the 2008 campaign, began reorganizing their Internet operations in preparation for the 2010 congressional midterm elections.

Meanwhile, the dominant U.S. role in the Internet's creation and in its content continues to raise concerns among foreign critics about the Americanization of their cultures. A French cultural minister, Jack Lang, echoed this theme when he described the Internet and other American information exports as "a real crusade — let's call things by their real names — this financial and cultural imperialism that no longer grabs territory, or rarely, but grabs consciousness, ways of thinking, ways of living."[10] Despite this and other elitist complaints, Internet access and its heavily American content are a global phenomenon, with users who include young Arabs hunched over desktops in smoky cybercafés and their counterparts in China, who make up one of the network's largest audiences overseas, tapping into foreign Web sites in defiance of government censors.

Despite the Internet's spectacular growth, its ability to influence the information age has yet to be fully tested. It is clear that the United States, as the major producer and user of Internet goods and services, is the center for strategic political decisions on information-age developments. The next phase of the transformation is already well under way, beginning with the introduction of a new generation of Internet capabilities. The network has gone through several technical upgrades in its short history. None of them comes close to matching the changes now being planned in obscure committees and working groups in Washington.

Much of this work involves phasing in new Internet capabilities, expanding its role as the basic highway to the digital age. Over a billion people worldwide are linked to its Web sites. VeriSign Inc., which tracks Internet traffic patterns, estimates that .com and .net messages on U.S. Web sites each day outnumber phone calls three to one. Nielsen/Net Ratings, an offshoot of the company that tracks television-program ratings, recorded 5.1 billion domestic Web searches in December 2005. At the same time, Nielsen reported that the number of Americans on the Internet topped the two hundred million mark for the first time.[11] Over thirty million of them had set up blog sites to advertise themselves and their opinions. Meanwhile, the proportion of Internet traffic taken up by junk e-mailers steadily increases. By the middle of the decade, these accounted for almost a quarter of all Internet traffic in the United States.

Americans increasingly use the Internet as a digital shopping mall. Forrester Research, a New York consultancy, estimated that 2008 Net retail sales reached $259 billion. This is a relatively small share of American retail commerce, but some analysts see the Internet influencing nearly half of all U.S. retail sales within a few years. This shift has particular meaning for the automobile industry, where potential buyers no longer just kick the tires in dealer showrooms. Eighty-five percent of online auto shoppers surveyed by JupiterResearch, a New York consultancy, said they go to the Internet first to compare new cars and other big purchases.[12] Another unique Internet marketing phenomenon is the online auction, involving merchandise of all kinds. EBay, the most extensive of the digital auctioneers, broke new ground in 2006 when it auctioned off the small town of Bridgeville, California.[13]

These trends are grist for strategic planners in Washington and elsewhere who are looking at the network's future. MIT research scientist David Clark, who helped design the original Internet and has since been involved in upgrading it, points out: "The challenging question is: can we conceive a vision of what a global communications network will look like in ten or fifteen years. To do that you have to free yourself from what the world looks like now. The Internet is so obvious that it is hard to contemplate what a non–Internet would look like."[14]

"What we need to do," Clark adds, "is to re-envision the future and stop thinking about the present, saying 'let's put a Band-Aid here.'" His vision is based on the coming giant leap in Internet technical capabilities. Consider this: at mid-decade, the current fourth technical generation of the network has a capacity of about 4.3 billion available addresses. One version being considered for implementation by National Science Foundation researchers, known as IPV6, is so capacious that it has to be expressed in exponents, namely 3.4×10 to the 38th power.

For those of us who are technology-impaired, this capacity means that there is no foreseeable limit to the amount of data the network can handle. Internet planners suggest that even present projections of the network's capabilities do not reflect future traffic requirements. A study by Frost & Sullivan, a leading analyst of technological trends, notes that the current surge in Internet usage could mean that the network will run out of transmission capacity sooner than expected. By 2012, there will be 17 billion devices connected to the Internet, Frost and Sullivan analyst Sam Masud predicts. He thinks that by that time the present network will begin to reach full capacity. Masud's message, along with that of other veteran Net-watchers, is that further upgrading the network's capacity cannot be delayed.

The Internet Innovation Alliance, an industry lobbying group, estimates that an "exoflood" of added Internet capability is needed. (Exoflood relates to exobyte, a word that describes 1,074 billion gigabytes of data.) Two exobytes equal the total volume of data generated on the Internet in 1999. By 2007, the Net was routinely transmitting one exobyte of data every hour. One popular Web site, YouTube, uses as much bandwidth as the entire Internet consumed at the turn of the century. "Preparing for the exoflood is critical to the nation's success," says Larry Irving, a Washington-based communications specialist. "The Internet infrastructure must be robust enough to handle all the new data; this is often a challenge because the Internet is really thousands of privately owned networks stitched together. It requires constant investment so that it will continue to grow and run smoothly."[15]

Washington plays a major role in dealing with this prospect. The National Science Foundation has sponsored two complementary groups on the subject, both burdened with bureaucratic titles. The first is the Global Environment for Network Innovations (GENI — or Jenny to its friends), which is planning an advanced test-bed network for examining new protocols and applications. The second group, Future Internet Designs (FIND), looks at ways to adapt the Internet's expanded capabilities to everyday needs. In particular, FIND envisions a network with capabilities well beyond its present emphasis on traffic initiated by individuals — sending e-mails and clicking on to Web sites — to a future in which Net traffic will increasingly involve machine-to-machine transactions, essentially between billions of chips located in everything from cereal boxes to medical devices implanted in human beings.

We will also deal with computers in different ways. In 2006, Microsoft unveiled a new version of its operating system for automobiles that includes digitally based music, telephony, and navigation devices, all of which will be voice-controlled. Computer chips are being downsized dramatically to carry out these new tasks. In August 2007, IBM announced a breakthrough in nanotechnology that, it said, could increase computers' data storage capacity by a factor of 1,000 and decrease the size of computer chips to no larger than a speck of dust.

The results of these research breakthroughs are showcased at the International Consumer Products Show, an annual Las Vegas extravaganza. The focus in recent shows has been on what its organizers call media place-shifting, which is geekspeak for making digital capabilities available anywhere. Clothing manufacturers, from Nike to Levi Strauss, are integrating digital devices into their products. Cell phone giant Motorola has introduced a clothing line that includes a parka with sewn-in stereo speakers. VivoMetrics, a start-up IT firm, markets a garment called LifeShirt with digital chips woven into the fabric. Data from the chips may help medical specialists remotely monitor vital signs and thirty other biometric readings of men and women who have potentially life-threatening conditions.[16]

These innovations are the thin wedge of a flood of digital products and services that are changing the ways in which we go about our daily business. A new generation, the post-baby boomers, will look back at present-day electronic devices as primitive artifacts of the early information age, suitable for display in a Smithsonian museum.

Washington will play a key role in determining the pace at which these new digital services are phased into the daily activities of Americans. As we have seen throughout this survey, the city and its surrounding region have evolved in recent decades as a major IT center. It is the home base of the world's largest user of digital goods and services, the federal government. More important, it is the political center where decisions being made are shaping the American information age, with ripple effects across the globe. In most cases, these decisions involve resolving current disputes between contending interests with political or economic stakes in the outcome. This process can result in less attention paid to anticipating changes down the road, a critical factor in an age where technical advances constantly outrace political and social realities.

Such an outcome occurred over a decade ago when, as noted earlier, Congress and the Clinton administration tried to draw a legislative map for the transition to the information age. The result was the Telecommunications Act of 1996, which sought to restructure national communications resources in order to deal with new digital requirements. It was an attempt at all-in-one master-plan legislation, and it didn't work. Although the 1996 legislation is still the law of the land, it has been modified extensively by rules designed to accommodate new technical breakthroughs. Happily, there is little taste in Washington these days for more grand-plan legislation to guide national information-age policy.

These pragmatic arrangements will serve the public interest if two considerations are kept in mind: first, to define the ground rules for adopting new technologies in ways that make universal digital service available for everyone in the country; second, to assure that First Amendment rights are protected in the process.

The goal of universal information services in the new age builds on a longtime national tradition. The United States is the most wired-up society on earth. This development traces back 140 years to the introduction of the first electrical communications utility — the Morse telegraph network. The decision was made then to build the network under private auspices rather than to make it a government monopoly, as has happened in most other countries. This pattern has been extended, with variations, to every subsequent American advance in public communications — telephones, radio, television, computer networking, cable systems, and the Internet, all managed with comparatively light government regulation. The result is the private network of networks that supports today's open information society in America.

Will this openness prevail in the digital age, empowering citizens with the communications and information resources they need to function and thrive? The question is still an open one, despite the obvious gains made in recent years in the availability of digital services, from cell phones to personal digital assistants like the BlackBerry.

Economist Robert Reich of the University of California has suggested that the new digital resources may not be enough to prevent a widening of the gap between the information-haves and information have-nots in American society: "No longer are Americans rising and falling together, as if in one large boat. We are, increasingly, in different smaller boats." The top one-fifth of working Americans take home more money than the other four-fifths combined. This affluent group is made up largely of professionals who create or otherwise deal with information. They inhabit a different economy from other Americans, Reich says: "The new elite is linked by jet, modem, fax, satellite, and fiber-optic cable to the great commercial and recreational centers of the world, but it is not particularly connected to the rest of the nation."[17]

The gap between racial groups in sharing the benefits of the new digital services is particularly disturbing. A Commerce Department study at mid-decade reported Internet access was available to only 45 percent of African-American households and 37 percent of Latino households.[18] This digital gap between the information-rich and the information-poor raises basic policy issues, beginning at the Washington level. The question is whether the gap can be sustained in an environment that makes access to digital information resources a necessity not only for individual needs but also for full public participation in a democratic society. Despite the enormous growth in digital resources in recent years, this prospect is still flawed.

The result has been to raise Internet access to the status of a major public debate. For Patricia Keefe, editor of *Information Week*, an industry trade paper, the question is whether the Internet is slated to be a next-generation public utility, in effect continuing a long American tradition of network resources supplied largely by competitive private organizations.[19] Although the idea of government-supported access to the Internet and other digital services is new, there is a long record of public-policy involvement in providing such services. The groundbreaking example, seventy years ago, was the Roosevelt administration's decision to subsidize electric power lines in rural areas, a service private utility companies could not or would not provide. (The plan was later expanded to include telephone services managed by rural cooperatives.) A more recent example of government intervention was the Clinton administration's decision in the 1990s to speed up computerization in school classrooms across the country through a small fee added to everyone's electric utility bills. The program has netted over $7 billion in annual subsidies in recent years.

In today's digital environment, new ways of providing full public access to the Internet and other information resources are taking hold. As noted in the previous chapter, one of these is Wi-Fi, a deceptively simple system for providing low-cost mail, voice, and video services. The technology relies primarily on shoebox-size radio transmitters mounted on streetlights or traffic signals, sending and receiving wireless signals from nearby laptop computers, cell telephones, and Blackberrys to the Internet and other networks. Wi-Fi links are relatively cheap to install, are technologically efficient, and are spreading quickly in American cities from coast to coast.[20]

Wi-Fi is also catching on abroad: London, Seoul, and other major cities already have extensive Wi-Fi services. Moscow city officials teamed up with Nortel, an American telecommunications firm, to build a Wi-Fi network to serve four million households. The government of India is planning a network serving 600,000 villages throughout the country, hopefully moving them from communications poverty to a full range of voice, print, and video services in one grand sweep. In Nepal, a primitive Wi-Fi network helps yak herders on remote mountains keep in touch with their villages.

There are many variations on how American Wi-Fi facilities are being set up and operated. Municipal governments have sponsored most of the early installations. In these cases, Wi-Fi is a public utility with access available to any digital information provider, such as AOL or Google, at one end and to any consumer with a wireless-enabled digital device at the other. For Wi-Fi enthusiasts, the technology offers the promise of narrowing the gap between the information-poor and information-rich in American cities. A more advanced version of Wi-Fi technology, known as Wi-Max, is already being installed around the country. Another prospect is to break Wi-Fi services out of their present urban settings and make them available in rural areas. Wi-Fi is already moving out of cities: in 2006, three neighboring Arizona towns — Gilbert, Tempe, and Chandler — announced plans to create a single network that would provide services in their suburbs as well as in downtown areas. Another project envisions high-speed Internet connections via Wi-Fi circuits in over 720 square miles of urban and rural areas in northern Michigan.[21]

Wi-Fi services started small in the late 1990s. The idea caught on at the turn of the century when Starbucks began offering Wi-Fi to its customers, who worked their laptops in between sips of coffee. It was a limited-range service but it worked. The decisive breakthrough in Wi-Fi development took place when Philadelphia inaugurated its citywide system. Its 135-square-mile network set a standard for other city systems, with transmitters on 4,000 city light posts maintained by EarthLink, a private contractor. The network also pioneered subsidies for low-income families, including free computers and a low $9.95 monthly fee. The system initially charged $20 a month for regular customers.[22]

Scores of other U.S. cities have followed Philadelphia's lead in planning Wi-Fi systems, including New York, Las Vegas, Corpus Christi, and Washington.[23] The District of Columbia got its first Wi-Fi installation in 2004, sponsored by the Open Park Project, a nonprofit group founded by communications lawyer Gregory Staple. Although it only covered the area around the Capitol, the project attracted enough attention to move the

District government to propose a more extensive system that could eventually serve 100,000 low-income residents, including free or subsidized services.[24]

Philadelphia's system played a special role in Wi-Fi development because Verizon, the local telephone company, initially challenged it in the courts as an unneeded facility, one that was an unfair burden on local taxpayers. The courts rejected the challenge, clearing a legal path for other cities to proceed with Wi-Fi systems offering advanced facilities that local telephone and cable companies were unable or unwilling to provide. The case for a municipal system has been stated by Dana Speigal, executive director of NYCwireless: "If a city decides for the benefit of all residents that everyone should have access to broadband services at an affordable rate and if the phone company is not doing that, then the city has the right to do it." In 2009, economic recession and other factors led many cities to postpone or cancel their Wi-Fi plans.

The new Wi-Fi municipal networks may only be a transitional stage in providing full-service access, until commercial firms can provide a similar service more cheaply and efficiently.[25] As the London *Economist* suggested in a survey of Wi-Fi prospects: "If city governments cannot even fill potholes, how will they be able to manage running a network?"[26] In 2005, Google offered to provide free wireless access to the entire city of San Francisco. Both Wi-Fi and Wi-Max are part of the new mix of wireless services that have to be factored into a national strategy for empowering citizens in the information age.[27]

Meanwhile, Washington will be the focal point for defining goals and practices for an advanced information-age society. As noted, there is little taste in the federal city for grand-plan legislation to guide this process. Any such attempts would probably suffer the same fate as the 1996 communications act, which tried to set rules for the new age. Its provisions were increasingly overtaken by the pace of technological change. A more realistic scenario involves defining a basic national goal — guaranteeing open access to electronic information to all citizens — and then negotiating flexible legislative and regulatory rules that can be adapted to changing technical and economic realities.

Whatever the outcome of these negotiations in Washington and elsewhere, they will include the Internet as the channel for greater involvement in the new digital environment. It is not too fanciful to suggest that today's Internet will morph semantically into The Network, with all the earmarks of a universal public utility. From a technical curiosity known only to a small group of computer buffs twenty-five years ago, the network has become an omnipresent reality in American life.

The pace of these changes will accelerate as the next generation of Internet technology comes on line. From the time the first primitive Internet-style network went on line in the late 1960s, engineers have tweaked it in piecemeal fashion, upgrading its capacities to accommodate technical changes. Today they are reinventing the network, taking advantage of the blazing speeds and awesome capacities made possible by new technical breakthroughs. Washington will play a major role in these changes, both as a policy maker and as a user of the new resources.

The eventual result will be what Internet groupies call Web 2.0, a capacious descendent of today's primitive Web. Tim O'Reilly, chief executive officer of O'Reilly Communications and convener of the first Web 2.0 conference in 2005, notes what he calls the essential difference between the original Web and the evolving one. Web 1.0 is an "architecture of consumption" and "read-only." Web 2.0 is an "architecture of participation." On the old Web, the user is the audience; on the new Web, the user participates. AOL, he adds, is a Web 1.0 company, mostly supplying one-way information. Google is definitely a 2.0 company, building its business on how users cross-link sites on the Web.

The shift to Web 2.0 is still in the early stages. This transition will depend heavily on economic and technical calculations by information-age industries from Hewlett-Packard on down to small start-up companies operating out of suburban garages, as Hewlett-Packard did a generation ago. Overall adoption of 2.0 standards will mean an Internet that is more interactive, customized, social, and media-intensive. "Twenty years from now, we will look back and say that this was the embryonic period.... The Web is only going to get more revolutionary," says Tim Berners-Lee, inventor of World Wide Web technology.[28] Lines are blurring between computers and traditional communications outlets such as phones, television, radio, books, and newspapers. Digital convergence among all information sources is happening in earnest.

Public policy will play a decisive role in this transition, centered heavily on Washington. As we have seen throughout this survey, the city and its surrounding region have changed dramatically in the early decades of the information age, with no quick-fix answers to either the opportunities or the barriers posed by technical advances. The attempts to legislate change, as in the Telecommunications Act of 1996, demonstrate the perils of trying to micromanage the passage to a new digital environment, as most of the provisions of that law have been overtaken by new realities.

This was particularly true of the government's attempt to end AT&T's virtual monopoly in domestic communications. A Justice Department decision in 1981 to break up the company into seven separate regional firms succeeded initially. AT&T appeared to be in its twilight years at the time. Twenty-five years later, however, the company roared back as the biggest telecom firm in the world, with its purchase of the last of the independent regional firms, Bell South, for $67 billion.[29]

In the new economy forming, thousands of private firms are huffing and puffing to keep up with leapfrogging technologies, resulting in a shifting mix of winners and losers. Early pioneers such as Microsoft and AOL are shedding some of their luster in the competition with feisty newcomers. A new generation of digitally savvy entrepreneurs increasingly sets the pace, while knowledge workers' brains replace brawn as the new economy's distinguishing characteristic.

Many old icons of American capitalism, from steel mills to downtown department stores, face downsizing or replacement. For the present, Wal-Mart rules in large part because it has fully embraced digital practices. The Internet and other new resources are also transforming the older mass-media industries — newspapers, television, films, and book publishing. Technology is changing the ways they assemble their products and, increasingly, send them down a single all-purpose digital channel.[30]

The media companies are responding to a massive shift in how consumers use their products. Newspapers began losing circulation over a decade ago, as readers turned increasingly to Web sites for their news. Radio and television broadcasters are also feeling the pinch.[31] This audience erosion is particularly noticeable among younger people, a critical group in terms of advertising revenues. "Newspapers have to change dramatically," says John Lavine of Northwestern's Medill School of Journalism. "Unless the public reads it, you're just chopping down trees."[32] In Washington, the venerable *Post* has suffered slow but steady circulation losses in recent years. Among other changes, it began producing a tabloid summary of its regular edition, distributed at subway stations, with stories targeted to a younger audience. The *Post* has also moved heavily into specialized Web sites and other digital channels. In the process it has rebranded itself as an "educational and media company," whose most profitable division is its Kaplan education services, delivered to students over the Internet.[33]

Traditional media advertising revenues are steadily eroding in the face of Net-based competition. The shift from older advertising models (thirty-second TV ads, among others) remains a small factor in the $800 billion global ad market, but the trend is accelerating. Internet advertising on Google and other Web sites increased by 30 percent by 2005 over the previous year, according to a survey by PriceWaterhouseCoopers, the accounting firm.[34]

The erosion has spread beyond newspapers to television, radio and films. In 2005, News Corp., a multimedia giant, spent more than a billion dollars buying up Internet-based companies as a hedge against further erosion of its film, television, and print-based properties. Rupert Murdoch, News Corp's head, puts the case for change in direct terms: "We're looking at the ultimate opportunity. The Internet is media's golden age."[35]

Other big media firms are also rushing to distribute their contents online. A more-than-symbolic point was reached in March 2006 when CBS television offered parts of one of its certified moneymaking programs, the annual NCAA college-basketball championships, live over the Internet free of charge. At mid-decade, revenues from online advertising and paid content still represented less than 10 percent of total earnings for U.S. media conglomerates, according to a Merrill Lynch survey. Exceptions like Time Warner, during the merger with AOL that ended in May 2009, counted on digital revenues for about 20 percent of its earnings. The one certain trend is that online revenues will increase steadily in the coming years as audiences turn away from traditional print, voice, and video channels.[36] The economic downturn in 2009 promises to accelerate this trend.

These changes have a major impact on America's international role. IT-based goods and services now constitute a major export area, challenging aircraft and agricultural sales in recent years. At the same time, the U.S. economy faces stiffer competition from savvy foreign companies: think Finnish cell phones and Chinese computers. Increasingly, U.S. companies are outsourcing goods and services operations abroad. IBM has moved its pace-setting Global Solutions Delivery Center to India as part of a shift that could result in locating 20 percent of its worldwide work force there within a few years.[37] One of IBM's purposes is to be closer to fast-growing foreign markets. In increasingly prosperous India, the country's middle class alone is larger than America's entire population of 304 million.

Among foreign policy issues that concern Washington policy makers is that of protecting the Internet's free-style independence from censorship and other restrictions. From the start, American organizations have managed the network's operations, originally by units within the federal government and more recently by ICANN, the awkwardly named private-sector committee whose primary purpose is to assure the network's technical and content integrity.

As noted, these commitments to universal openness are increasingly under attack in the United Nations and other international forums. Resentful of America's dominance of a network increasingly important in their own societies, many countries argue for restrictions on Internet content, usually under the dubious rubric of preserving local cultural integrity. Other countries, such as China, are more direct, enforcing political controls over local Internet transmissions, including prison terms for Web users who log on to forbidden sites. The persistent threat of some kind of international controls over the Internet surfaced in November 2005, when a "world summit" on global information sponsored by the United Nations issued a report that argued: "No single government should have a preeminent role in relation to international Internet governance."[38]

The United States will play a special role in setting the ground rules for the next phase of the digital age, both in big-ticket government decisions and in smaller bureaucratic actions such as the National Science Foundation's current deliberations on technical standards for an advanced high-speed Internet. Beyond the technical aspects of this search, these decisions have important social and political implications. The federal bureaucracy's ponderous pace of decision making, from the White House on down, constitutes a luxury in the new fast-paced digital environment. The Obama administration indicated early on that it intended to give this matter high priority as an ongoing policy concern.

The good news is that Washington is now better prepared to handle the problems of the new age. No longer just a "gummint town" but a major information-age center in its own right, it is now safely embedded among the top dozen or so global "knowledge economy regions," thanks in large part to the vibrant information-technology sector in its nearby suburbs.

Well-positioned to play a continuing role in the sector, the Washington area added more workers in one year, 2005, than the New York or Houston metropolitan areas managed in the previous five years. It has more college graduates and PhDs on average than Boston or Seattle. Regional employment is forecast to grow by 50 percent to 4.2 million jobs in the next quarter-century.[39] Increasingly, these jobs involve advanced digital facilities, based in part on the region's world-class research groups, focused heavily on emerging technical challenges in areas such as biotechnology and nanotechnology.

As never before, Washington is a magnet for newcomers eager to take advantage of these opportunities. They are succeeding aging baby boomers, pumping new energy into the region at both the government and private-sector levels. They have already earned a distinctive name: the Millennials. The other major regional demographic shift involves a new surge of immigration, notably from Latin America and Asia. This mix of races and talents presents challenging opportunities to demonstrate the flexibility of the American democratic experiment. An increase of nearly a half-million new arrivals in the first five years of the new century contributed to an 8 percent increase in the region's overall population. However, some ethnic groups increased at a much faster pace: Hispanics by 34 percent and Asians by 27 percent. By some estimates, the Washington region will expand by a million new households over the next decade.

Early indications suggest that the region may be reaching a tipping point in terms of future growth, a prospect it shares with many other U.S. cities. As Brookings urbanologist Bruce Katz points out: "An astonishing 83 percent of the American population lives in metropolitan areas which, together, drive and dominate our economy and house our wealth-generating industries, our centers of research and innovation, our ports of commerce, and our gateways of immigration."[40]

Greater population density brings other problems, including traffic jams and shortages of affordable housing, which push people further from their workplaces. The volume of daily car trips in the Washington area will increase by five million to nearly twenty million in the next quarter-century, according to some regional planners. Many urbanologists believe that relief will come only through higher-density crowding in the central city and close-in suburban neighborhoods. Some signs indicate that this is already happening.[41] In 2006, the Metropolitan Council of Governments, a loose federation of city, county, and state jurisdictions, joined with other planning groups in proposing a more robust regional approach to these problems.[42]

Continued reliance on America's democratic adaptability and innovation may be the only way to deal with these issues. As the political center of a society that, more than any other, is defining the shape and direction of the digital age, Washington faces what promises to be a roller-coaster century of change.

Cities have always been the staging grounds for the progress of civilizations. They are where great things happen, and they are changing now as never before. In 1900, there were 150 million city dwellers worldwide. By 2000, this had increased to 2.9 billion people. A decade later, more than half of the world's population live in metropolitan areas, making us for the first time an urban species. "Human history will ever more emphatically become urban history," says John Grimond, author of *The World Goes to Town*, a recent survey of this new prospect.[43]

Negotiating this transition successfully is one of the great challenges of the new century. Writing about politics twenty-three centuries ago, Aristotle declared: "Man is by nature a city beast." The difference now is that, thanks to the Internet and other digital breakthroughs, the changes taking place in the world's cities are global and swift. Washington is the political capital of a vibrant democracy that will play a special role in shaping this new environment. If it rises to this challenge, the city's greatest days are yet to come.

Afterword
Washington in the Obama Era

Future scholars exploring early twenty-first-century American events will give special attention to the 2008 presidential elections as a turning point in the nation's history. The most obvious reason for this was the elevation of the first black American to the White House. Significant as this event is, it will share another distinction: Barack Obama is the first chief executive to grow up in a time that witnessed the impact of computers and other digital technologies. He was immersed in this experience from childhood, and later as a law student, a community organizer, a college professor, and a state legislator in Illinois. From there he moved on to Washington where, as a junior senator, he was a fresh voice in dealing with the policies and practices of a digitally based society. In a real sense, he is the nation's first information-age president.

In these transitions Obama has followed the patterns of his generation. His early career helped him to understand the tone and direction of the new age, particularly in its power to connect people. London's *Financial Times*, commenting on this change shortly after his electoral victory, noted: "The prospect of a technologically literate president who believes in the positive impact of digital information and networking, not just on political campaigns and the conduct of government but also on the economy and society at large, has induced a strong sense of expectation for his administration."[1]

This prospect became a reality in the early months of the Obama presidency. As we have seen throughout this survey, the new president inherited a bureaucracy that had developed a formidable infrastructure of digital resources, replacing old paper-shuffling practices. Although a considerable achievement, this fell short of many of the possibilities computerization promised, particularly as it established digital networking as a vibrant link between a complex federal structure and the citizens it is meant to serve.

A formidable resource, this array of networks was often operated, however, without a sense that it could be a powerful democratic link between citizens and their government. Above all, no overall authority monitored federal policies and practices in this area.

In one of its first decisive moves, the Obama administration instituted new arrangements at the White House level to meet this need. Within weeks after the Obama team took over, it created an office to manage the government's computer resources and to plan for their more efficient use, both within the bureaucracy and as links to the public at large. It was the first time that the executive branch of the government achieved adequate policy and operational supervision of its vast computer resources.

This move to establish direct White House supervision of federal computer operations was the culmination of a series of earlier presidential attempts to deal with the problem, dating back thirty years. The first actions were piecemeal decisions, beginning with the 1964 executive order by the Lyndon Johnson administration encouraging federal agencies to take active steps to integrate digital technology into their operations. This initiative led to the first large wave of computerization within the government.

The next step was to fashion wider public policies encouraging computerization as a national resource, particularly in support of economic and social needs. This was an ill-defined area, well beyond the more obvious acceptance of computer resources as practical aids in business and other everyday uses. Within the federal government, Senator Albert Gore, an Arkansas Democrat, took the lead in the early 1990s in bringing computerization policy to a higher level. In policy papers and public speeches, he outlined a vision of the Internet as a digital "information highway" that would link all citizens to a wide variety of interactive services. He sponsored legislation setting up a commission made up of industry, labor and consumer leaders to recommend ways of integrating digital resources into federal operations. The result was the first substantive legislation, sponsored by the Clinton-Gore administration, on government-supported Internet services. Among the many projects it encouraged was the use of the Internet to provide enrichment lessons to primary-grade classrooms across the country. It was the beginning of a series of legal and administrative decisions within the federal structure that defined and implemented government responsibilities in the digital area. The two-term George W. Bush administration expanded on these initiatives in encouraging social uses of the Internet.

Enter the Obama administration in January 2009, brimming with ideas on broadening the public-service role of the Internet and other digital-distribution resources. The new president had made the subject a major theme during the election campaign, marking a policy distinction between Obama and his Republican opponent, Senator John McCain. The Obama strategy picked up on innovative ideas advanced four years earlier by Vermont governor Howard Dean in his primary campaign for the 2004 Democratic presidential nomination.

Although Dean was defeated in the primaries, his campaign had a critical influence on American election practices. Lacking strong support from regular Democratic Party organizations, Dean relied heavily on a maverick group of young political operatives conversant with digital operations. The campaign lacked most of the traditional get-out-the-vote practices such as leaflet mailings, television ads, and political rallies. Instead, his staff turned to the Internet, a channel that had become available to a majority of American homes. Dean was the first candidate in a presidential election campaign to exploit the Internet, both to explain his views and as a money raiser.

Joe Trippi, Dean's campaign manager, pointed out the Internet's significance as a political tool in a postmortem report on the campaign: "The Internet has been revolutionizing business and culture for years — and that was just a side effect. What's really going on is a political phenomenon, a democratic movement that flows naturally from our civic lives and spills over into the music we hear, the clothes we buy, the causes we support. But that's changing.... The 2008 election will be the first national contest waged and won primarily on line. The Web puts us over the tipping point; it's democracy's killer app."[2]

The Howard Dean campaign quickly faded from sight, but the implications of its innovative use of the Internet as a campaign resource did not. Both Republican and Democratic party strategists studied the lessons from what was otherwise a failed effort. It became increasingly clear to them that the Internet had a key role to play in the 2008 presidential campaign. Voters were beginning to go on line to learn about candidates, donate money, and join networking sites. Increasingly this change created a new breed of political operative — young computer-savvy men and women who understood how to manage the Internet for political purposes. They called themselves Online Political Operatives (OPOs), experts at setting up and operating sites on social networks such as MySpace and Facebook.

Typical of the group was Matthew Gross, who had worked on the Dean campaign as an Internet manager and later performed similar service for the Obama 2008 effort. Reviewing his experience as an electronic campaigner, Gross later pointed out: "In 2004, when campaigning online was a new thing, the Internet audience was relatively small, and everybody yielded the playing field to the Dean campaign. But the Internet audience is now much more mainstream and much more fragmented.... The challenge for everyone now is, how do you get your candidate into this whole new Internet audience."[3]

As the primaries for the 2008 presidential election approached, the major candidates reconfigured their campaign strategies to feature Internet appeals. Massachusetts governor Mitt Romney, a Republican candidate, offered a variety of Web sites, including "Ask Mitt Anything" and "Meet Mitt Romney." Senator John Edwards was the first Democratic candidate to set up an Internet site to get his message to voters in the contests. His chief opponent, Barack Obama, quickly followed with his own Internet sites, managed by a dozen staff members operating out of his Chicago campaign headquarters.

Other primary-campaign candidates, Democratic and Republican, soon had similar staffs of young tech-savvy workers convinced that the Internet was a whole new way of campaigning, with far more potential than the old print and television methods. Andrew Rasiej, cofounder of Tech-President, a bipartisan group that tracked online projects during the 2008 campaign, noted the mixed commitment that most candidates in both major parties had made in recognizing the Internet as an important organizing tool: "Every campaigner will tell you that they understand its power. But you have to look at where the power lies. How much influence do their online people have? Not much right now. Fact is, most campaigns, on both sides of the political aisle, think that the Internet is just a slice of the pie. They don't realize it's actually the pan."[4]

These ambivalent attitudes towards the Internet as an organizing tool changed as the 2008 campaign progressed through the primaries to Election Day. Online campaigning became an increasingly important activity in the organizational strategies of all the major candidates. In the many postmortems on the respective campaigns, there was general agreement that the Obama group was the most effective in integrating Internet resources with traditional election activities and capitalizing on the Internet's capabilities as a two-way social network. According to surveys released after the campaign, Internet viewers spent 14.5 million hours watching Obama campaign presentations on Facebook, YouTube, and Twitter sites. Obama's official Facebook application had 161,000 active users, who tapped into news items, blog posts, speeches, and videos. The Obama Twitter account had 123,000 subscribers, making it the most popular election site on Twitter, according to track site Twitterholic.[5]

Overall, the Obama campaign operated the most extensive of the Internet operations in the 2008 campaign. The social-networking strategy was a strong factor in his defeat of Hillary Clinton in the Democratic primaries, giving him a strong boost in the general election against his Republican opponent, John McCain. By April 2008, six months before Election Day, the Obama campaign had attracted 800,000 Facebook "friends," compared with 150,000 for Clinton and 117,000 for McCain. When Obama supporters signed up for the *mybarackobama.com* site, they provided information vital to campaign managers. This included details on age, occupation, and attitudes about foreign policy, education, energy, and other key campaign issues.

The Obama campaign's Internet sites turned out to be a formidable resource in the candidate's money-raising efforts. Some 3.2 million people donated funds through the Obama Web site, according to a post-election audit, providing an important part of the $750 million in contributions by Obama supporters during the campaign. As Ted Divine, a Democratic media consultant noted at the time: "We're talking about a fundraising network that will far surpass the dominance that Republicans held in the '80s and even into the '90s."[6]

The Obama election organization also used the Internet to organize local support groups in cities and towns across the country. This combination of online digital resources and volunteer activities became one of the hallmarks of the campaign's strategy. In the year before the election, Obama organizers created thousands of small groups linked to the national campaign by the Internet. Under the slogan, "United for Change," these groups met in homes across the nation.

The appeal was personalized. Once a potential member of a group signed up, he or she was given a detailed list of instructions, including driving instructions, measuring the distance between the new member's house and the location of the next meeting. The groups were often organized by social or professional categories. Thus in one Maryland suburb, Chevy Chase, support groups represented a wide range of interests, for example Fathers for Obama, Law Students for Obama, and Shanghai Ex-Pats for Obama.

The Obama campaign also deployed a range of other Internet-based methods to recruit and cement relationships with supporters. These included constant surveying of Web visitors, sending them regular text-message "blasts," and even announcing the selection of Obama's running mate, Senator Joseph Biden, in a text message. Using a customized social networking site, Obama supporters could log in and find lists of people to call and whose doors to knock on to persuade them to vote for the Democratic ticket. Social networks such as Facebook, YouTube, and Twitter were important channels for Obama's messages. According to one audience survey, YouTube users spent 14.5 million hours watching official Obama campaign videos. Adding that amount of TV network time for political commercials would have cost $46 million, according to one estimate.[7]

Another technique the Obama campaign exploited was the use of Web messages to stir up news-media interest, rather than through the purchase of expensive TV time. "Campaign ads-that-aren't are the oldest trick going," according to Kenneth Golding, a University of Wisconsin political scientist who tracks political advertising. "You call a press conference, announce the ad, then run it once or twice. It's like Lucy pulling the football from Charlie Brown."[8] Both Democratic and Republican strategists played this game during the 2008 campaign, reaping precious minutes of airtime from cable and local news stations that had given the ad a free ride.

As noted, the McCain campaign relied heavily on conventional electoral appeals, with an emphasis on television spots, mass mailings, and other traditional channels. As the campaign progressed, McCain headquarters increased its use of Internet channels, primarily as a way of countering the strong impact of the opposition's Web offensive.

Overall, however, it was a case of too little, too late. The McCain inability to reach out digitally, particularly to younger voters, was clearly a factor that weakened the Republican campaign effort.[9] In addition to outflanking the McCain election effort on the Web, the Obama strategy included frequent mentions of the candidate's commitment to strengthening national digital resources and making them available to all citizens. This subject came up less frequently in Republican appeals. At one point, John McCain admitted that he was not well acquainted with Internet practices.[10]

Overall, the general impression created by the candidates heavily favored Obama as the more technologically savvy of the two. In assessing the Internet's role in his election victory, *Information Week,* an influential trade paper, declared: "The 2008 presidential election crowned the Internet as the king of all political media, ending the era of the television presidency that started with John Kennedy. Barack Obama's pioneering use of social networking and other information technologies not only transformed campaign politics but could influence the way government and business work as well."[11]

Following the Obama victory, a group of young Republicans took steps to energize the party's messages, with an emphasis on more use of digital channels to reach voters. One of them was Mindy Finn, who had supervised Web strategies for Mitt Romney's primary campaign: "The Republican Party cannot reboot if it's viewed only as a party of old, crusty white guys. We need to face 21st-century politics with 21st-century tools," she declared. To this end, she teamed up with another computer expert, Patrick Ruffini, to create a new Web site, *RebuildTheParty.com*, designed to energize GOP digital messaging programs. They gained the support of Newt Gingrich, one of the party's elder statesmen, who had himself founded a group, American Solutions for Winning the Future, that was making heavy use of Web channels to reach the public with a Republican message.[12] At the same time, the Republican National Committee and its state affiliates stepped up their plans for employing the Internet and other digital facilities in the midterm congressional elections in 2010.

By the time Barack Obama took the oath of office in January 2009, it was clear that heavy emphasis on digital operations would be one of the many changes he would bring to his administration. He had made this promise many times on the campaign trail. Members of his campaign staff were hired on as White House officials to plan the details. Their task was twofold: to step up the pace of digitization within White House operations and to draw up plans for expanding overall government resources in the new administration. It was a project that figured high on the new president's crowded agenda, already burdened with such pressing issues as an economic recession and stubborn wars in Iraq and Afghanistan.

The preceding Bush administration had given information technology relatively little policy attention, despite pressure from such industry leaders as Mitch Kapor, founder of Lotus, one of the most successful early spreadsheet programs. Kapor had also created the Electronic Frontier Foundation, a political advocacy group, to lobby for a strategic approach to information-technology issues. Along with other IT-industry leaders Kapor advocated a more vigorous national policy for guiding the country into the information age: He believed that the issue involved basic concerns about national security and the role of the United States in the new digital order:

We're in the middle of the pack as a nation in terms of broadband deployment. We need to have policies that will enable us to catch up, and do so in a way that's ubiquitous and affordable. I also think that tech policies that stimulate innovation in the economy are very important because innovation is the engine of growth. Getting the balance in intellectual property law that will stimulate innovations is therefore very important. Net neutrality is also a huge issue in insuring that the Internet is not controlled by the people who own the wires, because that is just what is going to impede innovation.[13]

Kapor's comments were particularly significant, not simply because of his prominent position in the IT industry but also because he had been an important supporter of Obama in the election campaign. He continued in this role after the election as an adviser to the president-elect on overall technology policy. Among other issues, he argued for the creation of a stronger technology-policy presence within the White House. Obama had pledged such a move during the election campaign, saying that he would "appoint a national cyber adviser who would report directly to me."[14]

President Obama's first move in this area was to choose two officials who would monitor the details of White House technology policy. The first of these appointees was Vivek Kundra, who had been the District of Columbia's chief technology officer. Assigned to the Office of Management and Budget, Kundra's duties were to oversee the management of the $71 billion that the federal government was spending annually on computers and other information-technology resources. The other key appointment was Aneesh Chopra, Virginia's chief technology policy officer, who was assigned to the White House Office of Science and Technology Policy as senior adviser. IT industry leaders hailed both appointments as positive steps towards coordinating national technology policy. Under the Obama plan, both men are scheduled to report to a higher "cyber czar" who would coordinate overall policy at the National Security Council level. This is in line with recommendations by various groups that these two officials, while knowledgeable on technical details, did not fully cover the need for treating information technology as a strategic resource. A blue-ribbon report issued by the Center for Strategic and International Studies (CSIS), a leading Washington think tank, stressed the importance of this function. "The United States must treat cybersecurity as one of the most important national security challenges it faces," the report declared. To this end, it proposed a National Office for Cyberspace to oversee the issue and monitor the government's cyber operations.[15]

While the debate continued on the details of administering national cyber policy, the Obama White House proceeded to make vital decisions in other areas in which information technology was given a leading role. One of the most important of these was the plan for stimulating the economy in the face of a stubborn economic recession. The Obama strategy called for $7.2 billion to be spent on broadband programs, with at least a third of the funds aimed at extending high-speed Internet access to underserved areas of the country. The project specifically called for providing greater broadband resources in health care, environmental, and education undertakings.

A major task facing the White House IT group was supporting the bold plans for dealing with the growing economic recession that dominated White House policy in the early months of the new administration. In many ways, it was the first major test of the president's intention to use information technology as a social networking resource.

Central to this effort was a new Web site, *Recovery.gov*, to let citizens track the $787 billion in economic stimulus spending authorized in the American Recovery and Reinvestment Act passed by Congress and signed by the president within a month after his inauguration. The site permitted ordinary citizens as well as national, state, and local government officials to track the progress, or lack thereof, of this major initiative to restore the nation's economic health. The site had its origins in congressional legislation, the Federal Funding Accountability and Transparency Act of 2006, which authorized a federal Web site that would provide citizens and private organizations detailed information on the status of federal funding affecting their interests. Significantly the legislation had been sponsored by two senators, Tom Coburn, an Oklahoma Republican, and the junior senator from Illinois, Barack Obama.

Beyond the new Web site, the Obama administration laid out broader technology plans for transparent government, centered on Internet resources. One of these initiatives was a White House directive, the Open Government Directive, issued two months after Obama took office. It directed all federal agencies to harness digital technologies in ways that put their decisions online, to solicit feedback, and to use innovative tools, methods, and systems that provide citizens a clear picture of their policies and operations.[16]

Following this initiative, the new administration issued further directives authorizing a Web site describing specific projects initiated under the economic stimulus program and requiring contractors and subcontractors to specify how they are using funds allotted to them. States must report online in detail how they use the $92 billion allocated for educational projects and which schools benefit.

Given the high fiscal stakes involved in the economic stimulus program, private and public organizations responded quickly to these aspects of the program's activities. A survey by the Sunlight Foundation, a Washington public interest group, found that within weeks of the passage of the Recovery Act, twenty-six federal agencies had launched Web sites to track their own spending of stimulus funds. At the same time, forty-two states had set up their own recovery-related sites.

The most innovative of Obama's early efforts to make the Internet-enabled government transparency a cornerstone of his administration was the launch of *Recovery.gov*. This Web site lets citizens track the progress, or lack thereof, being made by the economic-stimulus program enacted by Congress in February 2009. While the president's use of YouTube, Facebook, and Twitter are important resources in this effort, *Recovery.gov* has been the administration's most substantial test of its ability to deliver more openness via technology.

The issuance of a White House "Open Government Directive" followed up these initiatives. It ordered all federal agencies to use digital technologies that will put decisions online and solicit feedback from citizens. These actions made it clear early on that the new administration intended to pursue an active strategy for bringing America fully into the information age.

Chapter Notes

Chapter 1

1. "World Knowledge Competitive Index," Robert Huggins Associates, Sheffield, England, April 2004. See also "U.S. Ranks High in Knowledge Economies," *Financial Times*, April 13, 2004.
2. Quoted in "2005 Regional Report," Greater Washington Initiative, Washington Board of Trade, 22.
3. "The Capital of Commerce," *Fortune*, November 17, 2005, 58.
4. "We Need to Be Dense," *Washington Post*, March 6, 2006, 17.
5. "Cracking IT Top 20 Takes More Revenue in 2005," *Washington Post*, May 9, 2005, BU-1.
6. Quoted in "Capital Gains," *Executive Decisions*, January–February 2006, 7.
7. Joseph Nolen, Jr., "Some Aspects of Washington's Nineteenth Century Economic Development," *Records of the Columbia Historical Society, 1973–1974* (Fall–Winter 2003–2004): 527.
8. "Lockheed to Lead Archives Project," *Washington Post*, September 12, 2005, BU-3.
9. "Confronting Digital Age Head-on," *Washington Post*, March 13, 2006, A-16.
10. "The Year at a Glance," *Library of Congress Information Bulletin*, February 2006, 34.
11. "Business Technology: Registry Web Site as Model of Cooperation," *Information Week*, September 20, 2005, 5.
12. "The Census Bureau Goes Wireless," *Information Week*, April 6, 2006, 5.
13. "Dead Electronics Going to Waste," *Washington Post*, January 21, 2005, BU-3.
14. "May I Download Your Passport, Sir?" *Wired* (November 2004), 50.
15. "Overview," *Congressional Research Service Overview* (July–August 1990), 2.
16. "Data Bunkers Protect Off-Site Sites," *Washington Post*, November 9, 1999, BU-3.
17. "Welcome to the Internet: The First Global Colony," *New York Times*, January 9, 2000, 18.
18. "Dreams Give Rise to an Industry," *Washington Post*, December 7, 1998, BU-7.
19. "Information Industry Overview," Greater Washington Initiative, Washington Board of Trade, June 2007.
20. "E-Mails Provide a Glimpse into 'Iron Triangle,'" *Washington Post*, December 2, 2004, BU-3.
21. "Lockheed and the Future of Warfare," *New York Times*, November 28, 2004, 16.
22. "Area Tops in Number of Software Workers," *Washington Post*, December 9, 2000, BU-3.
23. "DC Sprawl Crosses into a New State: Pennsylvania," *Washington Post*, February 11, 2003, A-15.
24. "Three Virginia Suburbs Near Top of U.S. in Growth," *Washington Post*, March 16, 2006, A-1.
25. "Fairfax County's Newest Overseas Office Is in India, *Washington Post*, August 9, 2004, BU-3.
26. Washington Survey," *The Economist*, December 11, 1993, 38.
27. "Talking the Talk of the Town," *Washington Post*, September 9, 2003, A-21.
28. "Big Apple Attack," *Washingtonian*, January 20, 2003, 28.
29. "Washington vs. New York," *New York Times*, June 20, 1988, 16.

30. "Big Apple Attack," *Washingtonian*, January 20, 2003, 28.
31. Richard Florida, *The Flight of the Creative Class* (New York: Harper Business Books, 2004). See also "Benchmarking the Creative Class in Arlington, Virginia," Arlington Economic Development Agency, Issue Paper no. 6, January 2005.
32. "Not Just a Government Town," *Washington Post*, March 23, 2007, A-22.
33. "Educated Minorities Flock to Region," *Washington Post*, October 5, 2003, A-1.
34. "DC Suburbs Top List of Richest Counties," *Washington Post*, August 8, 2006, M-1.
35. "The Truth about Men in D.C. Is a Tough Pill to Swallow," *Washington Post*, November 11, 2004, C-1.
36. "Women in Senior Executive Service Consider Themselves Influential, Study Finds," *Washington Post*, June 2, 2004, BU-3.
37. "U.S. Population Projections: 2005–2050," Pew Hispanic Center, Washington D.C., February 2008.
38. "Demographics, Markets Aid Latino Companies," *Washington Post*, March 22, 2006, BU-1.
39. In recent years, the most authoritative demographic studies of the Washington region have been sponsored by the Brookings Institution; see, for example, "The new metropolitan geography of U.S. immigration," February 2006.
40. "Of U.S. Children Under 5, Nearly Half Are Minorities," *Washington Post*, May 10, 2006, A-11.
41. "The Face of El Salvador's Charm Offensive," *Washington Post*, January 9, 2007, C-1.
42. For a useful survey of second-generation immigrants, see "The Rise of the Second Generation: Patterns in Hispanic Population Growth," Pew Hispanic Center, April 2007.
43. Jonathan Rauch, "Coming to America," *Atlantic Monthly*, July/August 2003, p. 30.
44. "Data Show Minorities' Movement to Majority," *Washington Post*, August 4, 2006, A-7.
45. "Immigration Keeps Population from Declining in D.C. Region," *Washington Post*, December 27, 2007, p. B-5.
46. "Leadership, Tax Issues Hamper Growth," *Washington Post*, November 10, 2003, A-1.

Chapter 2

1. This theme is explored in Leo Marx, *The Machine in the Garden* (New York: Oxford University Press, 1964).
2. Elizabeth Kite, *L'Enfant and Washington 1791–1792* (Baltimore: Johns Hopkins Press, 1929), 37.
3. Fritz Redlich, *The Molding of American Banking: Men and Ideas* (New York: Johnson Reprint Corp., 1968), 113.
4. Richard DuBoff, "The Rise of Communications Regulation: The Telegraph Industry 1884–1880," *Journal of Communications* (Summer 1984): 58.
5. Ibid., 61.
6. Menahem Blondheim, "Rehearsal or Media Regulation: Congress versus the Telegraph News Monopoly, 1866–1900," *Federal Communications Law Journal*, Vol. 56, No. 3, (September 2004): 324.
7. "Environs of an Invention," *Washington Post*, November 29, 1997, p. F-1.
8. James R. Beniger, *The Control Revolution: Technical and Economic Origins of the Information Society* (Cambridge: Harvard University Press, 1986), 403–407.
9. "Herman Hollerith: Punched Cards Come of Age," *Communications Week*, September 7, 1981, p. 33.
10. Claude Shannon and Warren Weaver, "A Mathematical Theory of Communications," *Bell System Technical Journal*, Vol. 22. (July 1948), 379–402.
11. G. Pascal Zachery, *Endless Frontier: Vannevar Bush, Engineer of the American Century* (New York: Free Press, 1997), p. 73.
12. Michael Shrage, "Vannevar Bush's Legacy: Alliances Among Industry, Academe and Government," *Washington Post*, May 25, 1990, p. F-3.
13. Bush outlined his vision of the new importance of science policy in an article. "As We May Think," *Atlantic Monthly*, July 1945, pp. 101–108.

14. "One of the Great Miscalculations in IBM History," *New York Times Magazine,* May 5, 1980, p. 23.
15. Karl W. Deutsch, *The Nerves of Government* (New York: Free Press, 1963).
16. Daniel Bell, *The Coming of Post-Industrial Society* (New York: Basic Books, 1973).
17. U. S. Department of Commerce, *The Information Economy* (9 vols.), Office of Telecommunications Special Publication 77–12, April 1977.
18. For a description of the political events leading up to the creation of Comsat, see Wilson P. Dizard, *Digital Diplomacy* (Westport, Conn.: Praeger Publishers, 2001), pp. 37–57.
19. "MCI Had Central Role in Telecom History," *Washington Post,* February 21, 2005, p. E-1.
20. Ibid.
21. Interview in "The Revenge of the Nerds," Public Broadcasting System documentary, July 1996.
22. "I'll Take One Slice of Cyberspace," *On the Internet,* March–April 1996, p. 47.
23. Jonathan Blake and Lee Tiedrich, "The National Infrastructure Initiative and the Emergence of the Electronic Superstructure," *Federal Communications Law Journal,* Vol. 46, No. 4, June 1994, pp. 397–431.

Chapter 3

1. "From a Government Town to a High-tech Hub," *Washington Techway,* June 26, 2000, 43.
2. *Human Capital,* a survey by the Greater Washington Initiative, an affiliate of the Washington Board of Trade, March 2007.
3. "Area Jobless Rate is Lowest in U.S.," *Washington Post,* April 10, 2007, D-1.
4. "Not Just a Government Town," *Washington Post,* March 26, 2007, D-1.
5. "Many signs point to an economic downer for the region in 2008," *Washington Post,* April 1, 2008, 8.
6. "A New Stage of Evolution," *Washington Technology,* May 14, 2007, 14.
7. "Perks Give Area Firms a Silicon Valley Feel," *Washington Post,* September 9, 2007, D-1.
8. "Rejuvenating Loudoun," *Washington Post,* September 17, 2007, D-1.
9. "A Bigger Slice," *Washington Technology,* March 7, 2005, 18.
10. "Many Factors Figure in Location Decision," *Washington Post,* October 10, 2004, E-1.
11. "Virginia, Fairfax Commit Funds to Help Lure New IBM Jobs," *Washington Post,* September 28, 2004, E-1.
12. "Fairfax County's Newest Overseas Office is in India," *Washington Post,* August 9, 2004, E-2.
13. "Dulles Clearly on Tech's Radar," *Washington Post,* December 13, 2004, E-1.
14. "National, Dulles Set Passenger Records," *Washington Post,* February 14, 2006, BU-3.
15. "Region's Job Growth a Centrifugal Force," *Washington Post,* June 18, 2006, A-1.
16. "Loudoun's Allure," *Washington Post,* September 4, 2006, B-1.
17. "D.C. Sprawl Crosses into New State: Pennsylvania," *Washington Post,* February 11, 2003, A-1.
18. "Milking the Web to Breed the Best," *Washington Post,* October 5, 1998, B-6.
19. "Muscular Defense Plan Buoys Contractors," *Washington Post,* February 11, 2008. D-1.
20. "War in the Pits," Report No. 6. Institute for National Strategic Studies, National Defense University, February 1996, 1.
21. "The Army's $200 Billion Makeover," *Washington Post,* December 7, 2007, A-1.
22. "High Costs Lead Navy to Cancel Lockheed Coastal Vessel," *Washington Post,* April 13, 2007, D-4.
23. "A Tougher Line on Government Contracting," *Washington Post,* October 8, 2007. D-1.
24. "Homeland Market Takes Off At Last," *Washington Technology,* March 7, 2005, 26.
25. "Feds Want Compatible Smart Cards," *Washington Technology,* April 5, 2004, 16.

26. "Privacy Advocates Criticize Plan to Embed ID Chips in Passports," *Washington Post*, April 3, 2005, A-6.
27. "Problems Slow Revival of Ground Zero Site," *Washington Post*, May 13, 2005, A-3.
28. "Now in Their Own Orbits, Carlyle's Stars Keep Rising," *Washington Post*, July 24, 2007. D-1.
29. "For Carlyle, Age-Old Missteps in a Too-Close Tango," *Washington Post*, May 9, 2007, D-1.
30. "Lobbying Glamorized," *Washington Post*, September 19, 2003, A-25.
31. "D.C. Law Firm's Big BlackBerry Payday," *Washington Post*, March 18, 2006, D-3.
32. "New Year, Not Much Change," *Washington Post*, September 11, 2007, A-15.
33. "The 2005 Wired Forty," *Wired*, May 2005, 110.
34. "Big Lobbying Spenders of 2007," *Washington Post*, April 15, 2008, A-13.
35. "The New Democrat from Cyberspace," *New Republic*, May 24, 1993, 18.
36. "On the Hill's Party Circuit," *Washington Post*, September 26, 2004, A-1. See also "To Understand Washington, Follow the Shrimp," *Washington Post*, February 21, 2005, E-1.
37. "Washington Gifts, or the 12-pound Ham," *New York Times Magazine*, June 29, 1958, 6.
38. "Jobs Remain, but Area Could Feel Major Loss," *Washington Post*, September 18, 2007, D-1.
39. "Climbing the Top 100 List: A Few Recipes for Success," *Washington Technology*, May 14, 2007, 22.
40. "Jobs Remain, but Area Could Feel Major Loss," *Washington Post*, September 18, 2007, D-1.
41. "Biotech Magnet," *Washington Post*, March 8, 2004, E-1.
42. "Biotech's Gains Again Outstrip Drug Giants," *Washington Post*, April 12, 2006, D-1.
43. "Being Better Off as Part of a Bigger Company," *Washington Post*, August 13, 2007, D-3.
44. "Profitless Prosperity," *Economist*, April 22, 2006, 63.
45. "Biotech Regulation Falls Short, Report Says," *Washington Post*, April 1, 2004, E-3.
46. "Small Wonders," *Economist*, January 1, 2005, special report on nanotechnology, 3.
47. "Downsizing Crossbar Nanocomputers," *Scientific American*, November 2005, 74.
48. "Small Wonders," *op. cit.*, 7.
49. "University of Maryland Gets an 'A' for Its Nanotechnology Research," *Washington Post*, July 7, 2005, D-1.
50. "Nanotech Is Booming, *Washington Post*, March 28, 2005, A-6.
51. "Nanofrontiers: Vision for the Future of Nanotechnology." Report of the Project on Emerging Technology, Woodrow Wilson Center for International Scholars, Smithsonian Institution, May 2007.
52. "Bring On the Nanobubble," *New Yorker*, March 15, 2004, 68.
53. "A Little Risky Business," *Economist*, November 24, 2007, 81.
54. "Can We Conquer Nanotech Fear?" *Financial Times*, January 15, 2004, 8.

Chapter 4

1. "Sunset Law for Agencies on the Horizon," *Washington Post*, July 26, 2005, D-1.
2. "Threshold of Interplanetary Internet," *Washington Technology*, November 22, 2004. See also "Hello, Neighbor," *Wired*, May 2004, 170.
3. "Agriculture Unveils Draft for Animal ID System," *Government Computer News*, May 6, 2005, 5.
4. "On High Alert," *Information Week*, May 3, 2004, 7.
5. "Data Storm," *Wired*, March 1994, 46.
6. "Researchers: Cost of Electronic Health Records Could Hit $200 Billion," *Information Week*, August 2, 2005, 5.
7. Darrell M. West, "State and Federal E-Government in the United States, 2006," Taubman Center for Public Policy, Brown University, August 2006, 19. For a useful overview of federal government digital operations, see Rowan Miranda, "The Building Blocks of a Digital Government Strat-

egy," *Government Finance Review*, October 2000, 47–58.

8. "EU is too late for lofty goals of global IT leadership," *Financial Times*, November 3, 2004, 23.

9. "Salary, Conflict-of-Interest Policies at NIH Are Questioned, *Washington Post*, March 25, 2004, A-21.

10. "Giving Cubicle Dwellers a Square Deal," *Washington Post*, August 29, 2004, F-5.

11. "Working from Home a Work in Progress," *Washington Post*, June 19, 2007, D-4.

12. "Washington Ranked Top 'Teleworking' City," *Government Enterprise*, March 30, 2006, 9.

13. Ibid.

14. "Report Criticizes OMB Oversight of IT Projects," *Washington Post*, April 21, 2005, E-5

15. "Managing Complexity," *Economist*, November 27, 2004, 71.

16. "Canada is Still No. 1 in E-Government," *Information Week*, May 6, 2004, 10.

17. John Arquilla and David Ronfeldt, "Cyberwar and Netwar," *Rand Research Review*, Fall 1995, 8.

18. "And Now, the War Forecast," *Economist*, September 17, 2005, p. 22.

19. "Keeping Secrets," *Economist*, January 28, 2006, p. 53.

20. "Why the U.S. Navy Needs an Urban Warfare Strike Force," *Financial Times*, May 11, 2005, 4. See also "Anti-terrorism Funds Buy a Wide Array of Pet Projects," *Washington Post*, November 23, 2003, A-1.

21. "Scope of Change in Military Is Ambiguous," *Washington Post*, August 1, 2004, A-6.

22. "Too Much Information," *New Yorker*, December 9, 2002, 45.

23. "Say Hello to Stanley," *Wired*, January 2006, 131.

24. "Attack of the Drones," *Wired*, June 2005, 134.

25. "Washington Tries to Staunch Wasteful Flow of Anti-Terrorist Funds," *Financial Times*, December, 2004, 4.

26. "Has Diplomacy Become Out-of-Date?" *New York Times*, January 6, 1983, 16.

27. "Lenovo PCs Score Big at State Dept.," *Government Enterprise*, March 20, 2006, 4.

28. Matt Bedan, "Echelon's Effect: The Obsolescence of the U.S. Foreign Intelligence Legal Regime," *Federal Communications Law Journal*, vol. 59, no. 2 (September 2004): 426–456.

29. "C-SPAN's Impact Gauged 25 Years after Its Launch," *Washington Post*, March 19, 2004, A-21.

30. "A Renewed Call to Televise High Court," *Washington Post*, February 12, 2007, 36.

31. "Bring Back the OTA," *Scientific American*, June 2005, 10.

32. "States Pushing for Web Sales-Tax Collection," *Information Week*, July 7, 2005, 7.

33. "On Capitol Hill, the Inboxes Are Overflowing," *Washington Post*, July 11, 2005, D-1.

34. "The Tech Lobby Calling Again," *New York Times*, July 25, 2004, BU-1.

35. "Where Lawmakers Look at Technology," *Washington Post*, February 23, 2004, E-1.

36. Gary Wolf, "How the Internet Invented Howard Dean," *Wired*, January 2004, 139.

37. "Of Slips and Video Clips," *Economist*, March 17, 2007, 32.

38. "Internet Donations Help Boost Obama," *Washington Post*, April 5, 2007, A-1.

39. "Online Firms Boot Up for Political Campaigns," *Washington Post*, March 17, 2007, D-1.

40. "Back to the Ballot Box," *AARP Bulletin*, June 2004, 10.

41. William Eggers, *Government 2.0* (Lanham, Md.: Rowman & Littlefield, 2005), 243.

Chapter 5

1. "The City America Loves to Hate," *Washington Post*, August 17, 1997, G-1.

2. "Washington, O Washington: A Capital Unsung," *Washington Post*, July 4, 2005, C-1.

3. "Bush Reviews Domestic Policy

Notes — Chapter 5

Scene," *Washington Post*, January 8, 2001, A-6.

4. "Only the Crazy Can Love This Town," *Business Week*, February 4, 2003, 28.

5. Ibid.

6. For an important study of the new role of metroplexes in the information age, see Richard Florida, *"Who's Your City?"* (New York: Basic Books, 2008).

7. "Soaring View of Tysons Centers on a Downtown," *Washington Post*, April 22, 2005, A-1.

8. Joel Kotkin, *The New Geography: How the Digital Revolution Is Reshaping the American Landscape* (New York: Random House, 2000), 23.

9. "Area Ranks Third Worst in Traffic Nationally," *Washington Post*, July 6, 2006, 2.

10. "N. Va. Leaders Decry Talk of Commuter Tax," *Washington Post*, July 16, 2003, B-5.

11. "Population Revision 'Big Deal' for D.C.," *Washington Post*, July 22, 2007, A-1.

12. "Rivlin Cites Need for District to Expand City's Population," *Northwest Current*, October 13, 2003, 4.

13. "D.C. Area a Magnet for Bright Singles," *Washington Post*, April 4, 2003, 1.

14. "Grant Invitation Prompts Look at Designation," *Northwest Current*, October 3, 2005, 1.

15. "Residents Chime In on Vision for D.C.," *Washington Post District Magazine*, June 2, 2006, 11.

16. "It's a Change, Not a Conspiracy," *Washington Post*, October 23, 2005, B-1.

17. "Grant Invitation Prompts Look at Designation," *Northwest Current*, October 3, 2005, 1.

18. "Revitalizing Washington's Neighborhoods: A Vision Takes Shape," Greater Washington Research Program, Brookings Institution, April 2003.

19. "High-level Debate on Future of D.C.," *Washington Post*, May 2, 2007, B-1.

20. "Residents Chime In on Vision for D.C.," *Washington Post District Magazine*, June 2, 2006, 1.

21. "Little Suspense at GOP Gathering," *Washington Post*, February 2, 2004, B-1.

22. "The Most Expensive ZIP Codes," *Forbes*, July 11, 2003, 45.

23. "The Right Side of the Tracts: Affluent Neighborhoods in the Metropolitan United States," *Social Science Quarterly*, Vol. 88(3), 2007.

24. "How Do You Spell Billionaire? B.E.T.," *Washingtonian*, November 2003, 51.

25. "Gap Growing between Rich and Poor in D.C.," *Washington Post*, January 27, 2006, B-1.

26. "The Virtue of Being Dull," *Economist*, March 4, 2006, 31.

27. "Turning D.C. into an International Cause," *Washington Post*, April 10, 2005, C-5.

28. "Only the Crazy Can Love This Town," *New York*, February 20, 1995, 25.

29. "Democracy Begins at Home, Says Washington DC," *Financial Times*, July 13, 2006, 6.

30. "About Those Election Promises," *Economist*, October 25, 2003, 27.

31. "Unified Communications Center," *ArchitectureDC*, Spring–Summer 2005, 15.

32. "Out of the Dark Ages," *Government Enterprise*, April 5, 2004, 3.

33. "The Electronic Bureaucrat: A Special Report on Technology and Government," *Economist*, February 16, 2008, 10.

34. "To Protect and Intrude," *Washington Post*, January 15, 2005, A-1.

35. "Moynihan's Legacy Is Written in Stone," *Washington Post*, July 10, 2000, C-1.

36. "Annual Session Touts District's Resurgence," *Northwest Current*, November 11, 2005, 5.

37. "D.C. Offers Tax Breaks to Boost Retail Growth," *Washington Post*, July 14, 2003, E-1.

38. "Fewer Travelers Spent More Cash in D.C. in '06," *Washington Post*, August 27, 2007, D-2.

39. "The Pull of Penn Quarter," *Washington Post*, September 2, 2003, E-1.

40. "Newseum's Debut Will Be a Late Edition," *Washington Post*, August 8, 2007, C-1.

41. "Coming Soon to NoMa: Life," *Washington Post*, February 2, 2006, D-1.

42. "14th Street's Architectural Evolu-

tion," *Architecture DC*, March 2006, 8. The revitalization of the city's neighborhoods was a major focus of a 2006 study, *Homes for an Inclusive City*, issued by the Brookings Institution's Greater Washington Research Program.

43. Stephen S. Fuller, *Washington DC's Technological Industry*. A study funded by the city's Office for Planning and Economic Development, the Morino Institute and the World Bank, February 2001.

44. "D.C. Area a Magnet for Bright Young Singles," *Washington Post*, November 4, 2003, A-1.

45. "Fides Means Faith," *Washington History*, Vol. 11, No. 2, Fall–Winter 1995, 31.

46. The phrase "secret city" was coined by historian Constance McLaughlin Green in her groundbreaking history of the city, *Washington: Capital City* (Princeton: Princeton University Press, 1963).

47. Jason C. Booza, Jackie Cutsinger, and George Galster, *Where Did They Go? The Decline of Middle-Income Neighborhoods in Metropolitan America*, Brooking Institution, June 2006.

48. "D.C. Boom Not Felt by All in City, Study Says," *Washington Post*, April 14, 2008, B-1.

49. "A Wreck of a Plan," *Washington Post*, July 17, 2005, B-1.

50. "Southwest Waterfront Will Finally Get Over the '60s," *Washington Post*, October 9, 2006, D-1.

51. "Poverty Rate Grows amid Economic Boom," *Washington Post*, October 24, 2007, B-1.

52. SOME Newsletter, August 2005, p. 1. See also "In D.C. Area, Even Subsistence Proves Pricey," *Washington Post*, September 1, 2005, B-1.

53. "The (Unaffordable) House We All Live In," *Washington Post*, July 20, 2007, D-1.

54. "Stronger Than Ever, But Not for Everyone," *Washington Post*, January 1, 2004, A-14.

55. "1 in 20," *Washington Post* editorial, August 17, 2005, A-18.

56. "DC Leads Nation in Per Pupil Spending," *Washington Post*, January 6, 2005, B-3.

57. "Many D.C. Teachers Lack Licenses," *Washington Post*, April 4, 2005, B-2.

58. "Illiteracy Aid Found to Lag in District," *Washington Post*, March 19, 2007, C-1.

59. "Cost of School Security Contract Questioned," *Washington Post*, June 2, 2005, B-2.

60. "Education Becoming Top Issue for D.C.," *Washington Post*, May 24, 2006, A-1.

61. "Armed Camp on the Hill," *Financial Times*, January 22, 2005, 2.

62. Alfred Kazin, "In Washington," *New York Review of Books*, May 29, 1986, 11.

63. Tom Wicker, "A Reporter's Memoir," *Saturday Review*, September 9, 1967, 49.

Chapter 6

1. "D.C. Area a Magnet for Bright Singles," *Washington Post*, November 11, 2003, A-1.

2. "Brain Gain Cities Attract Educated Young," *Washington Post*, November 9, 2003, A-1.

3. "Survey Captures D.C. in Transition," *Washington Post*, August 27, 2004, B-1.

4. "D.C. Tops Nation in Women's Pay, Equity with Men," *Washington Post*, November 17, 2004, 1.

5. "Laptops You Can Lug," *Information Week*, July 30, 2007, 45.

6. "Notebooks Surpass Desktop Sales for the First Time," *Information Week*, August 19, 2005, 6.

7. "Still Swiss and Still Sharp (Digital Memory Optional)," *New York Times*, May 1, 2005, BU-1.

8. "Watch This Space," *Economist Technology Quarterly*, September 17, 2005, 3.

9. "BlackBerries Are Not the Only Fruit," *Financial Times Information Technology Review*, June 29, 2005, 7.

10. "AT&T Completes BellSouth Takeover," *Washington Post*, December 30, 2006, A-1.

11. "Global Mobile Phone Use to Hit

Record 3.25 Billion," *Information Week*, June 27, 2007, 8.

12. "Verizon Loses Land-Line Customers, Profit," *Washington Post*, August 2, 2006, BU-3.

13. "Answer Man," *Washington Post*, January 18, 2004, M-9.

14. "Connecting with Kids, Wirelessly," *Washington Post*, July 7, 2007, A-1. See also "Disney Launches Parent-Controlled Mobile Phone Service," *Information Week*, June 14, 2006, p. 5.

15. "Skype Introduces Speakerphone, PC-Less Wi-Fi Phone," *Information Week*, May 1, 2006, 12.

16. "The Skype Hyper," *Economist*, October 6, 2007, 80.

17. "The War of the Wires," *Economist*, July 30, 2005, 53.

18. "Into the Pack," *Financial Times*, June 26, 2007, 7.

19. "The Third Act," *Economist*, June 9, 2007, 79.

20. "Cingular to Offer Phones for the 12-and-Under Set," *Washington Post*, November 17, 2005, D-12.

21. "Broadband in Suburbia," *Washington Post*, October 26, 2004, E-1.

22. "30 Million Blogs and Counting...," *Washington Post*, February 26, 2006, BU-4.

23. "Blogging the Block," *Washington Post*, June 6, 2007, M-4.

24. "Fighting Words," *Washington Post Magazine*, July 17, 2005, 13.

25. "Blogging Is All about Me," *Information Week*, July 19, 2006, 9.

26. "AOL's News Sites Adopt Look of Blogs," *Washington Post*, June 26, 2007, D-1.

27. "Two Kings Get Together," *Economist*, October 14, 2006, 67.

28. "A Loopy Deal That Actually Makes Sense," *New York Times*, October 15, 2006, BU-4. See also "The YouTube Gurus," *Time*, January 1, 2007, 68.

29. "Of Slips and Video," *Economist*, March 17, 2007, 32.

30. "Smart Wi-Fi," *Scientific American*, October 2005, 85.

31. "For Online Users, Change Is in the Air," *Washington Post*, July 23, 2005, B-3.

32. "New Dupont Listserv Debuts, Aspires to Connect the Circle," *Northwest Current*, April 6, 2006, 5.

33. "Trouble Clicks," *Economist*, November 25, 2006, 65.

34. "The Next Big Thing," *Economist*, October 6, 2007, 73.

35. "Music-selling Rivals Take Aim at iTunes," *Washington Post*, August 22, 2007, D-1.

36. "Cable Firms Try to Paddle Together," *Wall Street Journal*, September 28, 2007, B-3. See also "Networks Are Streaming into Prime Time Online," *Washington Post*, October 4, 2007, D-1.

37. "At One Billion, Music Sales by Download Come of Age," *Financial Express*, February 26, 2006, 15.

38. "Twenty-five Years Later, It's Still 9:30," *Washington Post Weekend*, May 27, 2005, 6.

39. "The Pleasures of Ibiza, a Metro Ride Away," *Washington Post*, July 6, 2007, C-1.

40. "For Bookstores, a Real Page-Turner," *Washington Post*, March 19, 2007, C-1.

41. "Mind over Muscle," *New York Times*, October 16, 2005, WK-12. See also "The Business Agenda Soon Will Be a Feminist One," *Financial Times*, September 27, 2003, 7.

42. "Best Geek Cities," *Wired*, January 2007, 155.

43. "Love in the Time of No Time," *New York Times Magazine*, November 23, 2003, 66.

44. "Do You MySpace?," *New York Times*, August 28, 2005, 1.

45. "Another Cup?" *Washington Post*, May 23, 2004, 15.

Chapter 7

1. Richard Florida, *The Flight of the Creative Class: The New Global Competition for Talent* (New York: Harper Collins, 2004) 68–74.

2. Quoted in *A City for the Nation: The Army Engineers and the Building of Washington* (Washington, DC: Historical Division, Office of the Chief of Engineers, Department of Defense, 1978), 6.

3. Jean King, "Alice Pike Barney: Bringing Culture to the Capital," *Washing-*

ton History, Vol. 2, No.1 (Spring 1990): 77.

4. Ibid., 89.

5. "A Global Salute to Mellon's Gift," *Washington Post*, March 20, 2007, C-8.

6. "Of Art and Salty Memories," *Washington Post*, Potomac Magazine, September 15, 1968, 41.

7. "The Heart of Washington Arts," *Washington Post*, October 13, 1999, D-1.

8. Richard L. Coe, "A Capital Idea," *New York Times*, August 31, 1958, 23.

9. "Another Stage in Life," *Washington Post*, November 1, 1996, G-1.

10. "The Kennedy Center's Open Invitation," *Washington Post Weekend Magazine*, February 2, 2007, 27.

11. "Fringe Fest," *Washington Times*, July 14, 2007, B-1; "The Washington Festival with the Fringe on Top," *Washington Post*, April 4, 2005, C-1.

12. "Improv Theater Hits the Streets, Video Cameras in Hand," *Northwest Current*, February 11, 2004, 15.

13. "Dancing In the Streets," *Washington Post*, December 12, 2003, D-26.

14. "The Unquiet Silence of Synetic's *Macbeth*," *Washington Post*, January 20, 2007, C-1.

15. "On 14th Street, Art Comes from the Inside Out," *Potomac Current*, June 27, 2007, 15.

16. "In a City of Monuments, No Room for the Howard?" *Washington Post*, April 25, 1999, B-3.

17. "Razzle Dazzle," *Washingtonian*, September 2004, 114.

18. "At Home in the Nation's Capital: Immigration Trends in Metropolitan Washington D.C.," Brookings Institution, June 2003.

19. "Home Is Where the Paycheck Is," *Washington Post*, March 4, 2008, B-1.

20. Samuel P. Huntington, *Who Are We? The Challenges to American National Identity* (New York: Simon and Shuster, 2004), 16.

21. "Brookings the Broker," *Time*, November 28, 1960, 42.

22. "Higher Education Degrees in Greater Washington: An Analysis by the Greater Washington Initiative," Washington Board of Trade, 2005.

23. "Hidden in D.C., a Constellation of Academic Stars," *Washington Post* District Extra, December 9, 2004, 10.

24. "GMU's Nurturing Potential," *Washington Post*, February 2, 2006, D-1.

25. "Hopkins Lab Focused on Mars," *Washington Post*, August 12, 2005, BU-3.

26. "To Size Up Colleges, Students Now Shop Online," *Chronicle of Higher Education*, June 10, 2005, A-25.

27. "The Cogs of Blogs," *Georgetown Alumni Magazine*, Fall 2005, 27.

28. "Technology Leads the Way as Online Learning Comes of Age," *Financial Times*, March 20, 2006, 9.

29. "Mapping the Terrain of Online Education," *Campus Technology*, April 2005, 6.

30. "Online Degree Programs Take Off," *Washington Post*, May 16, 2006, A-6.

31. "Troubles Grow for a University Built on Profits," *New York Times*, February 11, 2007, 1.

32. "Sylvan Learning Systems Renamed," *Washington Post*, May 18, 2004, BU-4.

33. "MIT Puts Everything Online," *Information Week*, March 19, 2007, 22.

34. "Washington's Egghead Quotient Keeps Growing," *New York Times*, April 24, 2005, WK-3.

Chapter 8

1. Karl W. Deutsch, *The Nerves of Government* (New York: Free Press of Glencoe, 1963), 120.

2. Marshall McLuhan, *Understanding Media* (New York: Mentor Publications, 1962), 32.

3. "Praise the Baud," *Economist*, September 9, 2000, 103.

4. Wilson P. Dizard, Jr., *The Coming Information Age* (New York: Longman, 1982), 131.

5. The commission's findings are summarized in J. Peter Grace, *Burning Money: The Waste of Your Tax Dollars* (New York: McMillan, 1984).

6. "Saving the Post Office," *Washington Post*, January 15, 2006, F-1.

7. "ICANN Turns Down XXX, but

Debate Continues," *Information Week*, May 11, 2006, 10.

8. "State Department Launches Internet Freedom Task Force," *Information Week*, February 14, 2006, 12.

9. "Revenues of $10Bn Forecast," *Financial Times*, June 15, 1995, 4.

10. "French Minister Cites U. S. Cultural Influence," *New York Times*, November 16, 1984, C-26.

11. "Google Grabs Half of Booming Web Search Market," *Information Week*, February 9, 2005, 9.

12. "Death of the Salesman," *Economist*, May 27, 2006, 60.

13. "Town to Be Auctioned on E-Bay (Again)," *Government Enterprise*, March 20, 2006, 4.

14. "Reinventing the Internet," *Economist*, March 11, 2006, 32.

15. "Bring on the Exoflood," *Washington Post*, May 15, 2007, 31.

16. "Wearable Technology Can Save Lives," *Information Week*, February 13, 2006, 3.

17. "Secession of the Successful," *New York Times Magazine*, January 20, 1991, 16.

18. "A Nation Online: Entering the Broadband Age," National Telecommunications and Information Agency, U. S. Department of Commerce, 2004, 14.

19. "Wishing I Was at the Web 2.0 Conference," *Information Week*, October 3, 2005, 3.

20. "Wi-Fi for the Masses," *Economist*, March 3, 2007, 38.

21. "Massive 720-Square-Mile WiFi Net in Michigan to Serve Urban and Rural Users," *Information Week*, January 26, 2007, 3.

22. "High-speed Internet Access for All? Not So Fast," *Financial Times*, June 3, 2005, 9.

23. "Sky's the Limit," *Information Week*, November 20, 2006, 23.

24. "District to Seek Wireless Internet That Aids the Poor," *Washington Post*, March 3. 2006, D-5.

25. "Hot, or Hot Air?" *Information Week*, May 21, 2007, 40.

26. "Wi-Pie in the Sky?" *Economist*, March 11, 2006, 22.

27. "Why Max?" *Economist*, February 24, 2007, 78.

28. "Next: A More Revolutionary Web," *International Herald-Tribune*, 23 May 2006, 7.

29. "Revival of the Fittest," *Washington Post*, March 7, 2006, BU-4.

30. "Big Media and the Internet," *Economist*, March 18, 2006, 61.

31. "Local Stations Struggle to Adapt as Web Grabs Viewers, Revenue," *Wall Street Journal*, June 6, 2006, 1.

32. "Newspapers in an Economic Storm," *Washington Post*, March 19, 2006, B-6.

33. "Out of Print," *New Yorker*, March 31, 2008, 48.

34. "Google's Ad-Grabbing Pushes Profits Up 60%," *Washington Post*, April 21, 2006, D-1.

35. "His Space," *Wired*, July 2006, 144.

36. "Online Ads to Outstrip U.S. Papers by 2011," *Financial Times*, August 7, 2007, 16.

37. "IBM's India," *Information Week*, March 13, 2006, 78.

38. "U.N. Body Endorses Cultural Protection," *Washington Post*, October 21, 2005, A-14.

39. "We Need to Be Dense," *Washington Post*, March 6, 2006, 19.

40. "A Much More Urban America," *Washington Post*, July 23, 2007, D-3.

41. "Growth Cooling in Suburbs, Census Data Show," *Washington Post*, March 22, 2007, B-1.

42. "More Cooperation Sought on Area's Future," *Washington Post*, June 21, 2006, B-5.

43. "The World Goes to Town: A Special Report on Cities," *Economist*, May 5, 2007.

Afterword

1. "The First IT-literate President," *Financial Times*, November 19, 2008, p. 3.

2. "Power to the People," *Wired*, November 2004, 97.

3. "Meet the OPOs," *Washington Post*, May 2, 2007, 8.

4. "Power to the People," *Wired*, November 2004, 97.

5. "Dawn of the Internet Presidency," *Information Week*, November 10, 2008, 17.

6. "Obama's Gigantic Base May Make Him Party's Power Broker," *Bloomberg News Service*, April 28, 2008.

7. "The Ads That Aren't," *Washington Post*, September 11, 2008, C-1.

8. Ibid.

9. "McCain Camp Hits Obama on More Than One Front," *Washington Post*, September 11, 2008, A-4.

10. "First IT-literate President," *Financial Times*, November 19, 2008, 3.

11. "Dawn of the Internet Presidency," *Information Week*, November 10, 2008, 17.

12. "To Rebuild, Pair Prods a Shortsighted GOP," *Washington Post*, November 28, 2008, C-11.

13. "Mitch Kapor," *MIT Review*, March 2009, 30.

14. "Obama Aides Debate Role of Proposed Cyber Czar," *Washington Post*, May 13, 2009, A-6.

15. *Securing Cyberspace for the 44th President* (Washington, D.C.: Center for Strategic and International Studies, December 2008), 34.

16. "Transparency 2.0," *Information Week*, May 11, 2009, 54.

Bibliography

Agar, Jon. *Constant Touch: A Global History of the Mobile Phone.* London: Icon Books, 2003.
Bender, Thomas. *The Unfinished City: New York and the Metropolitan Idea.* New York: The New Press, 2001.
Beniger, James R. *The Control Revolution: Technological and Economic Origins of the Information Society.* Cambridge: Harvard University Press, 1986.
Berg, Scott W. *Grand Avenue: The Story of the French Visionary Who Designed Washington D.C.* New York: Pantheon Books, 2007.
Ceruzzi. Paul. *Internet Alley: High Technology in Tyson's Corner, 1945-2005.* Cambridge: MIT Press, 2008.
Chadwick, Andrew. *Internet Politics: States, Citizens, and Newer Communications Technologies.* New York: Oxford University Press, 2006.
Clippinger, John Henry. *A Crowd of One: The Future of Individual Identity.* New York: Public Affairs Press, 2007.
Dizard, Wilson P., Jr. *The Coming Information Age: An Overview of Technology, Economics and Politics.* 3rd edition. New York: Longman Publishers, 1989.
Eames, Charles, and Ray Eames. *A Computer Perspective.* Cambridge: Harvard University Press, 1973.
Eggers, William. *Government 2.0.* Lanham, Md.: Rowman & Littlefield, 2005.
Florida, Richard. *The Flight of the Constructive Class: The New Global Competition for Talent.* New York: HarperCollins, 2005.
_____. *Who's Your City?* New York: Basic Books, 2008.
Fountain, Jane E. *Building the Virtual State: Information Technology and Institutional Change.* Washington: Brookings Institution Press, 2001.
Franda, Marcus. *Governing the Internet: The Emergence of an International Regime.* Boulder Co.: Lynne Rienner Publishers, 2001.
Hafner, Katie, and Matthew Lyon. *Where Wizards Stay Up Late: The Origins of the Internet.* New York: Simon and Schuster, 1996.
Hammer, Donald P. (ed.). *The Information Age: Its Development, Its Impact.* Metuchen, N.J.: Scarecrow Press, 1976.
Headrick, Daniel. *The Invisible Weapon.* New York: Oxford University Press, 1991
Hills, Jill. *Telecommunications and Empire.* Urbana: University of Illinois Press, 2007.
How Washington Has Changed. Special Issue. *Washingtonian* [magazine], October 1985.
Iriye, Akira. *Cultural Internationalism and World Order.* Baltimore: Johns Hopkins University Press, 1997.
Klotkin, Joel. *The New Geography: How the Digital Revolution Is Reshaping the American Landscape.* New York: Random House, 2001.
Kuhns, William. *The Post-Industrial Prophets.* New York: Harper Colophon Books, 1971.

Levinson, Paul. *Digital McLuhan: A Guide to the Information Millennium*. New York: Routledge, 1999.
_____. *Soft Edge: A Natural History and Future of the Information Revolution*. New York: Routledge, 1997.
The Making of Washington. Special issue. *Washingtonian* [magazine]. November 1987.
Marvin, Caroline. *When Old Technologies Were New*. New York: Oxford University Press, 1988.
Masuda, Yoneji. *The Information Society as Post-Industrial Society*. Tokyo: Institute for the Information Society, 1981.
Nilsson, Dex. *The Names of Washington D.C.* Rockville, Md.: Twinbrook Communications, 2000.
Nora, Simon, and Alain Minc. *The Computerization of Society*. Cambridge: MIT Press, 1981.
Rheingold, Howard. *Smart Mobs: The Next Social Revolution*. New York: Perseus Books, 2002.
Slack, Jennifer Daryl, and Fred Fejes (eds). *The Ideology of the Information Age*. Norwood, N.J.: Ablex Publishers, 1987.
Standage, Tom. *The Victorian Internet*. New York: Walker Publishing Co., 1998.
Tung, Anthony. *Preserving the World's Great Cities*. New York: Random House, 2001.
Van Agmentael, Antoine. *The Emerging Markets Century*. New York: Free Press, 2007.
Washington in Transition. Special issue. *American Institute of Architects Journal*. Washington D.C., January 1963.
Whitman, William B. *Washington D.C.: Off the Beaten Path*. Guilford, Conn.: Globe Pequot Press, 2003.
Williams, Andrew Paul, and John C. Tedesco (eds). *The Internet Election: Perspectives on the Web in Campaign 2004*. Lanham, Md.: Rowman & Littlefield, 2006.
Writers' Program of the Works Progress Administration for the District of Columbia. *Washington D.C: A Guide to the Nation's Capital*. Washington D.C.: U.S. Government Printing Office, 1937.
Zachary, G. Pascal *Endless Frontier: Vannevar Bush, Engineer of the American Century*. New York: Free Press, 1997.
Zysman, John, and Abraham Newman (eds). *How Revolutionary Was the Digital Revolution?* Palo Alto, Calif.: Stanford University Press, 2006.

Index

Abbott, Carl 31
Abramoff, Jack 68
Accenture Ltd. (IT firm) 52, 58
acronyms, D.C. use of 1, 20–21
Adam-and-Eve project (NIH) 13
Adams, Henry 37
Adams, John 33
Adams, Sherman 68
Advanced Research Projects Agency (ARPA) 3, 39, 45, 151
advertising, in old *vs.* new media 173–174
Afghanistan, U.S. invasion of 83
African Americans: as civic leaders 106, 107; as college graduates 137; in D.C. cultural life 143, 147; as D.C. residents 23, 28, 101, 105–106, 113–118, 123, 148, 149; Internet service to 96–97, 169; New Deal and 121; in U.S. population 149–150; wage disparities for 123; *see also* names of individuals
African Continuum Theater 147
"agglomeration economies" 22
Air Force, U.S. 83, 85
airport screening devices 86
Akin, Gump, Strauss, Hauer & Field (lobbyists) 64
Alien and Sedition Acts of 1798 33
Alpha Centauri, NASA project on 88
Amazon (online company) 65, 91, 136
America Online (AOL) *see* AOL (America Online)
American Management Systems (AMS) 16
American Perspectives (C-SPAN program) 91
American Recovery and Reinvestment Act of 2009 187, 188
American Solutions for Winning the Future (Republican Web site) 185
American Telegraph Company 35
American University 154
Anderson, Marian 143
AOL (America Online) 15, 17, 44, 45, 50, 54, 129, 132, 135, 170, 172, 173, 174

Apple Computers 3, 44, 65, 126, 129, 135
Applebaum, Anne 20–21
Arena Stage 144
Arizona (state), Wi-Fi in 170
Arlen, Gary 132
Army, U.S. Department of the 57, 83; *see also* U.S. Department of Defense
ARPA (Advanced Research Projects Agency) 3, 39, 45, 151
Arpanet 3, 15, 39; *see also* Darpanet; Internet
Artificial Intelligence Laboratory (Stanford University) 84–85
Asians, in D.C. area 24, 25, 26, 27, 101, 114, 118, 121, 123, 176
Associated Press 35
AstraZenaca (drug company) 71
AT&T Corp. 17, 37, 40, 41–42, 43, 50, 63, 81, 126–127, 161, 173
automobile purchases, online 165

Baker, Russell 99
Baltimore (Md.) 34, 35, 103, 137
Baran, Paul 81
Barney, Alice Pike 141–142
Barry, Marion 106, 107, 151
Bass, Randy 153–154
Bell, Alexander Graham 35–36
Bell, Daniel 41, 159
Bell Atlantic (phone company) 108
Bell Laboratories (AT&T Corp.) 37, 38, 40
Bell South (phone company) 127, 173
Bell System (AT&T) 42
Bellamy, Edward 37
"Beltway, inside the" 100
Beniger, James 36
Berners-Lee, Tim 163, 172
Biden, Joseph 184
Big Science, government sponsorship of 38–40, 42
Billings, John Shaw 36
biometrics 59, 70

203

biotechnology research 45, 53, 70–72, 157–158, 176
bird migration, digital tracking of 75
Black Entertainment Television (BET) 106
BlackBerrys (personal digital assistants) 1, 63, 67, 79, 89, 99, 125–126, 154, 168, 169
Blake, Peter 140
blogging 131–133
BlueGenel (IBM computer) 1, 14
Boeing Corp. 68–69, 83, 85, 86
BOGSAT ("Bunch of Old Guys Sitting Around a Table") 82
Boston (Mass.): homicides in 116; as IT center 1, 7, 9, 10, 18, 33, 41, 45, 49, 70, 74, 139, 157, 159; telegraph links to 34
"brain gain" in D.C. area 23, 121; *see also* Creative Class
Brains Trust (FDR appointees) 121
Brin, Sergey 134
Brookings Institution 151–152
Bruce, Edward 142
Brzezinski, Zbigniew 86–87
Buffalo (N.Y.) 34
Bush, George H.W., administration 46, 48–49
Bush, George W.: presidency of 10, 21, 75–76, 84, 117, 180, 185; as presidential candidate 100
Bush, Vannevar 37, 38–39, 159

cable companies 129, 130, 131
Caiazza, Amy 123
California 35, 71; *see also* San Francisco (Calif.); Silicon Valley (Calif.)
Cambridge (Mass.), IT research in 37, 38; *see also* MIT (Massachusetts Institute of Technology)
Canada, government IT projects in 80
Cantus, Charles 93
Carlyle Group 60–61
Carnegie Institution 45
Carter, Jimmy, presidency of 86–87
Case, Steve 17, 45
CBS television 174
cell phones 108, 124, 128–129, 130, 135, 153, 167, 168, 169
Census Bureau, U.S. 13, 26, 36, 78, 121, 122, 149
Center for Immigration Studies 101
Center for Public Integrity 62
Center for Responsive Politics 65
Center for Strategic and International Studies 186
Central Intelligence Agency (CIA) 14, 88
Cerf, Vinton 3, 82
Chamber of Commerce, U.S. 65
Cheney, Dick 94

Chesapeake Nanotech Initiative 72
Chicago (Ill.) 25, 28, 49, 60
China, People's Republic of 85, 87, 174, 175
Chopra, Aneesh 186
Cingular (telecom company) 130
cities, global changes in 176–177; *see also* IT centers; names of cities
civil liberties, potential threats to 59, 88–89, 175; *see also* First Amendment rights, protection of
Civil War, U.S. 11, 34, 100, 141
Clark, David 165
classified information, security concerns for 88–89
Clinton, Bill: campaign issues and 3–4, 18, 46, 48–49, 67, 157; as information-age president 48, 49, 51, 167, 169, 180
Clinton, Hillary 95, 183
cloning, as public policy issue 158
Coast and Geodetic Survey, U.S. 141, 151
Coburn, Tom 187
Cold War, and U.S. scientific research 40, 81
colleges, in D.C. area 152–155
Comcast 129, 130, 131
The Coming of Post-Industrial Society (Bell) 41, 159
communications satellites 41–42
communications systems, private ownership of 35, 42, 168; *see also* Internet; names of companies; telegraph; telephone
The Competitive Advantage of Nations (Porter) 22
computer firms *see* IT firms; names of firms
computers: as e-government resources 1, 41; memory chips for 40, 48, 56, 72, 167; pioneering work in 2–3, 11, 36–39, 158–159; for school use 117, 169, 188; social implications of 159; *see also* digital devices; IT (information technology)
Comsat (Communications Satellite Corporation) 42
Concord Law School 155
Congress, U.S.: arts initiatives and 142–143; AT&T monopoly and 42, 43, 63, 127; blogging in 131; citizens' privacy concerns and 91–92; colleges chartered by 152; computerization and 3, 8, 14, 16, 41, 89–90, 160; C-SPAN and 90–91; D.C. governance and 11, 33, 103, 106–108, 110; Dickens's impressions of 34; digital-age electioneering and 94, 164; digital devices and 126; electronic voting systems and 96; elite status of 120; e-mail traffic and 92; in L'Enfant plan 32; federal funding

accountability and 187; First Amendment freedoms and 33; Internet services regulation and 126, 167–168; IT-related public policy issues and 91, 158; lobbying and 18, 35, 58, 63, 67, 68, 69, 91, 93; logrolling and 85–86; negative image of 100; telecommunications law and 161; telecommuting and 79; telegraph funding by 34–35
consumer purchases, online 91
"control revolution," in communications technology 36
Corcoran Gallery of Art 20
cost overruns, in military projects 57, 58, 83, 84
Council of Advisers on Science and Technology 73
Cox Communications Cable 131
Creative Class 22–24, 138, 139, 148, 151, 156
C-SPAN (cable project) 90–91
cultural resources, as civic attraction 139
Customs and Border Protection, Bureau of (DHS) 58
"cyber czar," U.S. 4, 186
cyberspace, origin of term 162

dairy farming, IT applications and 55
Dallas (Texas) 10, 25, 49, 139, 157
Danner, Dan 68
Daou, Peter 164
DARPA *see* Defense Advanced Research Projects Agency (DARPA)
Darpanet 56–57, 81–82; *see also* Arpanet; Internet
DataStream Content Solutions 52
DD(X) series ships 57–58
Dean, Howard 93–94, 181, 182
Defense Advanced Research Projects Agency (DARPA) 56–57, 81–85
Democratic Party: computer-based electioneering and 4, 8–9, 96, 164, 181; in D.C. 105; direct political contributions to 62, 64; Michigan primary Internet voting by 97; *see also* names of individuals
Deutsch, Karl 40, 159
Devine, Ted 183
Dickens, Charles 33–34, 99
digital age: consumer phase of 48, 166–167; public policy for 161, 167–168, 169, 186; rapid rate of change in 158
digital devices: in clothing 167; obsolescence and 158, 160–161; professionals' reliance on 46, 124–126; safe disposal of 2, 14; student use of 153–154
diploma mills, online 154
Disney Mobile family cell phone service 128–129

distance learning, as educational alternative 154
District of Columbia: AIDS cases in 28, 116; anti-terrorism measures in 58, 86, 118; arts funding in 142–143; blogging in 131–132; building restrictions in 105; central city resurgence in 99, 109–113; commuter taxation and 103; cultural resources in 136, 139–148, 156; digital infrastructure of 108–109, 126, 127–128, 133–134; early years of 10–12, 20, 28, 29, 30–33, 140–141; elite groups in 120, 141–142; L'Enfant plan for 31–32, 53, 105, 109, 110, 140; films about 99; housing in 104–105, 111, 112, 113–116, 122, 176; income distribution in 106, 114; Internet access in 15, 126, 130; marketing strategies for 104, 112, 115, 116, 124; municipal governance in 106–109, 110–111, 122; as New York City rival 21–22, 31, 139, 140, 145; nightlife in 136; prejudices against 99–100, 139, 140, 145; public schools in 116–118; racial divisions in 2, 23, 28, 33, 105–106, 109, 113–118, 141, 143, 147, 148; riots of 1968 in 109, 112, 113, 146; social networking in 133, 134, 137–138; socioeconomic changes in 2, 19–20, 22–27, 28, 60, 99, 100–108, 112, 113, 118, 120–124, 136–137, 139–140, 148–151, 177; songs about 99–100; symbolic importance of 118–119; technological breakthroughs and 34–37, 177; tourism in 109, 111; urban problems in 2, 19, 27, 28, 113–118; voting rights in 33; women's status in 24, 123, 136–137; *see also* Washington, D.C. area
DLA Piper Rudnick Gray Cary (lobbyists) 64
do-not-call registry 92
DoCoMo (telecom firm) 131
Dodd, Jimmy 100
Dolan, Julie 24
Donavan, Dennis 53
"dot-com bubble" 18–19, 46, 51, 102, 160
Drucker, Peter 46
Dulles Airport 54
Dulles Corridor (Northern Virginia) 54
Duncan, Todd 143

"Early Bird" (communications satellite) 41–42
Earthlink (Internet service provider) 170
eBay (on-line auction company) 129, 165
Echelon (NSA communications monitoring project) 88–89
economic growth, cluster-based theory of 22–23
economic stimulus spending, Web sites

documenting 187–188; *see also* recession of 2008
"edge cities" 101–102
Edge Technologies, Inc. 55
education, economic stimulus spending and 187–188
education, higher: in D.C. area 152–155; digital age jobs and 121–122; gender gap in 137
Edwards, John 182
e-government 1, 14, 76–77, 97–98, 108–109, 162; *see also* Congress, U.S.; government, U.S. federal
Eggers, William 97, 162
Eisenhower, Dwight D. 68
elections, U.S.: ballot miscounts in 96; blogging and 131; computer-based techniques and 3–4, 8–9, 93–97, 100, 133, 163–164, 179, 181–185; computer-literate voters and 46; political consultants and 66, 181
Electronic Frontier Foundation 185
Ellington, Duke 147
e-mail messaging 40, 92, 165
Emerson, Ralph Waldo 29
employment, in D.C. area: forecasts for 175–176; at IT firms 16, 18, 19, 23, 27, 51; for knowledge workers 49–50, 78–79; for minorities 28, 123, 148; for women 24, 123, 136–137
Encyclopedia of Digital Government 97
Engelbart, Doug 82
ENIAC (computer project) 11, 39
Environmental Protection Agency (EPA) 14, 73
European Union (EU) 77

F/A 22 Raptor fighter jet project 70
Facebook 9, 96, 181, 182–183, 184, 188
FDA (Food and Drug Administration) 71–72
Federal Bureau of Investigation (FBI) 80, 88, 110
Federal Communications Commission (FCC) 17, 43
Federal Funding Accountability and Transparency Act of 2006 187
federal government *see* government, U.S. federal
Federal Reserve Board 11
Federal Trade Commission 92
Fenty, Adrian 107, 118
fiber-optic circuits 43, 108, 130
Fine Arts Commission (D.C.) 20, 142
Finn, Mindy 185
First Amendment rights, protection of 2, 29, 30, 33, 35, 46–47, 97–98, 168

Florida, Richard 19–20, 22, 139
Florida (state), ballot miscounts in 96
Fort Worth (Texas) 49, 100, 157
14th Street Northwest (D.C.) 112–113, 146
France, IT resource planning in 77
Frankfurt (Germany) 1
Franklin, Benjamin 29, 31
Fraunces Tavern (NYC) 30–31
freedom of information 29, 30, 33, 35, 46, 97–98, 168; *see also* First Amendment rights, protection of
Frey, William 23, 25, 104, 121
Fuller, Stephen 10, 54, 113
fundraising, political 9, 93–94, 96, 183
Future Digital System (GPO project) 13
Future Internet Designs (FIND) 166

GALA Hispanic Theater (D.C.) 113, 147
Gates, Bill 3, 44, 135, 162
gays, as D.C. residents 123, 150–151
Gehry, Frank 20
Genentech (biotech research company) 71
General Dynamics 83–84
GenVec (biotech company) 71–72
George Mason University 153
George Washington University 152
Georgetown (D.C. neighborhood) 100, 121
Georgetown University 152, 154
Gibson, William 162
gifts, politically motivated 67–68; *see also* lobbying
The Gilded Age (Twain) 62
Gilder, George 160
Gingrich, Newt 49, 185
Glauber, Robert 66
Global Environment for Network Innovations (GENI) 166
"global village" concept 29, 159
Goldberg, Arthur 110
Golding, Kenneth 184
good-government associations ("goo-goos") 66–67
Google (Internet search engine) 15, 132, 134–135, 170, 171, 174
Gore, Albert ("Al") 3–4, 49, 180
government, U.S. federal: African American employees of 148; arts sponsorship by 142–143; as D.C. economic engine 12, 74, 113; digital operations and 1–2, 3, 4, 8, 11–15, 38–40, 75–81, 97, 127, 158, 160–161, 162, 179–181, 185–188; equal employment laws and 123; as expanding bureaucracy 11, 18, 74–75, 77, 78–79, 157; Internet policy decisions and 167, 169, 171, 172, 180–181, 185–188; as IT industry customer 10, 15–16, 18–19, 41, 45, 46, 49, 50, 51–52, 56, 69–70, 73, 74, 77, 80–81,

126, 157, 161–162, 167, 186; IT network coordination and 83, 85, 87, 89; New Deal programs and 11, 37, 121, 142–143; as scientific research sponsor 11, 38–39, 40, 42, 45, 73, 151, 159; telecommunications overhaul for 81; transparency measures for 187–188; Web sites for 76–77, 187–188; *see also* Congress, U.S.; names of agencies and departments
Government Printing Office (GPO) 12–13
governments, state and local: economic stimulus spending and 187–188; IT firms and 52–53, 70–71, 72–73; Wi-Fi sponsorship by 170, 171
Grace, Peter 160
Greater Washington Initiative (GWI) 49–50
Green, Constance McLaughlin 114
Green Book *(The Social List of Washington, D.C.)* 120
Grimm, Ed 134
Grimond, John 177
Gross, Matthew 181–182
GSA (General Services Administration) 78, 79, 80–81

Hamilton, Alexander 31
Hampton, Barbara 78
Harbinger Technologies Group 59
Harman Center for the Arts 146
Hassell, John D. 64
Hayes, Patrick 143
Heath, Don 15
Help America Vote Act of 2002 96
Hewlett-Packard (HP) 17, 64, 172
Hill, Edward 27–28
Hingle, Judy 153
Hispanics: in D.C. area 23, 24, 25–26, 27, 101, 113, 114, 118, 123, 147, 148, 150, 176; Internet service to 96–97, 169; as largest U.S. minority 149–150
HIV/AIDS, in D.C. area 116
Hogan & Hartson (lobbyists) 64
Hollerith, Herman 36
Holt, Rush 91
Home Rule Act of 1974 103
Howard Hughes Medical Institute 10, 45, 53, 70
Howard Theater 147
Howard University 152
Huggins reports 7–8, 157
Hughes, Langston 147
Hughes Network Systems 17
Huntington, Samuel 149

Ibiza (D.C. nightspot) 136
IBM (International Business Machines Corp.): Chinese buy-out of 87, 158; Darpanet and 57, 81; D.C. area operations of 17, 52; early mainframes from 2, 8, 11, 13, 40, 158; federal contracts and 8; history of 36; nanotechnology and 72, 167; overseas operations of 174; supercomputers 1, 14; telecommunications laws and 161
identity card, proposed national 92
immigrants, to D.C. area 2, 24–27, 114, 148–150
India 170, 174
Industrial Partnership Program (Maryland) 52
influence peddling, abuses in 68; *see also* lobbying
information: convergence of digital sources of 172; freedom of 29, 30, 33, 168; haves *vs.* have-nots 168–169, 171; as source of political power 40–41, 159; *see also* IT (information technology)
Information Awareness Office 92
information economy, emergence of 41, 50, 168
information highway 3–4, 48–49, 51, 67, 180; *see also* Internet; World Wide Web
Information Infrastructure Task Force 49
information theory, pioneers of 37–39; *see also* names of individuals
Input (market research firm) 69
instant-messaging (IM-ing) 129, 132
InstaPundit (blog) 131, 132
intellectual property, concept of 30
Intelsat (global satellite network) 42
International Consumer Products Show 167
Internet: access to 15, 126, 130, 163, 164, 168–169, 170–171, 174–175, 187; advertising revenue for 174; federal government support for 180, 187; First Amendment rights and 35, 168; government surveillance of 88–89, 92, 175; interplanetary 75; Morse's foreshadowing of 34; pioneering work on 2–3, 38, 39, 81, 159–160, 163; political campaigning via 181–185; public-private management of 162, 166, 168, 169, 172, 173, 175; rapid growth of 161, 162, 163, 164–166, 171–172; retail sales via 91, 165; service providers 45–46, 126–131, 154; as social change driver 177; as social networking tool 9, 96, 132, 137–138, 179, 182, 183–184, 185; State Department use of 87; student uses for 153–154, 180; technologies of 3, 15, 56, 81, 82, 127, 159–160, 163, 172, 173; telephone service via 129; U.S. domination of 15, 163, 164, 175; in U.S. political process 4, 9, 46, 93–97, 163, 179, 180–185; upgrades to 172; *see also* World Wide Web

Internet Caucus 92–93
Internet Corporation for Assigned Names and Numbers (ICANN) 162–163, 175
Internet Innovation Alliance 166
iPhones 126, 129–130, 135
iPods (portable music players) 135
Iraq, U.S. invasion of 83, 89
Iron Triangle, definition of 18
IRS (Internal Revenue Service) 14, 77–78, 80
Irving, Larry 166
IT (information technology) 7; failed projects and 14, 80; as politico-economic catalyst 7–10, 40–41, 102, 180; rapid evolution of 48, 158, 171–173; *see also* digital age; digital equipment; Internet; knowledge economy regions; research facilities
IT firms: in D.C. region 1, 9–10, 12, 16, 17–18, 19, 22, 50–56, 69, 70, 72–73, 74, 83–84, 175; foreign competition for 174; lobbying by 17–18, 43–44, 50–51, 61–68; private investment in 61; space rocket projects and 68–69; *see also* names of firms
It's Just Lunch (dating service) 138
iTunes Music Store 136

Jackson, Andrew, presidency of 33
James, Henry 99
James, Lucian 133
Japan 1, 77, 157
Jefferson, Thomas 29, 31, 32, 33
JesuitNet (online network) 154
Jobs, Steven 3, 44, 129, 134
John F. Kennedy Center for the Performing Arts 144–145
Johns Hopkins University 153
Johnson, Lyndon B., presidency of 3, 8, 14, 77, 160, 180
Johnson, Robert 106
Joint Strike Fighter (JSF) project 83
Jones, James Earl 144

K Street Corridor 61, 63, 64, 100; *see also* lobbying
Kameney, Frank 151
Kaplan University 155, 173
Kapor, Mitch 66–67, 185–186
Katz, Bruce 121, 176
Kazin, Alfred 118–119
Keefe, Patricia 169
Kelly, Sharon Pratt 107
Kennedy, John F. 7, 42, 133, 144, 185
Kennedy Center *see* John F. Kennedy Center for the Performing Arts
Kennedy Onassis, Jacqueline 110, 144

Kerrey, Bob 100
Kerry, John 94
King, Colbert 115–116
Kinsley, Michael 62–63
Knight, Jerry 72
knowledge economy regions 1–5, 7–9, 12, 15–19, 22, 24, 27–28, 29, 33, 39, 40, 41, 42, 43–47, 49–54, 60, 69, 70, 72–73, 74, 101, 102, 103, 113, 152, 155–156, 157, 161–162, 167, 175–176; *see also* names of cities
Kotkin, Joel 102
Kundra, Vivek 186

Lafayette, Marquis de 31
LAKS (watchmakers) 125
Lamb, Brian 90
Lang, Jack 164
Lang, Robert 104
laptops, prevalence of 124; *see also* digital devices
Larides, Mike 125
Las Vegas (Nev.) 167, 170
Latinos *see* Hispanics
Laureate Education Inc. 154–155
Lavine, John 173
lawyers, in D.C. 63; *see also* lobbying
LCS (littoral combat ship) project 83–84
Leinberger, Christopher 105
L'Enfant, Pierre 31–32, 53, 105, 109, 110, 140
Lenova (computer company) 87
lesbians, as D.C. residents 150–151
Library of Congress 13, 22, 33, 89–90, 140, 141
Licklider, Joseph 2, 3
Lipman, Andrew 43
list-servs (Web-based bulletin boards) 134
lobbying: attempts to regulate 67–68; by IT industry 17–18, 43–44, 50–51, 61–67, 93, 185–186
Lockheed Martin Corp. 9–10, 17, 18, 55–56, 58, 68–69, 70, 83–84
logrolling, as congressional tradition 85
Los Angeles (Calif.) 18, 25, 26, 49, 103, 121
Lotus (software company) 66
Loudoun County (Va.) 19, 27, 31, 33, 35, 61, 62, 101, 109
Lowrey, Ying 25

Mahe, Henry E. ("Eddie"), Jr. 95
Mars family 106
Martin, Jurek 118
Martin, Rick 45
Marx, Leo 29
Maryland (state): African-American population in 106; IT firms in 9–10, 52, 53,

71, 72; Obama support groups in 183; regional growth in 19, 23, 27, 55; state government IT spending in 52; universities in 152–153; women's wages in 123
Masud, Sam 166
McCain, John 181, 183, 184
McGowan, William 17, 43–44
MCI Communications Corp. 17, 43–44, 50, 128
McLuhan, Marshall 29, 159
media, new *vs.* old 135–136, 158, 173–174, 182, 184; *see also* Internet
medical records, electronic 75–76
MedImmune, Inc. 71
Medlars/Medline network 78
Mellon, Paul 142
metroplexes, as national trend 100
Metropolitan Council of Governments (COG) 101, 176
Miami (Fla.) 25, 26
Michigan (state), Wi-Fi in 170
Microsoft 17, 44, 62–63, 65, 125, 166–167, 173
microtargeting 94; *see also* voter profiling
Miller, Harris 9
MIT (Massachusetts Institute of Technology): IT research at 2, 3, 37, 38, 45; online course offerings by 155
Moore, Arthur Cotton 21, 22
Moore, Gordon 48
Moore's Law 48
Morse, Samuel F.B. 34, 168
Motion Picture Association of America 66
Motorola 167
Mount Pleasant (D.C.) 113
Moynihan, Daniel Patrick 22, 110
Murdoch, Rupert 174
Muslims, as D.C. area immigrants 27
Musser, Philip 95
MySpace 9, 96, 181

Nano (multimedia device) 135
nanotechnology 72–73, 85, 153, 157, 167, 176
National Aeronautics and Space Administration (NASA) 13, 69, 75, 88, 153
National Archives and Records Administration (NARA) 1, 12
National Bureau of Standards 45, 151
National Endowment for the Arts 143
National Gallery of Art 142
National Institute of Standards and Technology (NIST) 87–88
National Institutes of Health (NIH) 10, 13, 45, 53, 56, 70, 78, 87, 151
National Oceanic and Atmospheric Administration (NOAA) 69

National Park Service 145
National Science Foundation 3, 39, 57, 88, 159, 166, 175
National Security Agency (NSA) 10, 69, 88–89
National Security Council 186
National Sex Offenders Public Registry 13
National Technical Information Service (NTIS) 77
Navy, U.S., Department of the 57–58, 83–84
Negroponte, Nicholas 162
The Nerves of Government (Deutsch) 40, 159
networking, of computers 2–3; *see also* Arpanet; Darpanet; Internet; social networking, Internet based
Neumann, John von 38
New Deal 11, 37, 103, 120–121, 142–143, 169
New York City (N.Y.): biotechnology research in 71; communications systems and 34, 170; immigrant population of 25; as rival to D.C. 21–22, 31, 32, 33, 49, 60, 111, 139, 140, 145
News Corp. 174
Newseum (D.C.) 112
Nicholson, Jim 94–95
9/11/2001 terrorist attacks 52, 58, 81, 83, 86, 102, 111, 118
9:30 Club (D.C. nightspot) 136
Nixon, Richard 23, 46, 105; in Watergate scandal 76, 152
No Child Left Behind legislation 117
Nokia Corp. 130–131, 174
Nortel (telecommunications firm) 169
Northrop Grumman Corp. 17, 55–56, 85
nuclear weapons, development of 39, 40

Obama, Barack: digitally-based electioneering and 4, 9, 94, 96, 100, 133, 163–164, 182–185; economic stimulus plan and 187; ethnic group support for 150; as first information-age president 133, 179; national technology policy and 4, 175, 180–181, 185, 186–188
O'Brien, Barbara 131
Office of Management and Budget (OMB) 69, 79–80, 86, 186
Office of Scientific Research and Development (OSRD) 38–39
Office of Technology Assessment (OTA) 91
O'Neill, Thomas P. ("Tip") 90, 95
Online Political Operatives (OPOs) 181–182
Open Access Card 59
Open Government Directive 187, 188
Open Park Project 170–171

Index

O'Reilly, Tim 172
Osaka (Japan) 1, 157
Owings, Nathaniel 110

Pacific Telegraph Act of 1860 35
packet switching (digital technology) 3, 15, 40, 56, 81, 159
Page, Larry 134
Papp, Joseph 140
passports, high-tech 14, 59–60
Patent Office, U.S. 30, 33
Patton Boggs (lobbyists) 64
Pearlstein, Steven 115
Peck, Suzanne 108
Pedigo, Stephen 50
Penn Quarter (D.C.) 111–112, 146
Pennsylvania (state), commuter suburbs in 55
Pennsylvania Avenue (D.C.) 109–111, 140
Pentagon *see* Defense, U.S. Department of
pharmaceutical industry 71
Philadelphia (Pa.) 31, 32, 33, 133, 170, 171
Phillips, Vicky 154
Phoenix, University of 154
pizza standard, in lobbying 68
pocketknives, digitized 125
podcasting 94, 135
political consultants, in D.C. 66; *see also* Online Political Operatives (OPOs)
PoliticalMoneyLine (research group) 62
pollution, computer disposal and 2, 14
Pool, Ithiel deSola 97–98, 158, 159–160
Porat, Marc Uri 41
Porter, Cole 99
Porter, Michael 22–23
postindustrial age 41, 159
Powell, Colin 87
Pressley, Nelson 146
Prince George's County (Md.) 106
privacy issues, digital technology and 59, 88–89, 91–92
private enterprise *see* IT firms; names of firms
public interest advocacy groups 66–67
public policy *see* Congress, U.S.; government, U.S. federal
public utilities, government subsidies for 169

Quinn, Sally 100
Qwest (telecommunications company) 81

racial divisions, in D.C. area 2, 23, 28, 33, 105–106, 109, 113–118
Rand Corporation 40, 81, 82, 162
Randall, Scott 95
Rasiej, Andrew 182

Rauch, Jonathan 26
Reagan, Ronald, presidency of 46
RebuildTheParty.com 185
receptions, as political tool 67
recession of 2008 50, 51, 61, 70, 187
Rechner, Suzanne 125
Recovery.gov 187, 188
Reich, Robert 168
Republican Party: computer-based electioneering and 4, 8–9, 164, 181, 182, 184, 185; in D.C. 105; direct political contributions to 62, 64, 183; IT advocacy and 49; IT lobbying and 64
research facilities, in D.C. area 3, 10, 37, 38–39, 45, 55, 72–73, 81, 87–88, 103, 141, 151, 153
Research in Motion (RIM) 63, 125
Reynolds, Glenn 132
Rich, Frank 21–22, 140
Riggs National Bank 60
Rivlin, Alice 104
RMA (Revolution in Military Affairs) 56, 82–83
Robert Huggins Associates, reports by 7–8, 157
Robinson, Boardman 143
robotics 57, 84–85
Rockefeller, Nelson 160
Romney, Mitt 182, 185
Roosevelt, Franklin D., presidency of 11, 37, 38, 42, 169
Rovere, Richard 99
Ruffini, Patrick 185

SAIC (Science Applications International Corp.) 83
Salt Lake City (Utah) 15
San Francisco (Calif.) 9, 15, 25, 103, 111, 121, 134, 171
satellites 83, 108–109; *see also* communications satellites; Sputnik
SBC Communications 127
Schrage, Michael 39
"Science—The Endless Frontier" (Bush) 39, 159
Science and Technology Policy, White House Office of 151, 186
scientific research, government sponsorship of 11, 38–39, 40, 42, 45, 73, 151, 159
security, for digital data 59, 88–89, 186
segregation *see* racial divisions
Selin, Ivan 16
semiconductor memory chips 40, 48, 56, 72, 167
Senior Executive Service 24
"sexiest city" survey (*Men's Health* magazine) 24, 137

Shahn, Ben 143
Shannon, Claude 37–38
Sherbeck, John 57
Silicon Valley (Calif.) 1, 7, 10, 12, 18, 19, 22, 41, 44, 45, 49, 51, 53, 66, 69, 70, 71, 73, 74, 122, 139, 157
Singapore (Malaysia) 157
Singer, Audrey 25
Skype 129
slavery, in D.C. area 31, 33
smart cards (biometric IDs) 14, 59–60
Smithson, James 142
Smithsonian Institution 142
SNAD (Social Networking Anxiety Disorder) 138
The Social List of Washington, D.C. 120
social networking, Internet based 9, 96, 132, 137–138, 179, 182, 183–184, 185, 188
Social Security Administration 78
solar power, military applications of 85
SOME (So Others Might Eat) 115
Souter, David H. 90–91
Southwest quadrant (D.C.) 114–115
speech, freedom of *see* First Amendment rights
Spiegel, Dana 171
Sprint Nextel Corp. 44, 128
Sputnik (satellite) 40
spy agencies, U.S. 88–89, 160
SRDS Direct Marketing List Source 93
Stanford University 45, 84–85, 122
Stanley (driverless car) 84–85
Staple, Gregory 170
Starbucks (coffee houses), Wi-Fi service in 133, 170
Steinhardt, Barry 59
Stern, Isaac 143
Sterne, Maurice 143
Stevens, Roger L. 144–145
Strayer University 155
Studio Theater 146–147
Sunlight Foundation 188
Suro, Roberto 150
Suter's Tavern (D.C.) 31–32
Swiss Army knives, digitized 125

Tabulating Machine Co. 36
Tactical Numerical Deterministic Model (TNDM) 82
tax returns, e-filing of 14; *see also* IRS (Internal Revenue Service)
TCP/IP (Internet software) 82
"technical czar," U.S. 4, 186
Tech-President (campaign tracking group) 182
Telecommunications Act of 1996 161, 167–168, 171, 172–173
telecommunications companies 42–44, 50, 126–131
telecommuting 79
telegraph system 34–35, 86, 158, 168
telemarketing, legal restraints on 92
telephone-answering machine 40
telephones 35–36, 41, 42, 76, 108, 126, 158; *see also* BlackBerrys, cell phones; iPhones
telework 79
terrorism: communications monitoring and 88–89; DHS spending to combat 52, 56, 58–59, 85–86, 102; U.S. military programs and 83–85
Texas Instruments Inc. 40
think tanks 151–152
time sharing, in computer operations 2
Time Warner (media company) 46, 174
Tocqueville, Alexis de 30
tolerance, as socioeconomic factor 139, 150–151
Tomlin, Lily 127
tornado spotting, digital systems and 75
Total Information Awareness Project 84
Trachtenberg, Stephen 152
trade associations, lobbying by 64–65, 66
traffic congestion 2, 103, 176
transistors, development of 40, 72
Trippi, Joe 133, 181
Truman, Harry 39
Trump, Donald 22
Twain, Mark 37, 62
Twitter (social networking medium) 182–183, 184, 188
Tysons Corner (Va.) 101–102

UAVs (unmanned aerial vehicles) 85
United Nations (UN) 175
United States: ideological premises of 29–30, 149; information age role of 1, 15, 163, 164, 174–175; as multicultural country 26, 149–150; national technology policies for 4, 175, 180–181, 185, 186–188; telegraph network in 34–35, 168
U.S. Department of Agriculture 75
U.S. Department of Commerce 41, 49
U.S. Department of Defense: acronym list at 21; computer networking technology and 3, 15, 40, 81–82; computer resources and 1, 13–14, 17, 160; IT firm lobbying and 18; personal data monitoring and 92; spending on IT projects 56–58, 68, 70, 81–85
U.S. Department of Energy 88
U.S. Department of Health and Human Services 75

Index

U.S. Department of Homeland Security (DHS) 52, 56, 58–59, 85–86, 89
U.S. Department of Justice 13, 126, 173
U.S. Department of State 14, 59–60, 86–87, 163
U.S. Department of Veterans Affairs (VA) 87
U.S. Postal Service 17, 30, 31, 33, 162
U.S. War Department 11
universities, in D.C. area 152–153
University of Maryland 10, 73, 152–153
U.S. Visit project 58

Valenti, Jack 66
Verizon (telecommunications company) 81, 127–131, 133, 171
Verne, Jules 37
Victorinox (company) 125
Virginia (state): DHS funding in 58; digital services in 130, 134; immigrant population of 25, 26, 27; IT companies in 17, 20, 52, 53, 54, 55, 72, 148; public universities in 152–153; regional growth and 19–20, 23, 54–55, 101–102; state government IT spending in 52; women's wages in 123
VivoMetrics 167
VOIP (Voice Over Internet Protocol) technology 129, 130
Voter Contact Services (polling company) 93
voter profiling 93, 94, 95, 96, 97, 183
voting, electronic 96–97

Walkman (portable cassette player) 135
Wal-Mart 173
Warner, Mark R. 58
Washington, George 28, 31, 32–33, 152
Washington, Walter 107
Washington, D.C., area: anti-terrorist funding and 58–59, 86; current extent of 19, 60, 100–103; educational levels in 23, 24, 27, 117, 175; employment figures for 28, 175; as financial center 60–61; higher-education resources in 152–155; immigrants to 2, 24–27, 114, 148–150, 176; Internet access in 126–131, 133–134, 170–171; as knowledge economy region 1–5, 7–9, 12, 15–19, 22, 24, 27–28, 29, 33, 39, 40, 41, 42, 43–47, 49–54, 60, 69, 70, 72–73, 74, 101, 102, 103, 113, 152, 155–156, 157, 161–162, 167, 175–176; local jargon of 20–21; research facilities in 3, 10, 37, 38–39, 45, 55, 72–73, 81, 87–88, 103, 141, 151, 153, 157–158, 176; traffic congestion in 103, 176; young professionals' impact on 157, 176; *see also* District of Columbia; government, U.S. federal; Maryland; Virginia
Washington Performing Arts Society (WPAS) 143
Washington Post (newspaper), diversification at 155, 173
Watergate scandal 76, 152
Watson, Thomas 36
Weaver, Warren 38
Web-MGI (Mating for Genetic Improvement) 55
Weiner, Norbert 37
Western Union (telegraph company) 34, 35
Wheeler, Douglas 136
Wheeler, Thomas 66
Who Are We? The Challenges to American National Identity (Huntington) 149
Wicker, Tom 119
Wi-Fi (wireless local area network) 133–134, 135, 169–171
Wiley Rein & Fielding (law firm) 63
Williams, Anthony 103, 106, 107
Wi-Max (wireless broadband network) 170, 171
wiretapping, by NSA 89
women, professional opportunities for 24, 123, 136–137
World War II: higher education expansion and 152; impact on D.C. of 100, 103; scientific research and 11, 38–39, 159
World Wide Web: basic technologies of 15, 163; 2008 presidential campaign and 182–185; Web 2 version of 172; *see also* Internet
Wornold Development Co. 55
Wozniak, Stephen 3, 44
wristwatches, digitized 125

Xerox copier 40

Yahoo (online company) 65, 132
YouTube 9, 96, 132–133, 166, 182, 184, 188

Zakaria, Fareed 163